GETTING RID
of
RITALIN

GETTING RID *of* RITALIN

How Neurofeedback Can Successfully Treat
Attention Deficit Disorder without Drugs

———————————

Robert W. Hill, Ph.D.
and Eduardo Castro, M.D.

HAMPTON ROADS
PUBLISHING COMPANY, INC.

Cover design by Marjoram Productions
Cover photograph © 2002 copyright Corinne Malet/PhotoAlto

Hampton Roads Publishing Company, Inc.
1125 Stoney Ridge Road
Charlottesville, VA 22902

(434) 296-2772
fax: (434) 296-5096
e-mail: hrpc@hrpub.com
www.hrpub.com

If you are unable to order this book from your local
bookseller, you may order directly from the publisher.
Call 1-800-766-8009, toll-free.

Library of Congress Catalog Card Number: 2001098003
ISBN 1-57174-254-9
10 9 8 7 6 5 4 3 2 1
Printed on acid-free paper in Canada

Contents

Introduction

The Neurofeedback Alternative

We have an exciting story to tell you. It's a story of heart-break and hope, of people devastated by a disorder who have found happiness and success, a story of brave and dedicated professionals swimming against the tide of conventional wisdom.

Attention deficit disorder (ADD) is discussed in many different contexts. Practically everyone in America has heard of it and it is often the topic of conversation among soccer moms. However, most people know very little about ADD. There are even professionals who think ADD is simply hyperactivity or a child's inability to pay attention in school. These professionals' "simple" solution is to place the child on stimulant medications like Ritalin. Ritalin stimulates the disinterested, lethargic child, and through what appears to be a paradoxical process, slows down the hyperactive child. So, the problem is solved and everyone is happy.

If it were only that easy. An estimated four million children are on Ritalin in our country alone, and the problem of ADD is increasing, not getting better.

ADD is not just a problem of inattention in the classroom. It is in a cluster group of problems that can only be described as serious, and may well be the first manifestation of life-long problems. Children who have ADD have a higher probability of developing aggressive, violent, and antisocial behavior. They are more likely to use drugs and alcohol when compared to children without ADD. In addition, children with ADD have a higher likelihood of exhibiting poor school performance, thereby ending up with less education than non-ADDs. They tend to be more hyper, have more failed marriages, less job success, more auto accidents, rockier personal relationships, and more trouble with the legal system. And we know scientifically that Ritalin does not fix the problem.

Slow brainwave activity is at the core of ADD. Ritalin is a stimulant and it speeds up the brain. It is, however, only a temporary treatment. Remove the stimulant and the brain slows down again. Not only does Ritalin not fix the problem, it has side effects, and we do not know the consequences of long-term use.

Slow brainwave activity is at the core of ADD. Ritalin is a stimulant and it speeds up the brain. It is, however, only a temporary treatment. Remove the stimulant and the brain slows down again. Not only does Ritalin *not* fix the problem, it has side effects, and we do not know the consequences of long-term use.

There is hope for people with ADD as well as its companions, hyperactivity, aggressiveness, violent behavior, and substance abuse: neurofeedback. Neurofeedback is a sophisticated form of biofeedback that actually trains the brain to speed up. It can do on a permanent basis what Ritalin can only do for a few hours, and there are no lasting side effects.

This is at last a quick, non-invasive, cost-effective treatment for attention deficit disorder and its cluster of companion disorders. So, without years of medical treatment, taking pills, or managing difficult diets, or without months of behavior modification, we can successfully treat ADD, reduce aggressive and violent tendencies, and effectively treat drug and alcohol abuse. Here is a case study from our practice that shows neurofeedback in action:

Seth was a nine-year-old. He was failing every third-grade subject and he had no friends. His mother gave him a birthday party and only two children showed up. Seth had been on Ritalin, but it did not seem to make any difference. We started neurofeedback treatment in the late spring and continued it through the summer. Although Seth had to repeat the third grade, his grades are in the "B" range and he has "lots of friends" even four years later.

Here is another neurofeedback case: Carolyn was a quiet, shy, sad-looking child. She was failing the sixth grade, oppositional at home, and had only one close friend. She was not diagnosed with ADD but should have been. In just twelve weeks of neurofeedback, Carolyn's sad personality began to brighten, her grades improved, she stopped writing gloomy poetry and started developing new friends.

These are just two cases out of hundreds we have treated. There were no medications, no major dietary changes, no endless behavior modification or psychotherapy—just neurofeedback. A simple treatment that involves two sessions a week, in which the patient is connected to a specialized EEG computer with a monitor to learn to speed up slow brainwave patterns while playing a sophisticated brainwave-oriented game. The treatment is easy, quick, and not costly. It involves no pain or discomfort—just playing a computer game with your brain.

ADD is certainly the disorder of public note in recent decades. Every child who misbehaves, is rambunctious, acts bored, or underachieves in school is now at risk of being diagnosed with attention deficit disorder, with or without hyperactivity. The vast majority of these children are placed on Ritalin by well-meaning clinicians. Adults who procrastinate, are disorganized, or become restless with routine promptly label themselves as ADD and frequently request stimulant medications from their physicians.

However, the attentional and behavioral disruptions seen in people with ADD are the symptoms of deeper problems. The problem is brain dysregulation, which makes so many of our children unable to access and utilize their inherent abilities and talents. There are not just inattention and hyperactivity to address; there are the frustration and anguish of academic underachievement, the lack of concern for the rights and welfare of others, the disregard of and contempt for order and authority.

An estimated four million children in the United States are prescribed Ritalin. What are the results? The consequences? Are we better off continuing this type of intervention? Is the problem substantially diminishing as a result of relying on stimulant medications? This book will address all of these questions. We will also cover nutrition, problems with toxic substances, the effects of television, violence and aggression in society, homework problems, and parenting strategies which we hope will help you in your quest for the best and highest functioning possible for your child or yourself.

The time is overdue for a serious look at our current treatment regimens and for a realistic approach to the cluster of problems that fall under the large umbrella of ADD. There is a pressing need to discuss the new treatment protocols ignored by mainstream medicine for the past two decades that frequently remedy not only ADD, but the problems commonly clustered with ADD, such as learning disabilities, depression, anxiety disorders, sleep disorders, headaches, delinquent behavior, aggression, and drug and alcohol abuse.

To achieve a clear understanding of the causes of ADD and ADD-type behavior, and to intelligently apply the best treatment methods available, we must begin by being honest about what ADD is according to the evidence. ADD is the result of brain injury. Sometimes the injury is obvious and sometimes extremely subtle. The dysfunction of ADD is most often a problem with the brain's self-regulation; the injured brain is usually too slowed-down for adequate functioning. A slowing of the brain tends to produce ADD-type symptoms. Mainstream medicine uses a simple "solution": speed up the brain with stimulants. Unfortunately this does nothing to correct the problem and often creates other problems.

In the 1930s, when the evidence pointed directly to brain injury, ADD was called "minimal brain dysfunction." In the 1960s, with nothing useful to offer patients, the diagnosis was changed to a descriptive term, "hyperkinetic syndrome," in place of the earlier one. By changing the term indicating that ADD is due to a brain dysfunction, it became easy for mainstream medicine to forget that anything which compromises proper brain functioning can produce ADD-like behavior.

Such factors as birth trauma, poor nutrition, toxic metals, physical injury, allergies, and genetics can play a role in how efficiently the brain functions. No doubt mainstream medicine did not wish to stigmatize children with a derogatory label like "minimal brain dysfunction," but the ability to keep a clear under-standing of the problem, and how to best address it, was lost when we changed the diagnostic label.

The recognized experts in the ADD field today are little more than exceedingly precise describers of the syndrome. They are very good at describing the problem; but beyond Ritalin and other medications, psychotherapy, and support groups, they have little to offer to successfully treat this syndrome. In contrast with this norm, we are not reluctant to address the brain-injury component of ADD, even though there are not many practition-ers who offer a treatment that effectively addresses this compo-nent. We do, in neurofeedback.

Neurofeedback is effective in 70 to 80 percent of those who receive this treatment. Not only does attention improve, but the associated behaviors usually resolve as well. Children typically sleep better, have less anxiety and depression, experience diminished learning difficulties, and are less aggressive. With neurofeedback, interactions with others improve, patients gen-erally act more appropriately in social situations, and self-esteem grows. If safety and efficacy are to be used to determine treatment, neurofeedback should be the treatment of choice for the entire cluster of problems.

Neurofeedback is a natural, self-regulating approach that helps restore the brain's ability to function in the manner in which it was designed to function. When the brain is restored to its proper functioning, it allows the achievement of all of its intrinsic capacities. Brains are exquisitely designed to be able to pay attention and to comprehend information, to achieve full human potential, to focus, think, reason, dream, and create. Brains should thrive on stimulation and information and grow in ability and proficiency.

Neurofeedback helps restore the injured brain's inherent abilities. Intelligent and widespread use of neurofeedback by cli-nicians and educators has the potential to heal some of the deep-est and most devastating wounds of our children and our society.

Mainstream opponents of neurofeedback, who are entrenched in the old medical paradigms or who are beholden to pharmaceutical firms for their research funding, state the wide ranging benefits we claim are anecdotal or temporary. This thinking is typical of those who are wedded to the use of drugs for the relief of symptoms. There is no drug that cures ADD—take away the stimulant medications and the symptoms are as predominant as ever.

While physicians were putting every disruptive child on stimulant medications, there were men and women who refused to settle for the notion that stimulants were the solution. Stimulants are what drug abusers refer to as "speed." For more than thirty years, practitioners of biofeedback have demonstrated that if you *feed back* appropriate information to the brain, the human being can change the functioning of any organ or system. Biofeedback is a treatment in which a person learns to reliably influence biological responses that are not ordinarily under voluntary control.

For example, a person attaches a thermometer to a fingertip, and by watching the temperature changes can learn mental techniques for voluntarily raising and lowering the temperature of the fingertip. In my (Robert Hill) practice, I have had eleven- and twelve-year-old boys who could consistently raise the temperature of a single finger to 103 to 104 degrees Fahrenheit. We have taught people with Raynaud's disease how to warm their cold hands with just the mind. We have taught patients with borderline hypertension to lower their blood pressure, thereby reducing the need for medications. We have taught people to use biofeedback to calm their anxiety or to relax or strengthen any muscle in the body. So, why not *retrain* the brain? Attention deficit disorder is a problem of brain function, so how do we train the brain to function properly?

When the notion of retraining the brain was first discussed, traditional physicians bristled. "You can't train the brain; we need a medication to speed it up or slow it down." Almost everything in medicine ultimately boils down to cutting something out or giving a pill—the cut-and-poison track. In contrast to this, there is a wonderful concept in complementary medicine: human potential. What are human beings ultimately capable of? Why can't humans learn to cure themselves by learning to unlock the secret of what is going on inside the body?

We can do this using biofeedback. We can feed back information to the thinking brain about inside-the-body events. The thinking brain can then learn to give subtle instructions to change these internal activities. As practitioners, we had been using biofeedback for years in traditional medicine, but you would have thought we were from another planet when we suggested you could do this with the brain, too.

The notion is simple. Just as your brain can learn to move your fingers across a piano or computer keyboard with ease, it can also learn to slow your pulse rate, lower your blood pressure, or have your immune system release more T-cells. We just have to let the thinking brain know how our internal organs or systems are responding to our subtle commands. This is not magic; it is a learning process. Biofeedback provides the brain with the information necessary to attain those skills.

Why can't humans learn to cure themselves by learning to unlock the secret of what is going on inside the body? We can do this using biofeedback. We can feed back information to the thinking brain about inside-the-body events. The thinking brain can then learn to give subtle instructions to change these internal activities.

Epilepsy was the key to understanding this feedback system. There are countless patients with epilepsy who are unresponsive to medication. They may have twenty, fifty, or even a hundred seizures a day, with medication offering no relief. For years, biofeedback therapists worked successfully with these uncontrollable cases of epilepsy. The therapist learned that by giving biofeedback information on a patient's electroencephalograph (EEG: a map of their brainwaves) back to the patient, he could actually change his brainwaves, thus reducing seizures.

Professor Joe Kamiya of the University of California at Berkeley got this approach started in the 1960s with his pioneering research in alpha brainwaves. Then, in the 1970s, Dr. Barry Sterman of the Sepulveda, California Veterans' Administration Medical Center Research Services did much of the early work on epilepsy. If you could change the brainwaves of a patient with epilepsy, then why not change the brainwaves of a person with attention deficit disorder?

This was the basic question asked by Dr. Joel Lubar, professor of psychology at the University of Tennessee. After all, there are similarities among the brainwave patterns in people with epilepsy and ADD. While Dr. Sterman worked tirelessly to help patients train their brains to be more resistant to seizures, in the mid-1970s Dr. Lubar and his wife, Judith, dedicated themselves to helping children train their brains to be more resistant to attentional lapses and hyperactive outbursts.

So much credit is due to pioneers like Joe Kamiya, Barry Sterman, and Joel and Judith Lubar. They had to stand up to tidal waves of professional neglect and peer ridicule. Yet, it is their work and courage that has inspired thousands of professionals to use neurofeedback in the treatment of ADD and many other disorders. Because of these pioneers, we are truly at a breakthrough point in human potential. Human beings have far more potential than traditional medicine has dared to consider.

Neurofeedback is perhaps the biggest breakthrough in noninvasive medicine in the last fifty years. It is a self-regulating process that offers the patient some control over his own recovery. Although patients are usually helped by such treatments as nutritional strategies, elimination of toxins, allergy treatments, homeopathy, and behavior modification, neurofeedback can stand alone as the safest and most effective treatment for ADD, aggressive and violent behavior, and addictions. Once brainwave patterns begin to normalize, all the symptoms in the cluster of problems begin to improve. When we treat a person for ADD, we find that attention, sleep disturbances, depression, nightmares, temper tantrums, tics, aggressiveness, anxiety, and a host of other symptoms improve.

Neurofeedback is the logical replacement for Ritalin because it works better, is safer, and addresses the core problem rather than treating a symptom.

Throughout this book, we have selected to use the term neurofeedback, but in the field of biofeedback, neurofeedback is used interchangeably with terms like EEG biofeedback, neurotherapy, and brainwave feedback.

We hope this book will acquaint you with the power and possibility of this exciting new treatment. We have also included other information that will help parents help their children to maximize their functioning and improve the quality of their lives. We have included chapters on nutrition, the effects of toxic substances, the influence of television on ADD-type behavior, the relationship of ADD to aggression and violence, how to deal with homework, and parenting strategies.

This book was put together from our clinical experience in treating hundreds of children and adults with ADD and the other difficult disorders that cluster around it. We hope our years of clinical findings help you to find answers for attentional and behavioral problems.

1

Attention Deficit Disorder (ADD): Defining What the Condition Is—and Isn't

Just like religion and politics, everybody has an opinion on Attention Deficit Disorder (ADD), from the woman who cares for the plants in our offices to the golfer at the country club. They tell you about their grandson or niece or neighbor who has ADD. Surprisingly, they can often recite a long list of symptoms. Recently, in a grocery store, we overheard two women discussing a grandchild with ADD. As one woman went into great detail about the child's behavior, she paused in mid-sentence to point out a child running by and casually inserted, "There goes one there." A week doesn't go by without a parent walking into our office with a child, announcing, "He has ADD." When we inquire who made the diagnosis, we get answers like "The teacher did," "Our minister," or "My mother saw it on TV."

Unfortunately these people are unhelpful diagnosticians, in that they frequently mislabel children, give erroneous advice, and form unwarranted opinions. With no disrespect to the teacher, minister, or talk show host, ADD is a complex disorder and cannot be diagnosed with casual observation or as a result of how annoying a child appears to be to an adult.

Even so, ADD is a topic of conversation at the dinner table, the bridge party, and with thousands of soccer moms. It is as though ADD is sweeping the country like a flu virus. The simple fact, however, is that ADD has been here forever. The human brain has always been vulnerable to injuries and disorders. However, we didn't start trying to label the symptoms we observed until the beginning of the twentieth century.

A typical scenario in our society is that Johnny is disruptive in class, so the teacher tells the parents, "He needs to be on Ritalin." The busy parents, both of whom work, take Johnny to the overworked pediatrician. They describe Johnny's disruptive behavior, poor attentional skills, and bad grades. Johnny is placed on Ritalin. Johnny's behavior changes enough to be noticed. The teacher is happy because Johnny is easier to handle in her overcrowded classroom. The parents have acted responsibly by getting their child the medical help needed. The pediatrician has offered Johnny the treatment most often prescribed for the presented symptoms.

We see this scenario over and over—children being prescribed Ritalin to treat *symptoms* while nothing is offered for the *cause*. But what about Johnny? Is he really ADD? Is he being helped by this treatment or have we just put a Band-Aid on a serious problem?

Far too often, the outcome of this scenario serves mostly the purposes of all the adults involved: the drug company makes money; the physician has prescribed the traditional treatment; the teacher has one less disruptive child to control; and the parents have done the responsible thing. What about the child? What about all of our children? Have we done the best we can for our children as their parents, teachers, or doctors? If there were a safer, more effective treatment, should we not incorporate it into our care of the children and adults with ADD?

The ADD Diagnosis

The diagnosis for ADD is made with the aid of a behavioral checklist. There is no blood test, imaging procedure (MRI or CAT scan), psychological test, or even an EEG (brainwave) test that can conclusively detect the brain injury of ADD. There are, however, two tests that are extremely helpful in the diagnostic process (see appendix C). Unfortunately, these tests are only commonly utilized by neurofeedback providers. So, at this point most clinicians still have to make the diagnosis on the basis of observable behaviors.

The layperson can certainly observe behaviors and recommend an evaluation. It is often the observations of parents and teachers that assist professionals in making the diagnosis. It is, however, the trained professional who can make the differential diagnosis between ADD and other disorders, distinguishing the symptom picture of ADD from other problems. The professional may determine if the observed behaviors are just a natural stage of development or a serious condition. It would be easy enough to label as ADD the manifestations of the "terrible twos" or an adolescent's first acting-out period, but that may not be ADD. There are normal stages of growth and many complex disorders that have similar symptoms to ADD. These disorders might include mild mental retardation, specific brain disorders, antisocial behavior, learning disorders, depression, anxiety, and others.

The "bible" of mental disorders is known as the *Diagnostic and Statistical Manual of Mental Disorders, Fourth Edition (DSM-IV)*.[1] This book is ostensibly the last word on what is and what is not a mental disorder. It lists ADD under "Disruptive Disorders," and clearly outlines the criteria for diagnosing ADD and ADD-type behaviors. However, by its very nature, *DSM-IV* does not cover all of the wide variations and presentations of this pervasive disorder. It does, of course, cover the more global aspects and the symptom highlights, including the most commonly observed behaviors.

The *DSM-IV* describes the essential features of ADD as "a persistent pattern of inattention and/or hyperactivity/impulsivity." The criteria listing includes the following:

- Fails to give close attention to details or makes careless errors

- Has difficulty sustaining attention

- Not listening when spoken to

- Not following through on tasks

- Organizational problems

- Avoiding tasks that require sustained attention

- Often loses things

- Easily distracted

- Forgetful

The category of hyperactivity includes the following common behavior characteristics:

- Often fidgets or squirms

- Often leaves one's seat

- Often runs or climbs excessively

- Often has difficulty playing

- On the go

- Talks excessively

The category of impulsivity includes the following:

- Often blurts out answers

- Has difficulty waiting one's turn

- Often interrupts or intrudes on others

The *DSM-IV* is critical to the diagnosis of ADD. It sets the standard measurement used by mental health professionals for diagnosing disorders. However, it does not expand on the wide variety of manifestations this complex disorder can take. ADD is more than just a list of symptoms from three categories to be checked off. ADD is a pervasive disorder that can present in dozens of different ways. One case can present so differently from another that you would not consider them the same disorder. So, in an effort to demonstrate this variety of manifestations, we will discuss some of the cases we have seen in our office in general terms. This should provide a clearer picture of how this disorder affects the day-to-day lives of people with ADD.

The Ups and Downs of ADD

Sporadic performance is common in ADD. The child may make 95 on one test and 45 on another, even though the parents knew the child prepared for both tests. It is as if his brain goes on vacation for the second test. Parents and professionals alike are often misled when the child can sit for hours playing video games. So they label the lapses during the tests as lazy or stupid behavior. But there are two things at work when the child (or adult) is engaged in something like TV or video games.

First, the game is in constant motion, which holds their attention, and secondly, these children have a quality of perseverance. Once they lock onto something like a video game, they have trouble turning themselves loose; they are unable to shift focus from one task to another.

On the other hand, they have much more trouble focusing on the teacher trying to give a lecture on pronouns. Teachers in today's classrooms have a hard time competing with the high-tech video world, particularly if the child is ADD. Pronouns or dates in history do not have the same high-attentional attraction as a video game or high-action movie.

Not all ADD children are bouncing off the walls. Some children quietly slip away into daydreaming and seldom cause trouble in school. They are often a great worry to parents who notice their detachment and aloneness. Such children are seldom labeled ADD, and they are never labeled hyperactive. A large number of these children are female, and they are often labeled lazy, depressed, dreamy, or unusual. The fact is, these children *are* ADD, but without the hyperactive component.

ADD children without hyperactivity never seem to make good contact with what is going on around them. They are very internal, quiet, and distant. They often miss social cues and are usually passed over for extra help or any other type of assistance.

They fall through the cracks and may only be diagnosed as ADD when brought in for treatment. Perhaps these are the saddest cases of all because they do not get recognized, diagnosed, or treated as often as the hyperactive children. They just get negative labels by peers, family, and school officials. Depression is common in these children, and the depression usually has to be addressed before addressing the ADD symptoms.

ADD: Over-stimulation and Overload

A normally functioning brain selects what to pay attention to and it takes an event of a certain magnitude to get it to change focus. If a non-ADD person is in the restaurant and a door slams, they may be slightly distracted but they do not necessarily lose their focus. The person with ADD can lose focus with the slightest distraction. For example, if someone wipes his mouth with a napkin, the person with ADD may completely lose the focus of what he is doing. People with ADD are often in sensory overload. It is hard to carry on a conversation with them. They keep breaking eye contact to follow other activity in the area. They laugh at what someone did across the room. They will often rejoin a conversation with inappropriate input. They may respond to something that was said by someone else five minutes ago, while they were off in their own world for a few minutes.

ADD has many components, and they vary in degree and intensity. Frequently, two different cases may not even look like the same disorder, when in fact they are just different manifestations of behaviors. The diagnosis must therefore include a wide-range checklist including symptoms from a variety of categories.

Several years ago we developed a behavioral checklist that includes behaviors from twelve different categories. These categories are: attention deficit, hyperactivity, impulsivity, immaturity, oppositional behavior, aggressive/sadistic behavior, tic disorders, depression, anxiety, low self-esteem, sleep disorder, and developmental and learning disorders. Our checklist can be found in appendix C.

We feel that ADD includes all of the above areas and perhaps more. For example, it is common for a child or an adult with ADD to have depression. Considering the trouble they have

learning and achieving, it's no wonder. In the case of oppositional and/or aggressive behavior, this can be a result of not
understanding the rules, missing social cues, or not caring about
the rules. When a child or an adult has this type of brain
injury/dysfunction, they may be unable to inhibit inappropriate
behavior. They talk when they should be quiet; they run when
they should sit; they cry when they should smile. They are angry
when they should laugh. They are oppositional when they
should comply. They are aggressive when they should be calm.
They are awake when they should sleep, and they are gazing out
the window when they should be looking at the blackboard.

Age of Onset: Early or Late

The *DSM-IV* diagnostic definition requires that some attentional or behavioral problem be present before the age of seven,
but it is easy to miss the cues. This is a disorder that may manifest in utero or may not be recognized until college. Children
with excessive hyperactivity frequently let their mothers know
they are ADD before they are born: they kick, squirm, and wig-
gle constantly in the womb. As one mother said, "He never let
me have a minute's peace from the time I conceived him until
today. When he was born he hit the ground running and hasn't
stopped since." Incidentally, she was right. Our office staff was
exhausted trying to keep up with this athletic nine-year-old. He
tumbled, flipped, jumped, and climbed from the time he arrived
until he left.

On the other hand, we frequently see the beginning college
student who "never had any problems until now." John was a
nineteen-year-old college freshman who had made average
grades in high school. He did okay until the work level exceeded
his persistence and dedication. Then John fell behind quickly.
His self-esteem dropped like a rock and he lost his motivation.
He had trouble focusing and remembering material he had
studied.

Like John, people with ADD are often bright and they often
compensate for attention problems with hard work, good study
habits, and persistence. But as the material gets harder and
harder, their compensation strategies begin to fail them. They

come into our office defeated and lost. Their families are in shock because, "He did well in high school," but the material finally got too hard and there was too much of it.

So, there are people with ADD who aren't identified until much later in life. One parent recently told us, "Now I realize I was ADD. I just thought I wasn't very smart." She was greatly relieved with her son's diagnosis and to be able to label her own childhood problems. We were able to successfully treat both child and mother, although it took much longer to treat the mother because her patterns of inattention were more ingrained.

ADD Affects More Boys than Girls

It is generally accepted that there is a much greater incidence of ADD in boys than in girls. The *DSM-IV* states that the ratio of males to females ranges from four to one to nine to one. We contend this is an incorrect notion and may reflect a misunderstanding of the disorder.

We agree that males have a higher incidence of hyperactivity, impulsivity, and oppositional and aggressive behavior, but when it comes to attentional problems, the ratio may favor girls. They sit quietly gazing out the window while the teacher lectures. A girl like this is labeled disinterested, stupid, or indifferent. She may never be given a diagnosis of ADD; she may never even come to the attention of a health-care professional. Yet everyone labels the "wild child" on the other side of the classroom ADD.

Incidentally "he"—the hyperactive boy—gets all the attention while "she" is often ignored. The quiet, *hypo*active child gets little, if any, attention, while the *hyper*active, impulsive ones get everyone's. We need to rethink this notion of ratios. We need to look more closely, and with fresh eyes, at the dull, bored, sleepy, disinterested child. That glazed-over look in her eyes may be as telling as the non-stop hyperactivity of another child.

The Problem Is Arousal, Not Attention

Let us first look at the underlying physiological problem of ADD. The bulk of scientific evidence accumulated since the

1940s indicates that the central feature of ADD is poor regulation of the brain's arousal state.

The most convincing argument to explain the role of arousal (how sleepy or awake the brain is) in hyperkinetic (hyperactive) syndrome came from two articles in the early 1970s—one by Satterfield and Dawson, and the other by Satterfield, Lasser, Saul, and Cantwell.[2,3] Satterfield and his colleagues proposed that hyperactive children had low states of arousal, that they habituated to sensory stimulation, and that they constantly sought new stimulation. By the late 1970s and early 1980s, this theory, known as the "Low-Arousal Hypothesis," was generally accepted in the medical community, and it remains so today. This is why a stimulant such as Ritalin has an effect on hyperactive children. It *speeds up* their low level of arousal. It appears to be a paradoxical effect: a hyperactive child is given a stimulant. But actually, the stimulant medication is used to wake up the sleepy brain.

The bulk of scientific evidence accumulated since the 1940s indicates that the central feature of ADD is poor regulation of the brain's arousal state. This is why a stimulant such as Ritalin has an effect on hyperactive children. It speeds up *their low level of arousal. The stimulant medication is used to wake up the sleepy brain.*

The brain can be either over-aroused (speeded up) or under-aroused (slowed down), and in either case it will not function the way it is designed to. If the brain is in over-arousal, we may be jumpy, hyper or anxious, looking at too much, trying to take too much in, paying attention to everything at once, nervous or upset. If, on the other hand, the brain is in under-arousal, we may appear sleepy, lethargic or disinterested, not taking in what's happening, not caring about what's going on around us. The hyperactivity can be an unconscious, automatic behavior to wake up the brain. The alert professional looks for ADD sufferers with characteristics from *both* categories. All cases do not look alike, but they all have problems with brain arousal states.

A way of conceptualizing brain arousal is to think of the intensity of light in a room. If a dimmer switch controls that light level, we can have every level of light from complete darkness to brilliant light. The "dimmer switch" of arousal in the brain is located in a part of the brain known as the thalamus. Like a dimmer switch that adjusts light levels in a room, the thalamus automatically adjusts the intensity of arousal for the task at hand.

For a restful sleep, the intensity is turned all the way down; for reading difficult material, it is turned to a more brilliant level. Most activities fall somewhere between sleep and intense thinking. This is done automatically, but in the case of many disorders, particularly ADD, the light (arousal level) usually stays adjusted to dim. Individuals with ADD are found to have inappropriately low physiological arousal. The set point for the dimmer switch (as in a thermostat) is set too low and does not automatically make the necessary adjustments. In disorders of low arousal, the individual is often so slowed-down he sits and stares, unable to focus or think clearly. Sometimes, however, he becomes hyper, trying to turn the arousal level up. This is an effort on the part of the brain to wake up or compensate for low arousal. As you can see, this can account for both the hyperactive person as well as the hypoactive (slowed down) person.

The chronic low-arousal state in ADD is like someone trying to work in a dimly lit room. It is hard to concentrate, stay on task, and complete the job. It is easy to become discouraged, frustrated, bored, and depressed. The chronically under-aroused brain may seek stimulation. Stimulation seekers are frequently hyperactive; there is often a lot of purposeless movement and out-of-control behavior. Frequently, the stimulation seeker acts externally with the larger world, demonstrating risk-taking and thrill-seeking behavior. Drugs and alcohol may play a major role in the life of the ADD risk-taker. Frequently, the professional treating ADD is dealing with many and varying symptoms at one time.

Thus, ADD and its concomitant behaviors often present the therapist with very complex problems. We frequently see ADD patients who are kicked out of school, in trouble with the law, angry, depressed, and using drugs and alcohol. Fortunately, neurofeedback can deal with all of these issues with remarkable speed and success because all of these problems relate to arousal levels of the brain.

If you would like a glimpse of what it is like to have ADD, just imagine someone walking into your room in the middle of the night, waking you from a sound sleep, and asking you to balance your checkbook. It is not that you do not have the intellect to do the task; you have the wrong level of arousal. Imagine the different emotional and behavioral reactions one might get from you in that situation. You are likely to be irritable, inattentive, disinterested, and stubborn. You could even be hostile and aggressive. This is how an ADD child feels when tasked with something requiring a higher state of brain arousal.

Most of us have experienced driving long distances at night while fighting off sleep. Look at what we do: We become hyperactive. We turn the radio up loud, sing, tap out the rhythm on the dashboard, talk to ourselves, bounce around, open the window, yell. That is exactly what the hyperactive individual is doing: fighting low arousal, trying to stay in the world, trying to wake up. There is nothing that wakes up the brain like risk-taking. This is a good hypothesis for explaining some criminal behavior. Committing a crime or being physically aggressive arouses the low level of functioning. The excitement wakes the person up, lets them know they are alive. The same is true of violent programs on TV and in movies or video games with high action and violent combat.

The Relationship between Arousal and Attention

Arousal and attention have a unique relationship. They are not the same but they are dependent on each other. Arousal is the level of intensity, how bright or dim the light is, whereas attention is how focused the light is. Compare an ordinary hundred-watt bulb to a hundred-watt spotlight. The ordinary light bulb illuminates the field around it, whereas the spotlight illuminates a specific spot on the field.

We can be very aroused but not focused on anything specific. Anxiety patients are a classic example, and so is the overaroused, bouncing-off-the-wall child. They are in a state of overarousal; they may be focused on everything. So, everything captures their attention, often moving quickly from one thing to another and back. Even with a very high level of arousal they cannot clearly attend or learn or have a sense of control. It takes focus to do that.

Focus is the "spotlight" that allows us the ability to pick out one object, task, or thought and work on it to the exclusion of other things. This is attention. People with ADD not only lack an adequate level of arousal but they often cannot focus on one specific task. This in part is arousal seeking, moving from thing to thing to stay aroused.

Try to do homework with the ADD child. They bounce from topic to topic, look at everything, find any excuse not to focus on the homework. For most of them it is painful to sit still, pay attention, and focus. Not only is it painful, it is exhausting. To get a sense of what their brain is experiencing, turn on every TV and radio in the house. Then have every family member talk to you at the same time. You will pay attention to everything and nothing at the same time. You cannot focus with all of this stimulation coming in. It is overload.

For many of these children it is not that they cannot pay attention—they are paying attention to everything at once. Therefore, nothing gets done, nothing gets absorbed, and nothing gets learned. It is just motion with no purpose. The level of arousal must be high enough to allow the brain to focus; if not, attention will be inadequate.

Arousal is the basic problem with ADD, but attention may play a major role in the person's dysfunction. If a child cannot attend, boredom is a chief complaint. Remember, boredom is always a result of inattention. An individual with good attentional skills can spend a long time examining a leaf; someone with poor attentional skills might not even notice the leaf.

Parents are often perplexed to see their attention-deficit child spend hours engrossed in cartoons or video games. Even uninformed professionals may say a child who can sit quietly for an hour watching TV or playing video games does not have ADD. Unfortunately, that is not the case. Children with ADD can spend hours playing a video game because the scene is changing, moving, bouncing, hopping, beeping, banging, hitting, and kicking. There is a constant stream of changing stimulation. Unlike the poor teacher who just has chalk and a blackboard, the video game or cartoon has kung fu, bombs, kicks, and blasts. The stimulation-starved, thrill-seeking child with ADD must have that rapidly moving, ever-changing stimulation to stay in the world.

Teachers, parents, and society in general cannot compete with the chaotic movement of video games. Yet, video games tend to drive the brain deeper into low arousal. Once the brain learns how to accommodate or deal with the video game, learning stops and the brain relaxes into "coast" mode. In a sense, it goes in neutral, requiring a very small part of the brain to be used on the game. Manual skills and physical quickness may improve because of practice, but the brain is lulled into inactivity.

The Different Faces of ADD Behavior

As you can see, ADD can present in many different ways even though the primary problem is inadequate arousal level. Because ADD looks different from one person to the next, some people do not think ADD is a real disorder. Others see it only as a disorder of hyperactivity. But ADD is a disorder, a real and often devastating disorder, and one that may present very differently from child to child, adult to adult.

When ten-year-old Gerald was brought to our office, everyone, including teachers, parents, doctors, and family friends had labeled him ADD. He was a classic case of Attention Deficit Disorder with hyperactivity and clearly met all of the diagnostic criteria of *DMS-IV*. He was hyper, inattentive, and impulsive. He had poor school performance and poor behavioral control in public. It was very difficult to begin the neurofeedback training with Gerald because he could not sit still long enough to train.

Neurofeedback requires being hooked up to a computer with sensor wires. After five or six minutes of training, he wanted to play with the sensor lead wires, sing, and ask dozens of questions, particularly, "Are we through yet?" So, we began by giving Gerald short sessions, limiting them to about ten minutes each. As his brainwaves began to improve, we were able to lengthen the sessions to twenty minutes, and eventually to thirty minutes. Gerald made an excellent recovery, but it took several months and approximately sixty neurofeedback sessions.

Gerald was an easy diagnosis compared to Karl, a fourteen-year-old truant. He was in trouble with school officials for fighting, had had a brush with the law for petty vandalism, and was a chronic marijuana smoker. He was the classic skinny little tough guy, yet no one considered him ADD. As it turns out, he used this tough, devil-may-care facade to cover his inability to focus and learn his schoolwork. Once during a training session this young Mr. Tough Guy looked up and said pitifully, "I hope this stuff can help me. I don't want to be a dumb shit." Karl's treatment was successful, and as his grades improved, so did his school attendance. He became much nicer to be around. He even developed friendships with peers that he had once tormented and terrified.

Neurofeedback training is a treatment where the patient's scalp is connected to a computer by sensor wires. The computer system amplifies and reads brainwave signals and a computer monitor feeds back information about how well the brainwaves are functioning. By watching the information on the monitor, the person is able to learn to change their brainwaves, thereby improving the level of arousal and reducing the ADD symptoms. Gerald and Karl, as well as most people we see, did very well with the training. Their ADD symptoms were dramatically reduced, their grades went up, and their social behavior improved.

Linda was the stereotype of the ADD child with hypoactivity. She sat in class daydreaming and doodled on her notebook paper. She would draw little cartoon characters and have them say funny things. Some cartoons were very clever, but the notepaper was devoid of classroom notes. Linda was sweet, polite, and pretty; she was also failing every class. Her parents declared she was smart but lazy. After evaluating her and discovering she was ADD, I began her on neurofeedback training. Linda and her parents were very cooperative and her grades soon began to improve. Linda may never be at the top of her class, but she is capable of doing college-level work. It would not surprise us if one day Linda ended up with a syndicated cartoon strip and made millions, all from those endless hours of doodling, which she now does after class.

These are three examples of how ADD presents with uniquely different behaviors in a given child. Although different, each behavior is caused by the same type of brain dysregulation. By the way, not every case that presents with symptoms like these three examples is ADD. There are many other disorders that must be ruled out before an ADD diagnosis can be made and training started. Disorders such as mental retardation, depression, anxiety, under- or over-stimulation in the environment, conduct disorders, grief, or anger should be considered before any treatment begins.

Some of these disorders are caused by an under- or over-arousal, but the treatment protocol/regime may be completely different from that of ADD. So we need to know what we are treating before we start. We frequently find we are not dealing with one problem alone, but two or more problems combined. This may necessitate a sequence of protocols to deal with the complexity of problems.

Refining the Distinctions: All Is Not ADD

Not everything that looks like ADD is ADD. Normal children and adults can have behavioral characteristics that can resemble ADD. We can all have bad days or even bad weeks. In our offices, if we juice up on a lot of coffee, our staff threatens to treat us for ADD. Frequently, we will get on a new project and our enthusiasm and behavior resembles an excited twelve-year-old child with ADD, but we are usually able to complete the project.

Linda Budd, Ph.D., a psychologist in St. Paul, Minnesota, has labeled many of these children as "Active Alert" children. Dr. Budd publishes an excellent newsletter called *The Active Alerter.*[4] She argues that many children who get labeled ADD are just Active Alert children, and we generally agree. We see many children who are vibrantly active and alert who are not ADD. We also contend that there are probably some children with ADD hiding out in her Active Alert group. However, we would like to see their brainwave patterns and see how they respond to neurofeedback before we totally agree with Dr. Budd's model.

We have on many occasions done a thorough evaluation of children who were labeled ADD and concluded that they were actually not ADD. Often we have recommended psychotherapy, family counseling, and even parent training to help these children.

There are many different problems that present to us as ADD, and these must be teased out before treatment begins. Due to all the attention on ADD, many individuals label normal childhood development stages as ADD. As Dr. Budd has pointed out, many bright, active children inappropriately get negative labels that can follow them for a long time.

Summary

This chapter may seem a bit confusing—we start off talking about adults, then we wander back to children, then adolescents, then back to adults again. Going from childhood to adulthood is a process on the same continuum. There are many adults who act like children and many children who act like adults. The best predictor of future behavior is past behavior, and since most children do not "grow out" of true ADD, behaviors we see in childhood are likely to be seen in some form when the person reaches adulthood.

The reason we have included discussion of adults with ADD is because this is not just a childhood problem. ADD is a pervasive disorder that starts in childhood, is carried through adolescence, and often becomes an adult disorder. By looking at how the disorder unfolds in individuals over decades, we get a broader picture of ADD. This helps us to realize that this is a much bigger problem than a child who cannot pay attention. It can, and usually does, grow into an adult who is likely to have failed marriages, poor job success, aggressive behavior, poor social skills, and problems with addictions. So, the next time you see or hear about someone with ADD, remember this is someone whose life is built on a telescoping history, levels and layers of similar behavior stacked up as the person advances in age.

2

Adults with ADD—The Problem Doesn't Automatically Go Away with Adulthood

Adults with ADD generally present with the same symptoms as children. However, the stakes tend to be higher and the ramifications of the problems are much broader. There is a long-held misconception, even among some professionals, that children will "grow out" of their ADD, thereby becoming "normal" adults.

In reality, ADD does not always go away as effortlessly as some predict. Long term follow-up studies on children with ADD have found that as many as 80 percent of children with ADD take their disorder into adulthood. Experts in the field indicate that 1 to 2 percent of the adult population, including men and women, have some degree of ADD.

This could mean as many as several million adults have the disorder. The hyperactivity component usually disappears, but the majority of

Long term follow-up studies on children with ADD have found that as many as 80 percent of children with ADD take their disorder into adulthood. Experts in the field indicate that 1 to 2 percent of the adult population, including men and women, have some degree of ADD. This could mean as many as several milliion adults have the disorder.

people with attentional difficulty take the problem into adulthood. This generally means we take the worst part of the disorder into the workday world, and unless someone is hyperactive, the problem may not be recognized.

The hyperactive child tends to be a problem for everyone around him, but the child may be having fun. They do not realize there is a problem; they are into everything, having a great time. The ADD component of the disorder is what causes the individual to have difficulty with academic success, job performance, and relationships. So, when it comes to something like schoolwork, the child begins to suffer. Their poor academic performance is usually followed by low self-esteem, loss of motivation, and even depression.

Since the adult usually continues to have the attentional problems rather than the hyperactivity, the ramifications are far-reaching. Low self-esteem, poor motivation, lack of follow-through, trouble sustaining attention, and depression become serious problems in adulthood. ADD interferes with every aspect of one's life. Let's look at how the adult with ADD may behave in the workday world.

I've Got a Great Idea!

Adults with ADD are often very bright and come up with great ideas. They tell us about these ideas and we often get excited for them. They take off like a whirlwind doing things, arranging things, setting things up. For those of us who love them, we feel they have finally found themselves. They're finally on track. They initially have boundless energy and cannot be stopped even by the most discouraging news. When they are in this phase it is impressive, but then, as the project progresses, these individuals go flat as a pancake. The work stops, the idea doesn't seem so good, and their failure is usually perceived by them as somebody else's fault.

Once again family and friends shake their heads in frustration. Adults with ADD are usually good "idea people" but need to have the backup of steady workers. They are good for short projects that do not require much follow through.

In the office we frequently put a stopwatch on children and monitor how long they can look at a TV monitor or carry on a conversation before they break away. Surprisingly, there are consistent patterns within the individual. Some children can hold on for twenty or thirty seconds, but many of them are in the five- to fifteen-second range. Adults with ADD are generally able to lengthen this time as a result of work experience, but they cannot always see projects through without a lot of help, encouragement, and supervision. Just like the children, they lose concentration and focus.

John was a thirty-nine-year-old independent contractor who built small single-family houses. He came to us because of a long history of ADD that he readily acknowledged was a condition which kept him from being more successful. He reported that he was sure his father was ADD and perhaps one of his brothers. He wanted help. He came to us because we had treated a neighbor's child and he was impressed with the changes he saw. "Can you help a grown man?" he asked.

We told him that although there were no guarantees, we thought we could. We then discussed the treatment plan and the probable outcome. He knew it would take longer for an adult to change, but he was willing to commit to the treatment plan.

The typical number of treatments for a child is thirty to forty. That translates to $1500 to $2000 for the total treatment at our office. John had almost fifty treatments before he began to report changes. First his depression lifted and he began to feel better about himself. Finally, after 65 neurofeedback sessions, he reported he was "catching up" in his work. He was no longer leaving jobs before he was finished, or starting new jobs that would go unfinished. He was finally able to stay with a job until it was completed. He said that before treatment, he would get "antsy" on a job and have to start something new. Although John ended up taking eighty sessions, he reported it was well worth the time and money it cost him. John spent nearly $4000 on treatment, but it was successful when everything else had failed. John said, "It was worth the money just to get rid of the depression." That was several years ago, and John still reports no depression and better job efficiency.

There Goes Another Job

People with ADD can be great workers but they usually lack staying power. They often change jobs because they see a new opportunity around every corner. Of course, new jobs do not always pan out the way they planned. The person with ADD has selective hearing: they may hear the part that says, "You can make more money," but miss the part that says "longer hours." If they have personality or character problems along with the ADD, then it is always somebody else's fault. "He did me wrong," "They lied to me," or "I intimidated them with my abilities."

After they are hired, things go wrong. They make lots of mistakes that "weren't my fault," and they are likely to say something like "the part you bought doesn't fit," or "the paint wasn't put on correctly" (as in the case of one ADD adult painter). There is no way to estimate the amount of money that is lost in the economy each year due to mistakes and inefficiency caused by ADD. There are people with ADD who are able to compensate well for it and be very productive, but many cannot, and struggle on a daily basis. They struggle with inattentiveness, easy distraction, excitability, poor focus, disorganization, and difficulty completing tasks.

Studies indicate that adults with ADD are less likely to fulfill work demands, work independently, and get along well with employers and supervisors. They are more likely to perceive the job as more difficult than non-ADD adults, so they quit their jobs more frequently. They are also fired more frequently. This correlates with early antisocial behavior. They tend to be more explosive and more difficult to deal with.[1]

Perhaps one day some forward-thinking company will address this type of inefficiency and neurofeedback training will be available to every employee. In the future it could be possible that we could have "peak-efficiency" industries without poor performers or alcoholics, and "peak-efficiency" sports teams where the players aren't in court or jail for off-the-field ADD behavior. People with ADD are like radio receivers with all the channels open. They hear and see *everything,* paying attention to all the stimuli in their environment. Athletics is often the perfect outlet for aggressive, hyperactive, risk-taking behavior. But off the field it is a different matter.

People with ADD frequently will leave a job when they feel the pressure to perform at a certain level at which they are unable to. These individuals are usually bright but at some level feel they don't match up. They say, "I'll look for another job." The adult work world becomes as frustrating as schoolwork was as a child—they may work hard, but the effort does not seem to pay off. For the spouse and family, it's one excuse after another, one disappointment after another. It is not easy for the person with ADD or the family living with that person, as the following example shows.

Philip came in to see us because his wife was leaving him. He reported depression, anxiety, and anger toward his wife. When we asked why his wife was leaving him, he had "no idea." "I guess she just doesn't love me," he said. Further questioning revealed Philip had had eight jobs in ten years. The family had moved three times in the ten years, and there was one period of eight months in which he had no job. Philip disclosed that he had hated school and that his grades had been "average." His wife later reported to us that he had had great difficulty in school. She also disclosed that she felt she could never depend on him, that she lived in constant fear of his being out of work again.

After a thorough evaluation, Philip was diagnosed with adult ADD. His treatment consisted of not only neurofeedback, but marriage therapy.

Don't Stand Up and Give a Talk

Adults with ADD are too easily distracted to give good talks. They are bright, enthusiastic, and witty, but they ramble. It is impossible for them to stay on track. If someone does something distracting, they are lost. For example, if asked a question, their answer is likely to go off in an unrelated direction, and they may or may not get back to their original topic.

Recently we attended a conference on healing. At one point a physician (who we are convinced has ADD) stood up to make a quick comment. He went on for ten minutes. The speaker tried politely to end the filibuster, but was unsuccessful. The audience became so impatient there was a mass cry for him to shut up and sit down. He missed those cues just as he had probably missed most social cues in his life.

Yes, there are ADD physicians. There are ADD engineers, dentists, therapists, and, frightfully, there are probably ADD airline pilots. Many people are able to compensate quite well by dogged determination. They become single-minded and hyper-focused, much like the child with ADD who plays video games. When the game starts they go into hyper-focus and it is hard to get their attention. You may ask them over and over to stop and do something else, but they will never hear you.

ADD in a Marriage—Problems in Organization

Adults with ADD have many more divorces than those without ADD. They go into marriage with the same zeal with which they come up with ideas. "This is perfect," or "This is what I've been waiting for" and then, "I can't understand why she wants a divorce."

ADD individuals bring the same disorganized qualities to a marriage that they take to work. They forget birthdays, don't remember anniversaries, or can't understand why their mate is upset. They are baffled at why their partners are not excited about their new jobs. They never seem to clean up their messes; they leave their clothes, shoes, cups, and golf clubs all over the house. A simple project takes forever and may never get completed. They never have the tool they need because they can't find it or it is in the other room, left there from the last project. Often, if they can't find the tool, somebody else lost it, misplaced it, or it was stolen.

Over time, the symptoms of ADD may cause a person to become quiet, withdrawn, depressed, and exhibit a beaten-down kind of personality. But they still continue to be inefficient, forgetful, and easily distracted; perhaps they have trouble mowing the grass or cleaning the house. Many adults with ADD qualities feel abused by the world and that functioning normally requires more energy than they can muster. Consider the following case:

Because we have a general practice, people frequently do not come in for neurofeedback, even though their problem indicates that neurofeedback would be the most effective treatment. Ann and Tom came in for marital therapy at Tom's insistence. He was ready to leave Ann if things did not change. Tom reported Ann was smart, loving, and pretty, "But she is a mess.

The house is always in a state of half cleaned; the laundry is always half done; dinner is always half fixed—*everything* is 'half.'" Ann could never finish anything she started; she was disorganized, bored, and unfocused.

For her part, Ann reported she had been this way as long as she could remember. "Tom thought it was cute at first, but over time he has become angry about it," she said. After the initial intake evaluation, Ann was diagnosed with adult ADD. Treatment in this case included neurofeedback and marital therapy. Neurofeedback could remedy the ADD, depression, and motivation problems, but it could not teach Tom and Ann how to communicate clearly with each other. As Ann's symptoms declined, the marriage became more fulfilling for both of them.

ADD and Driving—A Dangerous Mix

ADD people are individuals who can't see consequences. They have five times more auto accidents than people without ADD. Adults send adolescent drivers out at night with no medication because if they get the medication they can't sleep. So, a 3,500-pound automobile that will travel at speeds greater than a hundred miles per hour is in the hands of someone whose attention is poor. We believe no child or adult with ADD should ever have a driver's license without neurofeedback treatment.

If people are aware they are ADD, they may exercise more caution and be very careful, methodical drivers to compensate for their inattention. Others do not compensate or even realize their driving style is risk-taking. Many people who have ADD are often too distracted to know it, but they may be a driving nightmare for everyone else on the road. People with ADD are significantly more likely to have automobile accidents than people without it because people with ADD have trouble controlling their angry impulses. ADD likely plays a major role in what is now labeled "Road Rage." Individuals with ADD have less impulse control, so if they experience a sudden burst of anger, they are likely to act on that angry impulse rather than control it.

To give a person with ADD a driver's license is to put someone behind the wheel of a vehicle who, in varying degrees, may be disorganized, unfocused, forgetful, highly distractible, and possibly irritable. They have a low frustration tolerance and they may be hyperactive. They want to go quickly, do a lot, bounce from place to place, and they resent anyone slowing them down. These same symptoms apply to both teenagers and adults, and are likely to lead to problems behind the wheel, such as accidents, tickets, and road rage.

We have had countless conversations with parents of ADD teenagers about driver's licenses. ADD teenagers, like most other teens, want their driver's permits as soon as possible. They also like other motorized vehicles such as four-wheelers and motorcycles. Our advice is always treatment first, then when the behavior improves, get a driver's license. When it comes to four-wheelers and motorcycles, we never encourage use of these because of the high injury rates associated with them. When a parent disregards our advice on getting a driver's license for a teenager with ADD, we then recommend long periods of supervised driving, always accompanied by a parent.

It is even more important for the adolescent with ADD to establish good driving habits early. When the adolescent with ADD does start driving on his own, there need to be strictly enforced rules, such as no driving after dark and only one other adolescent in the car at one time. We have seen a disproportionate number of accidents and injuries, even deaths, from drivers with ADD. So we recommend a very cautious path.

Julie wanted her driver's license as badly as any other adolescent. She lobbied, pleaded, and negotiated from the time she turned fourteen. She had been diagnosed with ADD when she was in the fourth grade, and in spite of four years of medication, there was little change in her behavior. Julie's mother brought her in when she was fifteen because of poor high school grades. Her parents were afraid she would eventually quit school. Then the question came up about her driver's license.

We recommended treatment first, then getting the license. Her parents gave in to her constant pleading, and she got her learner's permit in a few weeks. On Julie's first drive she had a single-car accident. The car was a wreck, but fortunately Julie and her mother were not hurt. Julie came back to treatment with her confidence shaken. We were able to make more progress *after* the accident than we did before, and were glad the situation had not been much worse, as it could easily have been.

ADD Among the Jailed

Although this statement will probably invite challenge, we strongly contend that our jails, prisons, and juvenile detention centers are full of ADD adolescents and adults. After all, we are talking about risk-takers: individuals who have no fear but who cannot foresee consequences. It is easy to see that there is a recipe for disaster in that cluster of behaviors. The child who is prone to get in trouble and prone to accidents because of taking risks is now a late adolescent or adult who takes a different risk. The adult risks are bigger and the consequences greater.

There are not as many good follow-up studies as we would like to see, but the ones that are available are consistent in their findings. Brown and Borden did a study in 1986 which indicated that between 22 and 30 percent of hyperactive people engage in antisocial behavior.[1] That could mean five or six million, or even more, adolescents acting out in antisocial ways, and the best prediction for future behavior is past behavior. Gittelman and colleagues found that antisocial behavior may be present in 20 to 45 percent of ADHD (attention deficit/hyperactivity disorder, ADD with hyperactivity)[2] children by the time they reach adulthood. That study indicates that as many as 25 percent of adults with ADD or ADHD would meet the criteria for a psychiatric diagnosis of antisocial personality disorder. The *DSM-IV* states "the essential feature of Antisocial Personality Disorder is a pervasive pattern of disregard for, and violation of, the rights of others that begins in childhood or early adolescence and continues into adulthood." Behaviors of this disorder include lying, stealing, impulsivity, aggression, recklessness, and lack of remorse.

Weiss and Hechtman conducted a three-year study which looked at adults who had been diagnosed ADHD in childhood.[3] They found that those adults had much more likelihood of having trouble with the law and ending up in court. Approximately 20 percent of these adults committed physical acts of aggression.

No single childhood factor could be pinpointed as the predictor of adult criminal activity. Several factors played a role, but the chief factor to be considered was the diagnosis of ADD. Other factors included childhood aggression, intelligence, hyperactivity, conditions in the home, and parenting. We have a situation where not only genetics, but environmental factors and physical injury play a role in development.

Weiss and Hechtman conducted a three-year study which looked at adults who had been diagnosed ADHD in childhood. They found that those adults had much more likelihood of having trouble with the law and ending up in court. Approximately 20 percent of these adults committed physical acts of aggression.

Interestingly, the reason that many felons are behind bars is because they have ADD-type behavior, and it is often the ADD qualities that get them caught. They are forgetful, they are disorganized, and they can't pay attention. They leave behind clues, forget what they said before, and in general give themselves away. Sometimes there are police officers with ADD looking for lawbreakers with ADD; in fact, there are individuals with ADD in every profession. We contend that this undiagnosed, untreated population costs society a lot of money, to say nothing of the problems they cause and the pain they experience.

The Link between ADD and Drugs and Alcohol

Alcohol, drugs, and ADD are frequent companions. Virtually every study we have seen supports this conclusion, and it certainly holds up in our clinical practice. Using alcohol and drugs is an "easy" way to cope with difficult situations. As one of our twenty-year-old patients put it, "If you are numb, failure ain't so painful." Alcohol and drugs slow down the racing mind and provide a sense of calm.

More children with ADD develop problems with alcohol and drugs than do children without ADD.[4] This carries over into adulthood, as most late-adolescent substance abusers become adult substance abusers. Retrospective views of the problem reveal that alcoholics frequently have a history of childhood hyperactivity.[5]

Dale Walters, Ph.D., former director of training for the Menninger Clinic in Topeka, Kansas, traversed the U.S. during the 1990s teaching clinicians how to treat alcoholism and drug addiction with neurofeedback. He worked closely with Eugene Penniston, Ph.D., who developed a specialized treatment protocol for alcoholism. The treatment was later expanded to include drug addiction and to treat Vietnam veterans with post-traumatic stress. This treatment protocol has been shown to be the most promising treatment for alcoholism and drug addiction to date, with an astounding 20 percent relapse rate. Prior to this neurofeedback protocol, a 20 percent relapse rate was unheard of in the treatment of addictions.[6,7,8]

If you have a patient with alcoholism or drug addiction, it is a good practice to look for a history of ADD. If you have a patient with ADD, it is a good practice to teach coping skills that preclude the use of drugs and alcohol. Add alcohol or drugs to someone who is already impaired with ADD and there is potential for disaster. We seldom see an alcoholic who doesn't have a history of ADD. This, of course, increases the chances of auto crashes, failed jobs, failed marriages, and failed lives.

David Miller and Kenneth Blum, Ph.D., have done an outstanding job of looking at attention deficit disorder and the addictive brain in their classic book *Overload*.[9] We suggest this book go to the top of your reading list if there is any history of alcohol or ADD in your family.

It's Not Easy Being ADD

When we look at the personal lives of individuals with ADD, we often find them to be sad and frustrating. The child frequently has headaches, sleeps poorly, and generally doesn't feel good. These problems are dramatically worsened if the child is on the standard treatment—a prescription for stimulant medication.

The child and the adult miss many things. They do not pick up the normal social cues. For example, when we recently ushered a twenty-nine-year-old male into our office for an evaluation, he took the doctor's chair, never realizing the inappropriate nature of his behavior.

In sports, people with ADD can be both brilliant athletes and court jesters. They are fearless, and get into the thick of the fray with no hesitation; they often barrel over their teammates to get to the ball. If they are not knocking everybody down, interrupting the natural order of the game, or making a sensational play with pure ability, they are looking at flowers or some other distraction on the playing field, completely missing the game.

Frequently the only safe place for the ADD person is on the playing field. If they are able to combine all that hyperactivity with natural talent, they can become gifted athletes. Unfortunately, their lives off the field may be a mess. We have had college coaches tell us that three-fourths of their team members have ADD. The pro ranks are filled with adults with ADD.

Studies have estimated that 30 percent of people with ADD are depressed, 30 percent have an anxiety disorder, and 50 percent have conduct problems. This does not make for a happy life. Those with ADD usually receive a lot of criticism. It seems that someone is always critical of their behavior and performance. If it's not a parent, it's a teacher; if it's not a teacher, it's a sibling. They are even criticized by peers.

As a result, they either withdraw or develop a "stand-back-I'd-rather-do-it-myself" attitude, which of course generally gets them in more trouble. A great part of their conduct problem is the constant criticism which produces a lot of anger and hostility. They get tired of being seen as, or feeling like, "damaged goods," and they rebel. All of these problems, we emphasize, are a result of a dysregulated brain.

Correcting the Problem

Regulating the brain to a more functional pattern may not fix the individual stresses in one's life, but at least the brain can take a more active role in problem solving. Untreated, the individual may be driven ever deeper into nonfunctional and slow brainwave patterns.

Neurofeedback is a treatment that can normalize the dysfunctional or injured brain. For example, if the brain is too slowed down, causing a state of low arousal and ADD-type symptoms, neurofeedback can train the brain to speed up its activity level. This is done by feeding back information to the brain about how the brain is functioning, and rewarding the person with a sound or score for any improvement. Teaching appropriate behavior is called operant conditioning. With this simple operant conditioning procedure, the brain begins to regulate itself, and undesirable behaviors begin to modify. We will discuss this training procedure in detail in chapter 6.

3

What Causes ADD?

The big question haunting researchers and professionals who treat ADD is how does ADD start in the first place? There have been a number of theories and hypotheses over the years, but they generally explain only a part of the problem. The theories have ranged from the silly to the scientific, each having its basis in the assumptions of the observer. Let's explore some of the more popular theories.

Popular Theories of the Cause of ADD

The Bad Child: The earliest description that characterized ADD came at the turn of the twentieth century. In 1902, G.F. Still published an article in the British medical journal, *Lancet*.[1] He described in detail children who exhibited symptoms of ADD/ADHD and labeled them as having "abnormal defects in moral control . . . and wanton mischievousness and destructiveness." This was the notion of the "bad child," born "bad," and there was nothing you could do about it.

Even today, one hundred years later, there are still those who believe that some children are born with "deficits in moral control." The only factor that would offer even an element of credibility to this early theory is genetics. If this is the case, then the child is living out the genetic predisposition passed down to him. Regardless of genetics, a motto that every adult should consider is that if the child doesn't learn, then the adult has not taught. Adults cannot change the genetic code, but good teaching and good modeling can alter the course of most of these children.

Family Discord: A second theory that has a lot of support is the family discord concept. The theory suggests that a chaotic family life or marital discord in the family would cause the children affected by those stresses to become ADD.[2,3] In cases where the marital discord is affected by the psychiatric problems of one of the parents, the same would be true. Children need a stable environment, predictability, and an element of constancy. Families that have marital discord lose that sense of predictability, at least that sense of comfortable predictability. Often the children are left to parent themselves, and all too frequently, the parents are too busy taking care of themselves to take care of the children.

When the noise and chaos in a family reach a certain level, the child is likely to tune it out. They do this by slowing down their brain—the slowed brain is less alert to what is going on. It is slow brainwave rhythms that characterize ADD. When the brain slows down, it is less awake, less alert, and less aware. In our clinic, we have seen the same slow wave patterns in children who are yelled at constantly, and we have also seen this in verbally abused spouses. It is possible to conclude that anyone who lives in chaos and discord could suffer an emotional brain injury and would exhibit many classic ADD-type symptoms.

No ADD in the First Place: Perhaps the most interesting theory of all is the theory that proposes there is no such thing as ADD. Even today in our clinic, we have people to say, "There is nothing wrong with him; he just needs a good kick in the pants," or some other colorful phrase indicating there is no problem except not enough discipline. The idea that a child can be spanked out of this syndrome is not only offensive, but ludicrous.

In spite of articles like Schmitt's 1975 "The Minimal Brain Dysfunction Myth,"[4] ADD does exist. Schmitt and others propose that there is no such thing. He even went so far as to say it is a fabrication by distressed parents, teachers, and physicians to allow them to medicate disruptive children. We are the first to concede that thousands of children are needlessly medicated, but that does not mean that we are not dealing with a dysregulated brain. We agree that some children are actually medicated for the sake of adults, but ADD is not a myth conjured up by distraught teachers, parents, and physicians.

Poor Parenting: The theory that has the most popular support is that of poor parenting. It is difficult to discount the notion that poor parenting creates difficulties for children because, in fact, it does. Years of psychiatric and psychological work and countless research articles have been enough to convince us this is true. However, we do not believe parents are the root of all evil.

We have worked with ADD children who had great parents and others who had less-than-adequate parents. We are convinced that it is highly unlikely that poor parenting is the causative factor.

Now, before we go further, we would like to point out that ADD can become like a runaway train if parents are inadequate. Good parenting skills can dramatically alter the course of a child with ADD. This may be why ADD children can grow up, go to college, and lead normal, functional lives. Good parenting is able to set boundaries and teach children how to compensate; it can instill good values and model good behavior. In contrast, poor and neglectful parenting gives the ADD child a world with no boundaries in which risk taking escalates and respect is non-existent.

In general, poor parenting may lead to children who are uncontrollable, disrespectful, undisciplined, and neurotic. Their brain dysfunction may be a result of the way they interpret the world based on how it was presented to them by dysfunctional parents. However, they may not have the typical slow-wave brain patterns seen in ADD. Our conclusion is that poor parenting can dramatically affect the outcome of ADD children in a negative way, but it is highly unlikely to be the *cause* of ADD. On the other hand, children who are abused may in fact suffer the physical or emotional injury consistent with classic ADD-type behavior.

Environmental Influences: With a growing global awareness of how we are affected by toxins, synthetic substances, and pollutants in the environment comes the theory that ADD is caused by environmental factors. At this point in time, this theory cannot be completely ruled out or completely supported because nowhere near all the data is in. This is a theory that will be examined and reexamined for a very long time to come. New understanding in molecular biology, toxicology, and human sensitivities may lead to deeper insights into ADD as well as other problems.

However, to say with confidence that sugar, food additives, dyes, preservatives, and other such products do not cause ADD-type symptoms is not only scientific foolishness, but is ludicrous. We remember vividly an eight-year-old male who was very physically aggressive. During the intake interview, we noticed a constant runny nose. When we asked his mother about it, she reported that he always had a runny nose. We recommended no dairy of any kind for two weeks. The mother was very compliant, and she reported back to us that when he had no dairy, he had no runny nose, plus his aggression was dramatically improved. This is just one case in a complicated array of cases, but environmental agents can affect certain individuals.

We are just scratching the surface of how some individuals are affected by certain products. We are well aware of how humans and wildlife are affected by deadly toxins like lead, dioxin, and mercury, but we suspect that that is just the tip of the iceberg.

The notion of allergies and toxic reactions causing problems such as ADD got a big boost in the mid-1970s when Dr. Ben Feingold's book, *Why Your Child is Hyperactive,* was published.[5] Since that time, the Feingold Association has done much to promote the idea of feeding children pure foods. We are in sympathy with this cause. Even if red dye #3 or some other product does not cause ADD, it could be a contributing factor in some other diseases and disorders. Even if not causative, it could exacerbate ADD symptoms. The jury is still out on this connection, so in the meantime, we think it is best to keep our water, air, and food as pure as possible.

Theories of environmental causes for ADD are receiving increasing interest over time. Though no single factor has clearly been shown to cause ADD, ultimately some of the environmental factors may. Environmental theories include nutritional causes, toxic chemical exposure, TV, video games, video monitors, fluorescent lighting, chemical additives, and other environmental hazards. Even though we have no direct cause-and-effect relationships yet, we want to know as much as possible about the child's lifestyle, eating habits, and exposure to the aforementioned environmental factors.

Knowing about these factors may help to direct our treatment protocols and parental recommendations. We hope all parents and treating professionals will examine not only the child's eating habits but also such things as TV viewing and exposure to chemical additives and other environmental factors.

> *Theories of environmental causes for ADD are receiving increasing interest over time. We hope all parents and treating professionals will examine not only the child's eating habits but also such things as TV viewing and exposure to chemical additives and other environmental factors.*

Genetics: The idea that ADD is a genetic disorder is well grounded in the scientific literature. We in the mental health field have long accepted the notion that certain psychological problems such as alcoholism, depression, anxiety, and antisocial problems, seem to run in families. Beginning in the 1970s, research data began to support this observation.[6,7] What is clear though, is that the genetic relationship of ADD is not as strong as the genetic relationship of conduct disorders and antisocial behavior. When you have a person with ADD and conduct disorder, the genetic relationship appears to be a strong one.

In a study examining the parents of fifty-nine hyperactive children, James Marlson and Mark Stuart concluded that fathers of ADHD children had a greater incidence of antisocial personality disorder when compared to the control group; mothers had a greater incidence of histrionic personality disorder.[8] Histrionic personality disorder is characterized by excessive emotions and attention-seeking behavior. There was a much higher incidence of alcoholism for both parents. This study lends support not only to the genetics theory but also to the family discord and poor parenting theories.

Looking at brothers and sisters of ADD children, there are a number of studies that indicate that if one child is ADD, there is approximately a 30 percent chance that brothers and sisters will be ADD. Again, studies like those not only support the theory of genetic transmission, but they also leave open the question of learning behaviors. Did the child inherit the ADD or conduct disorder, or did the child *learn* the behaviors from watching the parents exhibit such behaviors?

The most convincing evidence for the genetic theory comes from a large study of twins. Goodman and Stevenson compared 127 monozygotic (identical) with 111 dizygotic (fraternal) pairs of twins.[9] They found 51 percent of the monozygotic twins to be hyperactive, compared with 33 percent of the dizygotic pairs.

We believe that genetics play a role in ADD. The susceptibility to acquiring brain dysfunction can get passed from generation to generation, but injuries can be sustained from growing up in a toxic family environment. In a disorder that is as disruptive and pervasive as ADD, all types of injury and dysfunction must be considered.

In more thoroughly examining the case for genetics in ADD, Dr. David Comings has written a classic work, *Tourette's Syndrome and Human Behavior*.[10] Dr. Comings has taken our understanding of the role of genetics in these disorders to new heights. This is a complex text but is well worth reading, particularly for health professionals. Dr. Comings clearly outlines the role of genetics in ADD as well as other disorders, including Tourette's, alcoholism, bad conduct, anxiety, depression, schizophrenia, obesity, sleep problems, and personality disorders. Many of these other disorders are closely associated with ADD.

When working with children, we frequently spot ADD in the parents, usually undiagnosed. Our staff will frequently tell us which parent has the ADD before we even see the child for evaluation.

Brain Injury: The last major theory, which has a strong scientific basis, holds that we can experience a brain injury that will cause ADD-type behavior. This injury can be structural, functional, or both. A structural disorder is when the brain is physically damaged, as with a heavy blow to the head. These injuries usually show up on hospital diagnostic imaging such as MRIs. The functional injury relates to how the brain is functioning. For example, there may be no structural damage, but the brainwaves are dysregulated. These disorders usually do not show up on MRIs or CT scans. We believe that the functional type of injury is much more prominent in ADD. The brain's physical structure may appear normal on conventional diagnostic imaging.

As a matter of fact, almost all of the ADD patients we have seen over the years have had normal CT scans and normal EEGs. But when we break the EEG down into functional bandwidths (a specific range of the EEG) at specific sites on the head, we usually see abnormal patterns in people with ADD. Examples of functional bandwidths are the dominant brainwaves in the low bandwidth range of four to seven cycles per second or the higher bandwidth of fifteen to eighteen cycles per second. The dominant bandwidth will have a profound effect on the behavior of the individual.

A functional injury generally relates to the timing of the brain. Is it producing the appropriate brainwaves for the task at hand? What if the brain is slowed down or is too fast? How will this affect behavior? For example, what if the person is trying to go to sleep and the brain is producing a faster, alerting-type wave? What if a child is trying to pay attention in class and his brain is producing a slow, sleep-type wave? Will the person be able to accomplish the task at hand? Not likely. So, in a functional injury, although the structure of the brain appears normal, it is functioning at an inappropriate level. This would be much like having a new car whose timing is wrong. The car looks great, but it does not function properly.

The idea that ADD is a manifestation of a brain injury was the first and most productive theory about this disorder. This theory was reflected in the diagnostic term minimal brain dysfunction (MBD). The term MBD was later changed to the descriptive term attention deficit disorder, to describe the nature of the dysfunction rather than to reflect the etiology of the disorder.

Brain injury can occur from many different factors. The first and most commonly thought of injury is physical trauma. We have seen many ADD children with histories of head bangs, hits, falls, and accidents. One adult female with severe ADD reported a concussion as a result of a minor motorcycle accident. After the accident she became even more risk-prone, and consequently suffered three additional head injuries. Most of the ADD children we have seen did not report what we would term "significant head trauma," but many reported jolts, hits, and bangs that could be sufficient to alter their brain's rhythmic functioning.

Other types of injury that could be responsible for functional problems are toxic exposure, nutritional deficiencies, hypoxic/anoxic trauma (an interruption in the flow of oxygen to the brain), genetics, pregnancy or birth complications, and infections. The severe influenza epidemic of 1918 resulted in many children who developed influenza-related encephalitis. In the 1920s, researchers began to notice an increase in ADD-type behavior and conduct disorders.[11] The increase in these disorders was attributed to the influenza epidemic, and this gave credence to the idea of infection-related brain injury. Often in our clinical work, parents will report the child as having had severe infections, usually accompanied by high fever.

We contend that brain injury from toxic metals and other pollutant exposure is much more commonplace than people realize. Toxic levels of such heavy metals as lead and mercury have long been known to cause behavioral problems in children. We will discuss the implications of exposure to other toxic materials in chapters 9 and 10, along with the role of nutrition.

Pregnancy and birth trauma have been suspected in this causative hunt for a long time. The research generally supports the theory that there is a higher incidence of ADD-type behavior in children who have had some problems during the gestational period or during delivery.[12] Our clinical findings indicate that the problems are often related to such phenomena as a difficult pregnancy, long or hard labor, fetal distress, forceps delivery, anoxia, and jaundice. However, clinical observations are what the treating professional sees in the clinic and are not always confirmed by research data.

Parents of our ADD children often relate stories like, "The cord was wrapped around his neck two times," "He was blue as could be," or "I was in hard labor for 26 hours." More often than not the APGAR scores (a way of measuring a newborn's progress in terms of coloring, heart rate, respiration, reflexes, and muscle tone) were normal, but parents report some kind of difficulty occurred at birth. APGAR scores are given to newborns at one minute and five minutes after birth. The higher the score, the better the condition of the infant.

The fact that some children go through difficult births and have no problems while others experience difficulty and become ADD may suggest a genetic predisposition or a vulnerability to such difficulty. The fact remains, however, that there is a greater incidence of ADD in children who experience such birth difficulty.

Stress Injury: Stress may play a greater role in ADD than previously considered. The EEGs of people under stress show that these individuals begin to produce faster brainwaves (15 Hz and higher) in the beta range. This busy activity is designed to problem-solve and reduce feelings of stress. In essence, the brain kicks into a higher gear, becoming more alert and aroused. If the brain adapts to the stressor or solves the problem, it appears to become more comfortable and moves down to a lower frequency range. This seems to be good for the ego; there is now an element of positive self-esteem knowing one has solved the problem. There is a calming of the stress response, and the person produces more relaxed, alpha-type waves.

If, however, the brain does not adapt to the stressor but instead feels assaulted, it ceases its busy activity and slips far down the continuum to the very low-frequency ranges. It goes into that foggy theta (4 to 7 Hz range) type world (pre-sleep). In some cases the brain keeps increasing its activity until the busy work becomes anxiety. So, under chronic unsolvable stress, the brain either goes to pre-sleep and sleep or to anxiety and worry. In the low-frequency ranges we find reduced alertness, difficulty learning, reduced quality and quantity of thought, depression, attentional problems, and learning deficits. These are all consistent with the ADD symptom picture. For a more thorough look at brainwave states and the correlating behavior, see the chart in chapter 7.

In our clinic we see a recurring pattern, namely, children and adults who are constantly exposed to stress develop a slowing of the brain. The brain begins to make more low-frequency (slow) brainwaves and less mid-range frequency (somewhat faster) brainwaves. It appears that children and adults exposed to chronic yelling, threats, critical remarks, or tasks that seem overwhelming go into low-range, slower waves. In other words, exposure to stress causes us to either zone out or become hyper and anxious.

We decided to test this hypothesis, of stress causing a slowing of brainwaves, in our office. We took two children with whom we were doing neurofeedback and asked their parents to assist with the training. We purposely selected two children who had what we considered demanding, autocratic parents. (Incidentally, both fathers were professionals—one was an attorney, the other a physician.) We invited the parents to sit in on their children's training sessions.

A short time into the first training session, both children began to increase theta waves and decrease beta waves. This reflects a slowing down of brainwaves. The parents' "coaching" of their children with typical remarks like, "pay attention, sit up straight, don't talk, don't look at me," drove the children straight into theta. In this slowed-down state, they zoned out to escape the obsessive-compulsive training style of their parents.

A milieu of continual demands and threats placed upon children and adults appears to dramatically exacerbate ADD-type symptoms. It either makes them dull and unproductive or anxious and unproductive. Life is not fun in theta, but at least it is quiet and not threatening.

We can hypothesize that much of the depression and ADD-type symptoms are a result of the individual feeling overwhelmed, threatened, or constantly faced with tasks that seem too large or too difficult. It is easier to let the brain slow down so the person can "zone out" or, as we call it, "go underground." Many children who feel overwhelmed become depressed over time, and they appear to have ADD. They often end up diagnosed with ADD and are prescribed Ritalin and/or other stimulant medication, which can make their condition worse.

Genetic Brain Injury: A genetic brain injury is an injury or a dysfunction that is passed from one generation to another. In working with ADD children we often feel we are working with second- or third-generation pathology. Because our office staff frequently gets to observe the parents while we are treating the child, it has become commonplace for us to ask them which parents of the ADD child has ADD. By watching their behavior in the waiting room, the office staff frequently observes ADD-characteristic behavior.

Many times we have ended up treating both the child and a parent, and this usually produces a profound change in the family dynamics. After treatment, we no longer have a person with obvious ADD symptoms parenting a child with ADD symptoms, so things at home go more smoothly. In cases like this we usually recommend brief family therapy or parent training to go along with the neurofeedback.

Characteristic EEG Rhythms in the ADD Patient

Since there appear to be no differences in the brain structure of people with and without ADD,[13] how does the injury show up, other than in their behavior? In 1938, Jasper, Solomon, and Bradley published an article demonstrating that there were abnormalities in the brainwaves of "minimal brain dysfunction" children.[14] This was the first evidence of a functional injury as opposed to structural damage. Over the next thirty years, there were a number of articles indicating that the EEGs of people with ADD and conduct disorders were abnormal. The general findings were that they had brainwaves similar to people with epileptic seizures and a generalized slowing of the brainwaves, meaning that the brain was slowed down, not as active or alert as it should be.

Dr. Lubar and his wife Judith began training children using brainwave biofeedback to reduce the four- to seven-hertz range and increase the brainwaves above 14 hertz. When the ADD children learned this, there was a significant reduction in ADD-type symptoms, indicating ADD is a functional disorder caused by dysfunctional brain rhythms.

The idea that the brainwaves of people with ADD are slower than non-ADD people helped to explain why children were improved when Bradley administered the stimulant amphetamine sulfate.[15] Even today, that is the basis for administering amphetamine drugs such as Ritalin to people with ADD. There is a generalized slowing of the brainwaves in people with this type of disorder, so amphetamines speed up the brain, and the problem is temporarily "solved." But of course it is not solved at all.

It was not until 1971, when Satterfield and Dawson, and Satterfield, Lasser, Saul, and Cantwell proposed the "low-arousal hypothesis" that other treatment modalities were looked at seriously.[16,17] The low-arousal hypothesis basically said that hyperactive children were in a low state of arousal, not very awake or aware of what is going on around them, so they move around to wake up, to be in the world.

Dr. Barry Sterman's work had a profound impact on the development of a theoretical model for ADD. His work consisted of using neurofeedback to train people with seizure disorders to produce different brainwaves, thereby reducing their seizure activity. Dr. Sterman demonstrated that people with the low-frequency brainwave burst that produces seizures can be trained to produce higher frequency brainwaves. Rather than producing excessive brainwaves in the slow four- to seven-hertz range, they were trained to produce more brainwaves in the area of 14 hertz. Since there are some common brainwave features between seizure disorders and ADD, Dr. Sterman's work added more credibility to the theory that ADD is a functional disorder, involving the timing of the brain.[18-23] (See figure 3-1.)

Dr. Joel Lubar at the University of Tennessee saw this relationship very clearly, and after working with Dr. Sterman for several months began applying his model to children with ADD. Dr. Lubar and his wife Judith began training children using brainwave

Figure 3-1.

cps = cycles per second, or Hertz

DELTA Less than 4 cps	THETA 4–8 cps	ALPHA 8–12 cps	SMR 12–15 cps	BETA 15–18 cps	HIGH BETA more than 19 cps
Sleep	Drowsy	Relaxed Focus	Relaxed Thought	Active Thinking	Excited

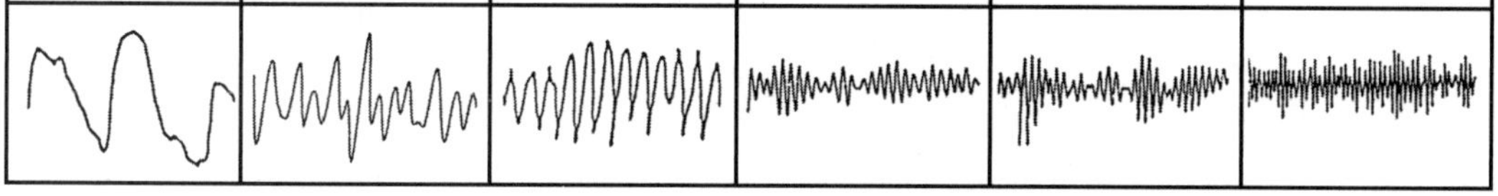

Depression, ADD, and seizure activity in this range.

We train the brain to move into this range to modify symptoms of depression, ADD, and improve seizure activity.

biofeedback to reduce the four- to seven-hertz range and increase the brainwaves above 14 hertz. When the ADD children learned this, there was a significant reduction in ADD-type symptoms, indicating ADD is a functional disorder caused by dysfunctional brain rhythms.[24-26]

So What Is the Cause of ADD?

After all this research, what is the cause of ADD and ADD-related behavior? It is injury of some sort. It may be a genetic predisposition to brain injury passed from one generation to another. It may be a traumatic brain injury caused by a kick, knock, bang, hit, or fall. It may be a result of some injury sustained in utero or during delivery. It may be an injury sustained during exposure to a toxic environmental element. It could also be emotional injury resulting from growing up in a family where stress and chaos reign. ADD and ADD-type symptoms are manifestations of a slowing of the brainwaves, and this slowing is a functional result of an injury.

4

A Practical Checklist for Assessing ADD in Children and Adults

When a person receives treatment for any disorder, they should know, with some degree of certainty, whether the treatment had any effect, positive or negative. All too often, people receive treatment for some problem and end up just guessing as to whether or not it helped. In order to help diagnose ADD and to evaluate the progress of treatments, we developed a practical checklist. It was important for us to know how good this new treatment was. We wanted a simple checklist that would give us a clear picture of the problem areas and assess the severity of the problems in one easy-to-read chart.

With much trial and error, over time we were able to develop a checklist that could be used by parents, teachers, and health care professionals alike. It is not designed to replace the *DSM-IV,* but rather to give concerned individuals and treating professionals a picture of what they are dealing with.

Before we discuss the checklist, we would like to give you the background on how we started treating ADD with neurofeedback and how we developed the checklist.

In the early 1980s, I (Robert Hill) was treating attention deficit disorder and conduct disorders with psychotherapy and behavior modification. Ed Castro was writing prescriptions for

Ritalin and other psychotropic medications for these disorders. Neither of us believed we were making any progress. In frustration with lack of any consistent and long-term results, I quit seeing children with these disorders and started referring them to other psychologists and psychiatrists. Ed continued to write prescriptions, but he was just as frustrated as I was.

I had been a long-time practitioner of biofeedback, using mostly thermal biofeedback and EMG (electromyography) for relaxation. I was well aware of the therapeutic value of biofeedback for relaxing and calming tense, anxious patients. I also knew that there had been biofeedback experiments on hyperactive children using EMG to relax them. However, the results were not particularly impressive, and I did not want to go back to the frustration of not being successful with these children. Psychology and psychiatry were failing a large number of bright, active children with ADD. In the back of my mind I knew there had to be an answer.

In the mid-1980s, I came across an article by Joel Lubar and Margaret Shouse in which they described using EEG biofeedback, which we now call neurofeedback, on an eleven-year-old hyperkinetic child.[1] Neurofeedback, as we have discussed, is a treatment in which the patient learns how to change the frequency of his brainwaves. The results were impressive, but I was skeptical. It just sounded too good to be true. I knew we could change a person's temperature or relax muscles with biofeedback, but changing brainwaves with biofeedback was too much to grant. This was a time when medicine was just beginning to accept the notion that humans could actually have some control over such things as their temperature, muscle tension, heart rate, and blood pressure. The idea of changing something as central as brainwaves seemed too farfetched.

Although I didn't do anything with that article or the idea of EEG biofeedback for some time, I kept thinking about it. Every time a child would come in with ADD or conduct disorder and I would refer him out, that article crossed my mind. After several months, I conducted another literature search and began to find other articles on EEG biofeedback in the treatment of ADD and other disorders. Barry Sterman's articles on the use of EEG biofeedback in the treatment of seizure disorders were impressive. It was obvious that researchers like Sterman, Lubar, and Tansey were good scientists. They were doing solid research with remarkable results. I continued to follow the work in EEG biofeedback with particular interest in Barry Sterman, Joel Lubar, and Michael Tansey. Over time, I began to feel that maybe they had developed a safe, effective way of treating attentional and behavioral problems.

I finally decided to investigate further and enrolled in my first training course. The instructor was not a leading researcher or practitioner, but he heightened my interest. This led to a long series of training courses taught by the top people in EEG biofeedback. This list included Joel and Judith Lubar, Barry Sterman, Michael Tansey, Les Fehmi, Sue and Siegfried Othmer, and others. I joined a biofeedback organization and started attending conferences. Initially, I was not using this new therapy in my practice, I was just reading and going to training workshops. Ed was doing the same thing. He had followed the same path, researching but not practicing EEG biofeedback. He was still frustrated with the drug treatment options available to him for his patients with ADD.

It was not until 1989 that I purchased my first EEG biofeedback machine. It was a bulky computer that was attached to an amplifier. The amplifier was fed by wires and a harness which were attached to the patient's scalp. When the person was hooked up, the amplifier received and amplified the brainwave signals and sent them to the computer. The computer software program analyzed the brainwaves, calculated their activity, then separated them into discrete ranges, and the information was fed back to the patient on the monitor. With practice, the patient could use the information to learn the subtle skill of changing the brainwaves. If the person improved the brainwaves, they got a score in a little box on the monitor screen and a tone would ring. Eventually, the patient could learn to voluntarily change their brainwaves, thus changing their feelings and behaviors.

The first machine was very expensive, and I felt overwhelmed with computer, amplifier, harness, and wires. All of a sudden, I was dealing with skin preparation, pads, electro paste, sensors, cotton balls, alcohol, and miscellaneous articles that I was not familiar with. The task seemed too big to be worth it, but I had invested the money. For several weeks I could not get the machine to work properly, so my sense of frustration grew. I was on the phone with the supplier daily until finally I began to get a proper EEG signal. Now it was time to learn how to use it. Could I take the information I had learned in all of those training courses and use it to treat attentional and behavioral problems? Could I hook a person up to this machine and train them to improve their brainwaves so that they no longer were controlled by their ADD behaviors? I was not sure.

For weeks on end I played with the machine. I hooked up everyone in my family and all the office staff, including their children. My son was my first hookup and in my zeal to get a good hookup, I rubbed his skin too hard. The preparation pad has an abrasive on it which can injure the skin if applied too roughly. He had a weeping sore spot for several days, but he recovered and I learned a valuable lesson. After three months I felt properly prepared to try it on my first patient. Because I was still unsure of the treatment benefits, I could not charge a fee.

This first patient was a ten-year-old who had been diagnosed attention deficit/hyperactive disorder, and he had been on Ritalin for three years. After I told his mother about EEG biofeedback and offered to treat him free of charge on an experimental basis, she agreed and I began the treatment.

After twenty sessions, his mother began to report positive behavioral changes. In less than ten weeks we were seeing real behavioral changes in the boy. I then took on a second, then a third, then a fourth experimental patient. After a time, I became more comfortable with the equipment, but I was still unsure of its lasting benefits. One by one, the successes began to mount up and my confidence in the treatment began to grow.

For the first two years, I did not charge anyone for the treatment. Fortunately, the other areas of my psychological practice were successful and I could afford to buy better equipment and continue to treat some children for free. After two years I had four biofeedback systems, some good, some not so good, and I had treated approximately thirty children for free. I was comfortable with my equipment, more confident in my skills, and completely sold on neurofeedback for attentional and behavioral problems. (As a note, the name of the treatment is more of a preference than anything else. Even today, at any conference, some say neurofeedback, some say EEG biofeedback, some say neurotherapy, and some say brainwave biofeedback.)

We began to routinely offer neurofeedback for children with these types of problems. Because insurance companies frequently do not pay for biofeedback, we set our rates for the treatment very low, beginning by charging forty dollars a session. If you consider it may take forty sessions, we were talking about $1,600 to treat a child for a very disruptive disorder. Today neurofeedback sessions can vary in price from sixty-five dollars to over one hundred dollars per session, depending on such things as practice location, insurance, and practitioner. However, it is still generally less than putting braces on a child's teeth. Business was slow at first, but word got out. We did not advertise, and all of our patients came by word of mouth. Once things got rolling, we had people coming from all over our region, and soon I was seeing more people for ADD than for other psychological problems.

I met Ed Castro in the early 1990s at a conference. He was a practicing psychiatrist in Charlottesville, Virginia. He was gaining more interest in EEG and was becoming more discontent with prescribing Ritalin. We had many lengthy discussions about the new treatment. When I got a call from Ed asking to visit my practice, we set a time and made a day of it. He picked my brain, analyzed my practice, and went back to Charlottesville. Shortly after that, Ed phoned to tell me he was going to buy an EEG biofeedback machine and asked my recommendations. After we discussed his needs, he moved forward with his purchase plans. We stayed in close contact as his practice continued.

Ed phoned me one day to say he was closing his practice in Charlottesville and moving to Indianapolis, Indiana. He had been offered an opportunity to set up a neurotherapy treatment program in a hospital setting. I expressed my regret and offhandedly said, "Gee, I thought you were calling me to tell me what color carpet you wanted in your new office here with me." We laughed and hung up the phone. A few days later, Ed phoned back and said, "I thought you were kidding about the carpet, but I just wanted to make sure." For the first time we examined seriously the possibility of joining practices. In 1996, Ed moved to the Abingdon, Virginia, area and we began working together.

We have had as many as nine neurofeedback machines working at one time, and treating fifty children a week is not uncommon. We have seen children from Virginia, D.C., North Carolina, West Virginia, Kentucky, and Tennessee. We estimate we have a 75 to 80 percent success rate, based on improvement ratings by parents using the checklist and test scores.

In the beginning, when we were unsure of the efficiency of this treatment, we wanted a way to monitor patient progress. We looked at the available checklists for determining ADD symptoms. They were all much alike and covered the major symptoms listed in the *Diagnostic and Statistical Manual of Mental Illness.* We believed that attentional problems like ADD, ADHD, and conduct disorders were much more pervasive and broader than those lists, so we developed our own checklist, revising it as we went along. We not only wanted it as an assessment tool, but we wanted to be able to measure our clinical progress and use it as an indicator of what specific neurofeedback treatment protocol to use; i.e., what brainwaves to increase, what to decrease, and where to place the sensors. Our treatment protocol is generally to increase the faster (more alert) brainwaves and decrease the slower (drowsy, dull, sleepy) brainwaves.

In the checklist we included the symptoms that were most often seen in our clinic. After all the revisions, we ended up with our current "Checklist for Attention Deficit and Related Disorders." This checklist includes the following categories:

- Attention Deficit
- Hyperactivity
- Impulsivity
- Immaturity
- Oppositional Behavior
- Aggressive/Sadistic Behavior
- Tic Disorders
- Depression
- Anxiety
- Low Self-Esteem
- Sleep
- Developmental and Learning Disorder(s)

We later created the adult version, which reflects some minor behavioral changes but is basically the same checklist. Instead of learning disorders, we list other problems and have changed some of the wording to eliminate purely childhood problems such as developmental coordination disorder.

We wanted a checklist that gave percentages rather than cut-off scores. Checklists with cut-off scores tend to be more absolute; i.e., if the score is above a certain number you have the disorder, if the score is below that number you don't. By using a percentage score you can more easily assess the severity of the problem. For example, if a person has a score of 85 percent on the Impulsivity category, you can conclude the problem is severe. Whereas, if the score was only 27 percent, you can conclude there is some impulsivity but it is not severe.

We also wanted a checklist that gave a broader overview of how the person is functioning in many different areas of their life. The checklist is relatively simple to use and is usually completed by parents, guardians, and/or teachers. The consistent pattern that emerged in our completed checklists was that Mom rated the child the worst, teachers second, and Dad did not see as many problems. This seemed to relate directly to time spent with the child— the more time a parent spent with a child, the worse they rated them. Often the parent who was paying for the treatment, particularly non-custodial fathers, saw very little wrong with the child.

In the case of adult ADD, we like to have the patient and a spouse or family member fill out the checklist. You may use this checklist to score your child or have a family member fill it out for you. Our complete checklist appears in appendix C.

Instructions for Using the Checklist: Each category is scored on a scale of "not present," "very mild," "mild," "moderate," "severe," or "very severe." Tally the score in the block by adding the blocks together, and figure the percentage. For example, if you end up with a score of 70 in category I, divide the 70 by 110. That gives you 63 percent. If you have a 63 percent problem rating in that symptom category, you have a clue as to how severe the symptoms are in this category. If 100 percent is very severe, the 63 percent figure would be in the moderate range. If the score were 22 percent, that would be in the very mild range. If the percentage were 93 percent, the symptoms would be very severe. Although this is subjective scoring, it gives you an idea of the level of severity you are working with in each category.

The checklist is also an excellent way of measuring progress. We frequently have parents tell us their child has made no progress, that "he still doesn't do his homework." When we point out that he no longer has all the tics and has not been in a fight for weeks, they often acknowledge that they had completely forgotten about all of those symptoms. Remember that parents sometimes have adult ADD and memory remains a problem for them.

If math isn't your strong suit, don't figure the percentages. Just "eyeball" the checks; you'll still see the areas of dysfunction. You don't need a percentage figure when you see most of the checks are in the severe range. You also do not need to be told the child's problem. You can see everything for yourself. This checklist provides a graphic representation of the symptoms.

This scoring method is not beneficial in tic disorders and developmental and learning disorders. If a child licks his lips until they are red and sore, that is a severe or very severe problem. Parents have to use their own judgment and look at the checklist sensibly. Once you have evaluated the person, take the checklist to the physician and/or hopefully to the nearest neurofeedback therapist. (See appendix A for listings.) The checklist will help them to know where to start with the neurofeedback training. It also gives clues and indications to the well-trained neurofeedback therapist as to where to place the EEG sensors and what EEG brainwave frequency or frequency bands they want to increase or decrease.

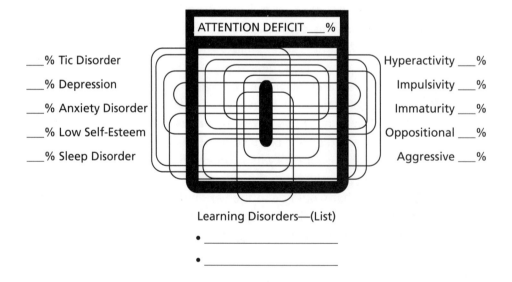

ATTENTION DEFICIT ___%

___% Tic Disorder   Hyperactivity ___%

___% Depression   Impulsivity ___%

___% Anxiety Disorder   Immaturity ___%

___% Low Self-Esteem   Oppositional ___%

___% Sleep Disorder   Aggressive ___%

Learning Disorders—(List)

• _____

• _____

Figure 4-1. ADD Checklist Summary Chart

This is the summary chart for the checklist. At a glance, you will be able to determine the problem areas and the severity of the problems. For example, if you end up with a 0% Tic Disorder and 86% Depression, you can assess the relative severity of the problem category.

Figure 4-2 (pages 52-53) is an actual checklist on a nine-year-old male. He was brought in by his mother with complaints of poor school performance and hyperactivity. The mother had been told by the child's teacher that he was ADD and should be put on Ritalin.

In reviewing the checklist, the Attention Deficit percentage score is at 48 percent, with a score of 53 points out of a possible 110. This score falls roughly in the moderate range of Attention Deficit. On both the Hyperactivity and Impulsivity categories, the child scored at 58 percent. You will notice that in the Hyperactivity category, most of the checks were in the "severe" column; in the Impulsivity category, he even had one check in the "very severe" column.

Without going any further, we can conclude that this child is experiencing attention deficit disorder with hyperactivity in the moderate to severe range. Even if you did not figure the percentages, the checklist gives a graphic view of how this child functions in daily life.

The checklist would indicate that the parent felt the child acted generally in an age-appropriate manner and had some oppositional characteristics, though not enough to be of major concern.

When we examine Aggressive/Sadistic Behavior, Tic Disorders, Depression, Anxiety, Self-Esteem, and Sleep problems, this child is relatively unaffected emotionally by the attentional and behavioral problems he is experiencing. A visual examination would indicate the focus of treatment should be centered on Attention Deficit Disorder and Hyperactivity. The mother did check two tic symptoms in the moderate column, but close observation of the child convinced me that he did not have any actual tics.

We chose a treatment protocol specifically designed to treat ADD and Hyperactivity.

This next checklist (see figure 4-3 on pages 54-55) is one that was filled out by a forty-six-year-old, self-employed male. He had separated from his wife the year before. His oldest child had started college and his youngest was living with his estranged wife. He came in because he had self diagnosed his condition as ADD.

Because he lived alone and had no close friends or family, he did the checklist himself. My clinical observation indicated he

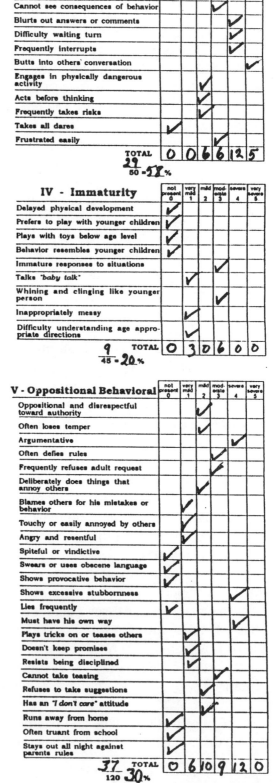

Figure 4-2. Checklist
for Nine-Year-Old Boy

VI - Aggressive/Sadistic Behavior

	not present 0	very mild 1	mild 2	moderate 3	severe 4	very severe 5
Bullies, threatens or intimidates others	✓					
Often initiates fights	✓					
Has used a weapon that could harm others	✓					
Has been physically cruel to others	✓					
Has been physically cruel to animals	✓					
Has stolen while confronting victim	✓					
Has forced someone into sexual activity	✓					
Deliberate fire setting	✓					
Broken into the property of others	✓					
Lies to obtain goods or favors	✓					
Stolen without confronting victim	✓					
Does not respect anyone	✓					
Bosses others around	✓					
Makes derogatory remarks about others	✓					
Seems to enjoy being in trouble "a hero"	✓					
Delights in failure of others	✓					
Pushes or shoves others	✓					
Cheats at games	✓					
Preoccupied with death, guns, killing	✓					

TOTAL 0/95 = 0 %

VII - Tic Disorders

Motor Tics (sudden jerky type motions)	not present 0	very mild 1	mild 2	moderate 3	severe 4	very severe 5
Facial tic: eye blinking, eye rolls, squinting, grimacing, lip licking, biting tongue, grinding teeth		✓				
Head and neck: hair out of the eyes, neck jerking, tossing head around, shoulder shrugging		✓				
Arms and hands: Flailing arms, extending arms, biting nails, finger signs, flexing fingers, picking skin, popping knuckles		✓				
Diaphragm: unusual inhale, exhale, gasping for breath		✓				
Legs: Kicking, hopping, skipping, jumping, bending, stooping, stepping backward				✓		
Feet: tapping, shaking, toe curling, tripping, turning feet				✓		
Others: blowing, smelling, twirling hair, jerking, kissing, hitting self, chewing, scratching, shivering, pulling						

Vocal Tics	not present 0	very mild 1	mild 2	moderate 3	severe 4	very severe 5
Throat clearing, coughing	✓					
Grunting, snorting, animal noises	✓					
Yelling, screaming			✓			
Sniffing, burping	✓					
Barking, honking	✓					
Motor or jet noise						
Spitting	✓					
Squeaking, "huh"	✓					
Humming	✓					
Stuttering	✓					
Deep breathing, sucking breath in	✓					
Repetitive cursing, "fu", "sh"	✓					

TOTAL 11/95 = 11 % | 0 | 3 | 2 | 6 |

VIII - Depression

	not present 0	very mild 1	mild 2	moderate 3	severe 4	very severe 5
Seems sad, does not smile very much	✓					
Seems unusually quiet	✓					
Poor sense of humor	✓					
Grouchy, irritable	✓					
Sullen	✓					
Looks flat	✓					
Withdrawal from family/activities	✓					
Tearful	✓					
Frequently seems lonely	✓					
Moodiness, unpredictable mood swings	✓					
A loner, withdrawn	✓					
Depressed	✓					
No interest	✓					
Problems with sleep	✓					
Thinks about death or dying	✓					
Suicidal	✓					

TOTAL 0/80 = 0 %

IX - Anxiety

	not present 0	very mild 1	mild 2	moderate 3	severe 4	very severe 5
Panic attack type symptoms	✓					
Frequently nervous	✓					
Often upset	✓					
Is fearful of many things	✓					
Fearful of being alone				✓		
Fearful of a specific object	✓					
Jumpy, hypervigilance	✓					
Timid	✓					
Worries excessively	✓					
Persistent thoughts				✓		
Repetitive behaviors (hand washing, counting)	✓					
Exaggerated startled response	✓					
Shaking, trembling	✓					
Tearful	✓					
Fear of death or dying	✓					
Tense muscles	✓					
Always on edge	✓					

TOTAL 6/85 = 7 % | 0 | | | 6 | | |

X - Low Self Esteem

	not present 0	very mild 1	mild 2	moderate 3	severe 4	very severe 5
Doesn't trust themselves	✓					
Frequently put themselves down		✓				
Refuses to try new things		✓				
Poor performance even when they have the ability		✓				
Always takes a back-seat position	✓					
Timid and reserved	✓					
Often shy around others	✓					
Trouble answering questions in front of others	✓					
Sees the worst in self	✓					
Hangs around with less capable friends	✓					
Easily embarrassed	✓					
Seems satisfied with poor school performance	✓					
Does not compete with others	✓					
Gives up easily	✓					
Shows no self confidence		✓				

TOTAL 4/75 = 5 % | 0 | 4 | | | | |

XI - Sleep

	not present 0	very mild 1	mild 2	moderate 3	severe 4	very severe 5
Difficulty going to bed	✓					
Difficulty going to sleep	✓					
Wakes up frequently	✓					
Early awakening	✓					
Restless sleep	✓					
Talking in sleep		✓				
Walking in sleep						
Wakes up in terror						
Restless legs		✓				
Bed wetting or soiling	✓					
Nightmares		✓				

TOTAL 4/85 = 7 % | 4 | | | | | |

XII - Developmental & Learning Disorder(s)

	not present 0	very mild 1	mild 2	moderate 3	severe 4	very severe 5
Mental Retardation	✓					
Reading Disorder						
Mathematics Disorder						
Disorder of Written Expression						
Developmental Coordination Disorder		✓				
Expressive Language Disorder	✓					
Mixed Receptive/Expressive Language Disorder		✓				
Phonological Disorder (articulation)		✓				
Stuttering		✓				
Autistic Disorder	✓					
Retts Disorder		✓				
Childhood Disintegrative Disorder	✓					
Aspergers Disorder		✓				

(List any learning disorders on the front)

I - Attention Deficit

	not present 0	very mild 1	mild 2	moderate 3	severe 4	very severe 5
Does not seem to listen when spoken to			✓			
Makes careless errors				✓		
Avoids or dislikes tasks requiring sustained attention				✓		
Short attention span					✓	
Disorganized					✓	
Loses things				✓✗		
Procrastinates				✓		
Easily distracted		✓	✓			
Forgetful in daily activity			✓			
Difficulty completing tasks				✓		
Gets bored easily				✓		
Stares into space/daydreaming				✓		
Low energy, sluggish or drowsy					✓	
Apathetic or unmotivated					✓	
Frequently switches from one activity to another					✓	
Trouble concentrating			✓			
Falls asleep doing work		✓				
Failure to meet deadlines						✓
Underachiever					✓	
Trouble following directions		✓				
Excited in the beginning but doesn't finish				✓		
Difficulty learning/remembering			✓			
Works best under deadlines/pressure						
TOTAL		2	6	24	32	10

74/115 = **64** %

II - Hyperactivity

	not present 0	very mild 1	mild 2	moderate 3	severe 4	very severe 5
Fidgets with hands and feet			✓			
Squirms in seat			✓			
Frequently leaves seat inappropriately			✓			
Moves excessively		✓				
Difficulty working quietly			✓			
On the go				✓		
Driven				✓		
Talks excessively		✓✗				
Can't sustain eye contact		✓				
Needs a lot of supervision	✓	✗				
Pays attention to everything						
Frequently "rocks"		✓				
Excitability		✓				
Lacks patience			✓			
In trouble frequently		✓				
Restless			✓			
TOTAL		2	12	6		

20/80 = **25** %

Figure 4-3. Checklist for Forty-Six-Year-Old Man

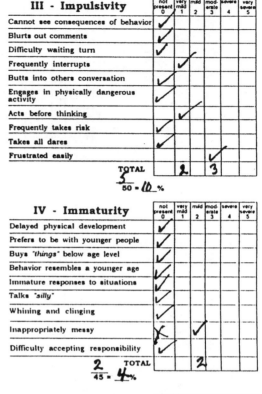

III - Impulsivity

	not present 0	very mild 1	mild 2	moderate 3	severe 4	very severe 5
Cannot see consequences of behavior	✓					
Blurts out comments	✓					
Difficulty waiting turn	✓					
Frequently interrupts		✓				
Butts into others conversation	✓					
Engages in physically dangerous activity	✓					
Acts before thinking				✓		
Frequently takes risk	✓					
Takes all dares	✓					
Frustrated easily				✓		
TOTAL		2		3		

5/50 = **10** %

IV - Immaturity

	not present 0	very mild 1	mild 2	moderate 3	severe 4	very severe 5
Delayed physical development	✓					
Prefers to be with younger people	✓					
Buys "things" below age level	✓					
Behavior resembles a younger age	✓					
Immature responses to situations	✓					
Talks "silly"	✓					
Whining and clinging	✓					
Inappropriately messy	✗		✓			
Difficulty accepting responsibility	✓					
TOTAL			2			

2/45 = **4** %

V - Oppositional Behavioral

	not present 0	very mild 1	mild 2	moderate 3	severe 4	very severe 5
Oppositional and disrespectful toward authority	✓					
Often loses temper		✓				
Argumentative	✓					
Often defies rules	✓					
Frequently refuses request	✓					
Deliberately does things that annoy others	✓					
Blames others for his mistakes or behavior	✓					
Touchy or easily annoyed by others		✓				
Angry and resentful	✓					
Spiteful or vindictive	✓					
Swears or uses obscene language	✓					
Shows provocative behavior	✓					
Shows excessive stubbornness		✓				
Lies frequently	✓					
Must have his own way	✓					
Plays tricks on or teases others	✓					
Doesn't keep promises	✗		✓			
Resists being disciplined	✓					
Cannot take teasing	✓					
Refuses to take suggestions	✓					
Has an "I don't care" attitude	✓					
Doesn't come home on time	✓✗		✓			
Often absent from work	✓					
Frequent trouble at work	✓					
Can't hold a job	✓					
TOTAL		4	2			

6/125 = **4** %

VI - Aggressive/Sadistic Behavior

	not present 0	very mild 1	mild 2	moderate 3	severe 4	very severe 5
Bullies, threatens or intimidates others	✓					
Often initiates fights	✓					
Has used a weapon that could harm others	✓					
Has been physically cruel to others	✓					
Has been physically cruel to animals	✓					
Has stolen while confronting victim	✓					
Has forced someone into sexual activity	✓					
Deliberate fire setting	✓					
Broken into the property of others	✓					
Lies to obtain goods or favors	✓					
Stolen without confronting victim	✓					
Does not respect anyone	✓					
Bosses others around	✓					
Makes derogatory remarks about others	✓					
Seems to enjoy being in trouble *a hero*	✓					
Delights in failure of others	✓					
Pushes or shoves others	✓					
Cheats at games	✓					
Preoccupied with death, guns, killing	✓					

TOTAL $\frac{0}{95} = 0\%$

VII - Tic Disorders

Motor Tics (sudden jerky type motions)

	not present 0	very mild 1	mild 2	moderate 3	severe 4	very severe 5
Facial tic: eye blinking, eye rolls, squinting, grimacing, lip licking, biting tongue, grinding teeth	✓					
Head and neck: hair out of the eyes, neck jerking, tossing head around, shoulder shrugging	✓					
Arms and hands: Flailing arms, extending arms, biting nails, finger signs, flexing fingers, picking skin, popping knuckles	✓					
Diaphragm: unusual inhale, exhale, gasping for breath	✓					
Legs: Kicking, hopping, skipping, jumping, bending, stooping, stepping backward	✓					
Feet: tapping, shaking, toe curling, tripping, turning feet	✓					
Others: blowing, smelling, twirling hair, jerking, kissing, hitting self, chewing, scratching, shivering, pulling	✓					

Vocal Tics

	not present 0	very mild 1	mild 2	moderate 3	severe 4	very severe 5
Throat clearing, coughing	✓					
Grunting, snorting, animal noises	✓					
Yelling, screaming	✓					
Sniffing, burping	✓					
Barking, honking	✓					
Motor or jet noise	✓					
Spitting	✓					
Squeaking, "huh"	✓					
Humming	✓					
Stuttering	✓					
Deep breathing, sucking breath in	✓					
Repetitive cursing, "fu", "sh"	✓					

TOTAL $\frac{0}{95} = 0\%$

VIII - Depression

	not present 0	very mild 1	mild 2	moderate 3	severe 4	very severe 5
Seems sad, does not smile very much				✓		
Seems unusually quiet				✓		
Poor sense of humor			✓			
Grouchy, irritable			✓	✓		
Sullen			✓			
Looks flat				✓		
Withdrawal from family/activities					✓	
Tearful			✓	✓		
Frequently seems lonely					✓	
Moodiness, unpredictable moodswings		⋅		✓		
A loner, withdrawn					✓	
Depressed				✓		
No interest				✓		
Problems with sleep			✓	✓		
Thinks about death or dying	✓					
Suicidal	✓					

TOTAL $\frac{36}{80} = 45\%$ 0 1 12 15 8

IX - Anxiety

	not present 0	very mild 1	mild 2	moderate 3	severe 4	very severe 5
Panic attack type symptoms	✓		✓			
Frequently nervous	✓					
Often upset	✓					
Generally fearful		✓				
Fearful of losing control		✓				
Fearful of a specific object or event	✓					
Jumpy, hypervigilance	✓					
Timid	✓					
Worries excessively			✓			
Persistent thoughts			✓			
Repetitive behaviors (hand washing, counting)	✓					
Exaggerated startled response	✓					
Shaking, trembling	✓					
Tearful	✓					
Fear of death or dying	✓					
Tense muscles	⋅			✓		
Always on edge				✓		

$\frac{10}{85} = 11\%$ TOTAL 0 4 6

X - Low Self Esteem

	not present 0	very mild 1	mild 2	moderate 3	severe 4	very severe 5
Doesn't trust self	✓					
Frequently puts self down			✓			
Refuses to try new things			✓			
Poor performance even when they have the ability				✓		
Always takes a back-seat position			✓			
Timid and reserved				✓		
Often shy around others			✓			
Trouble answering questions in front of others					✓	
Sees the worst in self			✓			
Hangs around with less capable friends				✓		
Easily embarrassed				✓		
Seems satisfied with poor performance	✓					
Does not compete with others		✓				
Gives up easily/expects failure		✓				
Shows no self confidence					✓	

$\frac{34}{75} = 45\%$ TOTAL 2 12 12 8

XI - Sleep

	not present 0	very mild 1	mild 2	moderate 3	severe 4	very severe 5
Difficulty going to bed				✓		
Difficulty going to sleep				✓		
Wakes up frequently			✓			
Early awakening	✓					
Restless sleep			✓			
Talking in sleep	✓					
Walking in sleep	✓					
Wakes up in terror	✓					
Restless legs	✓					
Night sweats/Hot flashes	✓					
Nightmares				✓		

$\frac{10}{55} = 18\%$ TOTAL 1 4 6

XII - Other
(List on front page)

	not present 0	very mild 1	mild 2	moderate 3	severe 4	very severe 5
Mental Retardation	✓					
Learning Disorder (list type)	✓					
Studdering	✓					
Autistic Disorder	✓					
Allergies	⋅	✓				
Chemical Sensitivity	✓					
Addiction(s) (list)	✓					
Anorexia (nervosa)	✓					
Bulimia (nervosa)	✓					
Stroke	✓					
Seizure Disorder	✓					
Head Injury	✓					
Migraine Headaches	✓					
Tension Headaches			✓			
PMS	✓					
Menopause	✓					
Other:						

did a good job of accurately assessing his symptoms. I did feel, however, that he had underestimated his depression and low self-esteem.

A visual examination of his Attention Deficit category indicated he was experiencing moderate to severe problems in this category. The 64 percent score confirms this. There was some mild Hyperactivity, but only in the 25 percent range. He reported that he was "very" hyperactive as a child but outgrew it as he aged. It is typical for adults to outgrow hyperactivity but not the Attention Deficit Disorder.

When we looked at the categories of Impulsivity, Immaturity, Oppositional Behavior, Aggressive/Sadistic Behavior, and Tic Disorders, there were no problems. However, when we came to Depression and Low Self-Esteem, he was experiencing a moderate level of discomfort. There was very little anxiety, but some difficulty sleeping.

In selecting the protocol for this individual, we wanted to make sure we addressed not only the ADD but the depression and low self-esteem as well. We began by selecting a protocol that trained the brain to make more brainwaves in the beta range (15-18 Hz). This frequency would not only result in more efficiency but also elevate the sad mood.

5

A Closer Look at Ritalin: Is It Really a Desirable Solution to ADD?

In conventional medicine the first, and often only, treatment intervention for ADD is medication. The categories of drugs used for ADD are psychostimulants (drugs that increase brain arousal and attention), antidepressants, and antipsychotics (powerful tranquilizers which are prescribed for people who lose touch with reality). There are even an antihypertensive (a drug that lowers blood pressure) and two anticonvulsants (drugs that reduce seizure activity) in use. So why do we single out Ritalin?

We do this for two reasons. First, because Ritalin has come to symbolize the medication-for-bad-behavior thinking that is pervasive in conventional medicine. Who has not heard someone joke, "He needs his Ritalin," when referring to someone's high energy level? This is not so amusing, however, if it is your child who is being steamrollered onto a medication by well-meaning teachers or clinicians.

The second reason to focus on Ritalin more specifically is that since its producers own approximately 80 percent of the ADD drug market, they are the most active in managing and micromanaging the thinking about ADD and its treatment. This chapter is an effort to provide additional information to balance that picture.

Let us be clear from the beginning that it is not the proper use of Ritalin, its generic equivalent methylphenidate, or the other medications used to treat ADD that we dispute. It is the *unbridled* use of Ritalin in an attempt to treat virtually any and all behavioral or academic problems that we question. It is also the neglect of other, quite possibly better and safer treatment interventions, that we protest. We believe that if parents inform themselves of the benefits and risks of the true range of treatment options, their child will not be merely treated with the knee-jerk response of a prescription for Ritalin. Rather, the parents will choose safer, more natural treatments, such as neurofeedback.

> *It is the* unbridled *use of Ritalin in an attempt to treat virtually any and all behavioral or academic problems that we question. It is also the neglect of other, quite possibly better and safer treatment interventions, that we protest.*

Let's address the question of how children get put on Ritalin in the first place. Typically, a child exhibits behaviors that are disruptive at home or school. As stated in chapter 1, these behaviors may include hyperactivity, impulsivity, inattention, aggression, immaturity, or learning problems. A parent initiates, or a teacher may suggest, an evaluation of the child for possible ADD. This evaluation may be only a ten-minute discussion by the parents with a busy pediatrician or family doctor, who may quickly go down a checklist of questions, or the child may be referred to a psychologist for an extensive evaluation and battery of psychological testing.

A concern at this point is whether the family doctor or pediatrician is adequately trained to diagnose the other psychological problems that may result in the child's behavior. For example, conduct disorder, anxiety disorder, depression, and childhood post-traumatic stress may be confused with ADD. None of these disorders should be treated with Ritalin. On the other hand, will the psychologist be in a position to recognize underlying *medical* problems that may be the cause of the child's symptoms? Possibilities include seizure disorder, hypothyroidism (underactive thyroid gland), or any of a variety of toxicities. And how many people can afford a comprehensive medical and psychological evaluation? Medical insurance companies will not foot those bills. Parents who inform themselves and ask the necessary questions help increase the chance that their children will be adequately evaluated and not merely rubber-stamped with a diagnosis and handed a prescription. It may be useful to take the checklist from appendix C with you to the doctor's office to help you organize your thoughts and better understand their evaluation of your child.

Since the diagnosis of ADD is predominantly descriptive, that is, about behaviors that are observed, it is not surprising that a large number of children will be diagnosed with ADD no matter what route their behaviors take. This invariably results in a trial of medication, and this almost always means a prescription for Ritalin.

If the child does not respond well to the Ritalin, an increase in dose is usually the next step, and this step may be repeated several times. If there is even a hint of improvement, a child is usually left on the current dose, even if side effects have emerged. Desperate to help the child, parents and physicians cling to the hope that the medication will eventually work better for the child. If they are knowledgeable and comfortable with prescribing it in children, some physicians may switch to another medication such as an antidepressant. The child who initially responds well to Ritalin is also likely facing an increased dose for any behavior that may be attributed to ADD. For instance, if the child gets into a fight or is not doing her homework, the dosage is likely to be increased. If this seems like a trial and error approach with your child as the guinea pig, it is.

This same scenario is happening over and over throughout the country. There are an estimated two million children on Ritalin today. Is this the best we have to offer them? To consider this for a moment, let's take a look at Ritalin's pros and cons. Then we will take a step back and consider the larger picture that addresses why conventional thinking on ADD is so entrenched and self-protective.

The Pros: Ritalin is approved by the FDA for treatment of ADD, and it can be nothing less than a godsend to many children and their families. There is no question that some children do well on Ritalin.

Ritalin is thought to work by activating the brain. As we suggested earlier, Ritalin increases the brain's physiologic arousal level as though turning up the lights in the brain. This increase in the brain's arousal is artificial and temporary, but it is an increase nonetheless. As a result, a child with ADD may be able to pay attention for a period of time. To continue with the analogy that arousal is like the intensity of the lights, then attention is like a spotlight. When the lights are turned up the spotlight works fine. Ritalin turns up the lights for a few hours.

During this period of increased arousal and adequate attention, a child may be observed to sit still and pay attention in class, complete tasks, even interact better with peers and teachers. It is no wonder that teachers appear to be clamoring for a Ritalin trial for their disruptive students.

Numerous studies have been done on the use of Ritalin for ADD, and there is good scientific support for its use. The results of the largest study of its type were recently published. This study was conducted at six medical centers and was sponsored by the National Institutes of Health. This study was called the Multimodal Treatment Study, or the MTS.[1] Roughly 600 children diagnosed with ADD, aged seven to nine years old, were assigned to one of four treatment groups. The findings show that the children treated with medications or with medications plus intensive behavioral treatment showed fewer ADD symptoms than those treated without medication. It is regrettable that no one was treated with neurofeedback in this study.

Medication was indeed our approach before we learned of other options for children with attention, behavioral, or learning problems. We gave every benefit of doubt to a diagnosis for which there was an established treatment. After all, we thought, how could a trial of Ritalin possibly hurt? It might even help. We quickly learned, however, we were not doing children or their parents any favors with our well-meaning but limited approach.

The Cons: It appears there is a rather narrow range of people for whom Ritalin is useful. Over half the children who have ADD and hyperactivity respond to Ritalin with improved behavior, but less than one in four who have ADD without hyperactivity respond favorably. In those who do not have ADD it is not beneficial. Once the diagnosis of ADD is established or suspected, the rush to prescribe Ritalin is not supported by the medical literature. Further attention should be given to the accuracy of the diagnosis and to the type of ADD.

There are numerous reasons to not be cavalier about giving Ritalin a try. We can begin by looking at how Ritalin is classified as a drug. Since Ritalin has similar effects and side effects on the brain to amphetamines and cocaine, the U.S. Controlled Substances Act classifies Ritalin as a Schedule II drug. Medications in this category are the most strictly controlled as they are deemed to have a very high potential for abuse and/or severe dependency. Other Schedule II drugs include amphetamines, morphine, barbiturates, and anabolic steroids.

Ritalin is so carefully controlled that refills are not permitted when a physician writes a prescription. It may be written for only a one-month supply, and must be written anew each month. This degree of caution is not unwarranted.

The rigorous control over Ritalin is not an outdated anomaly. Patented in 1950, Ritalin use did not begin to escalate until the late 1980s. In 1994, the American Academy of Neurology and the largest support group for ADD, Children and Adults with Attention Deficit Disorder (CHADD), petitioned to have the regulations on Ritalin reduced. The U.S. Drug Enforcement Agency (DEA) then researched this issue. They examined the use patterns, abuse potential and actual abuse data, and the diversion and trafficking of Ritalin. Their findings are not equivocal.[2,3] They concluded that Ritalin is indeed a drug with a high potential for abuse and that it has use patterns characteristic of cocaine and amphetamines. Consequently, the FDA continues to classify Ritalin as a Schedule II drug based on the findings by the DEA.

Ritalin for recreational use can be taken orally, pulverized and snorted, or dissolved in water and injected to achieve a rush or high. It has been found to be one of the drugs commonly obtained in street sales and drug trafficking rings. The source of Ritalin that makes its way to the streets for abuse is the kind made by the pharmaceutical industry rather than that by way of illegal manufacture. It is one of the most commonly *stolen* controlled drugs and one of the most commonly forged prescriptions. The numbers of adolescents who report Ritalin abuse are escalating, as are emergency room visits for Ritalin toxicity.

Those who abuse Ritalin commonly exhibit tolerance and psychological dependence characterized by an escalation of dose and frequency of use. The toxic effects are similar to cocaine. Psychomotor overactivation with tachycardia (rapid heart beat) and palpitations, elevated blood pressure, and agitation may occur and lead to psychosis, seizures, and death.

Despite these data, there are reports in the medical literature describing Ritalin as having a low potential for abuse. These studies should be read carefully, and it should be noted that although their conclusions are valid, their scope is limited—no doubt to reassure everyone that Ritalin is not likely to lead to substance abuse.[4] These reports primarily discuss the proper use of Ritalin in children with ADD. We do not dispute their findings, indeed, the proper dosing of Ritalin does not produce a high or drug-seeking behavior, nor does the proper dose of morphine in a patient who has post-surgical pain.

Not all the problems that stem from Ritalin arise from abuse. Numerous side effects may occur: insomnia, loss of appetite, nervousness, abdominal complaints, anorexia, tics, increased risk of drug abuse or dependence, and increased risk of seizures.[5] These are not minor problems. Let's look at the ramifications of some of these.

To avoid severe insomnia, for example, the last Ritalin dose must be given early enough in the day for the effects to wear off before bedtime. This renders many children less able to attend to their homework in the evening, and more frightening, it means that teenagers with ADD who drive are essentially in an untreated state with respect to symptoms of inattentiveness and impulsivity when they drive around at night with their friends.

Loss of appetite may lead to poor nourishment. There is evidence to suggest children who take Ritalin have a shorter stature, and perhaps, smaller brains.[6]

Tics may emerge, and are suggestive of Tourette's syndrome.[7] The tics often disappear if Ritalin is discontinued, but there are many cases of permanent tic activity after discontinuation of the drug. Apologists for Ritalin believe these tics would have emerged and persisted anyway, but that is not known at this time. Medicine has already experienced such an unexpected problem with other drugs. There is a permanent, often disfiguring, movement disorder called tardive dyskinesia that may result from taking antipsychotic medications. This was of course not known when antipsychotic medications were being touted as wonder drugs for schizophrenics and were extensively pre-scribed, beginning in 1952.

Even when Ritalin improves attention and is dosed properly for ADD, it often does not come without cost to the child. The type of attention improved by Ritalin is a narrow, focused kind. It is not uncommon to hear reports from adolescents that although their schoolwork is improved while on Ritalin, they feel less creative and less spontaneous. This appears to be one of the primary reasons older adolescents stop taking Ritalin on their own—they want their brains and their uniqueness back.

The potential immediate benefit of taking Ritalin for sup-posed ADD can confuse the prescribing physician if he or she assumes a positive response to Ritalin confirms the ADD diag-nosis. Anyone who takes a psychostimulant, such as Ritalin or an amphetamine, may work more attentively on an otherwise tedious task for a period of time. This does not confirm a sus-pected diagnosis of ADD, nor does it mean that a person should continue to take stimulant medication. After all, cocaine users also exhibit a similar improvement in attention for a period of time.

Also of concern is that even those children who do respond well to Ritalin do not acquire a better prognosis. Research has shown that the rates of occurrence of adult antisocial behavior, criminality, alcoholism, and suicide are no different in those treated for ADD with medications and those not treated.

Another significant limitation to be aware of is that children who respond well to Ritalin rarely exhibit improvements in the problems that commonly accompany ADD—learning disabili-ties, conduct problems, anxiety, depression, bedwetting, headaches, and sleep disturbances. Children who have ADD are much more likely to also be diagnosed with another, distinct problem. Thirty percent of children diagnosed with ADD are also diagnosed with an anxiety disorder. Yet another thirty percent are diagnosed with depression. Ritalin may actually worsen these problems, especially anxiety and sleep problems.

Regarding the increased risk of drug dependence, it is not a stretch of the imagination to worry that raising a generation of children who are medicated for behavioral control will result in a generation of adults who continuously turn to pill bottles or alcohol to modulate their moods. This may not be limited to just those teenagers who abuse Ritalin.

Ritalin may lower the seizure threshold in a child with epilepsy.[8] A child taking Ritalin who has seizures will be placed on yet another brain-altering drug to control the seizures.

Side Effects and Long-Term Effects: Not reported in the *Physicians Desk Reference (PDR)* is an important side effect— many children have a period of marked difficulty each day as the effects of Ritalin wear off. Teachers frequently see a deterioration in behavior in late morning before the noon dose is given, and it is common for parents to report unusually irritable behavior in their children in the late afternoon and early evening. The reality for the family may be a terrible dilemma of trying to keep a child on Ritalin because of the improved attention at school while dealing with a daily crisis at home which may disrupt the entire family.

What are the long term effects of Ritalin on the brain? Unknown—we repeat: *unknown*. We will have to wait a few-score years to answer this question. One area of concern is that Ritalin may prove to have similar long-term effects to those of cocaine on a short-term basis. Cocaine increases certain brain chemicals but leads to depletion states in others. Depletion of brain chemicals not only produces serious psychiatric symptoms, it can alter regulatory mechanisms and create a need for medication to regain normal chemical levels in the brain. This translates into becoming dependent on medications to function normally. It may well prove to be regrettable to give a powerful chemical brain stimulant like Ritalin to a child whose brain is in the vital process of development.

One potentially crippling long-term effect of relying on Ritalin to treat ADD is that it may sustain a child's brain in the condition of ADD. This is equally true for those children who receive the most benefit from taking Ritalin. How? Since Ritalin is not curative, its use may preclude other treatments that offer long-term solutions—neurofeedback, heavy metal detoxification, and optimal nutrition, which we discuss later in the book.

Though we know of no reported cases of human cancer induced by Ritalin, animals fed Ritalin have developed liver cancer.[9] The National Institutes of Health reported that Ritalin produced liver cancer in mice when given at thirty times the normal human dose for a two-year period. The risk does not seem insignificant when we consider some people take ten times the normal dose, and many are being advised they will need to take Ritalin for the rest of their lives.

Other animal studies that raise serious concerns show that the heart tissue of rats and mice is affected by Ritalin. Lesions of unknown effect have been found to appear on membranes in heart muscle.[10,11] The conclusions thus far suggest that there is a persistent, cumulative effect on the heart muscle tissue. Whether or not this occurs in humans, or will prove to be significant, will take years to determine. In the meantime, a million or so American children are the laboratory guinea pigs who will provide the definitive data. We can only hope the news will not be bad.

Other Drugs Used to Treat ADD

Ritalin is of course not the only drug in question with respect to what we are doing to our children in an effort to help them. There is an assortment of medications on the ADD drug treatment menu that includes, but is certainly not limited to, the following:

Psychostimulants: Like Ritalin, these raise the arousal level in the brain, and include Dexedrine, otherwise known as "speed," and Cylert, which has caused liver toxicity. Concerta, the newest medication to be approved for ADHD, is nothing more than a timed-release Ritalin. The primary benefit is eliminating one or two of the scheduled daily doses. The cost is more than that for individual doses added together.

Antidepressants: These increase neurotransmitter levels, the brain's chemical messengers. The more commonly used are Wellbutrin, Prozac, Effexor, Paxil, and Desipramine. The more common side effects include anxiety, insomnia, headache, dry mouth, dizziness, constipation, blurred vision, and nausea, depending on which of these the doctor prescribes.

Antihypertensives: Clonidine, a blood pressure-lowering drug, is used for its sedating properties and is commonly given to reduce hyperactivity, tics, or insomnia. It is frequently used in very young children. More common side effects include listlessness, dizziness, and constipation. The scary thing is that the FDA has received over 140 reports of serious adverse effects from Clonidine, including five deaths, yet they contend that there is not enough information to draw any conclusions, and this for a drug that has almost no studies done on children or in ADD. Had these results occurred from the use of an herb or vitamin treatment, there is no doubt the FDA would have acted swiftly and decisively.

Antipsychotics: Haldol is the most commonly used, though there are dozens, while Risperdol is the newer kid on the block. These are major tranquilizers and are usually reserved for more serious disruptive or aggressive behavior. They are also used to suppress the tics of Tourette's syndrome, even though they can cause a permanent movement disorder called tardive dyskinesia.

Anti-anxiety drugs: Buspar is actually a relatively mild and safe medication that can help relieve disturbing levels of anxiety. It does not treat ADD, however, and only helps with one of the symptoms that often accompanies ADD or is caused by medications used to treat ADD.

Anticonvulsants: Depakote and Tegretol are the drugs used in this category. Side effects include dizziness, abdominal cramps, and nausea. Liver function testing needs to be performed regularly due to potential toxicity of this drug.

Why Is Ritalin Use So Widespread?

If the preceding information is accurate, then why is the use of these medications so widespread? It is no coincidence that the thinking surrounding the causes of ADD and its treatment is so entrenched. The DEA reported that in 1996, pharmaceutical firms producing Ritalin and other stimulants used to treat ADD reported an annual profit of $450,000,000 from these drugs. From 1996 through 2000, the annual rate of Ritalin production was more than ten tons per year. The ramifications of this much money being involved are inescapable.

For any industry, pharmaceutical or otherwise, half a billion dollars a year in profits means using all the available hardball tactics to keep those profits up—waves of lobbyists, major political contributions, media spin management, and large confer-ences for "support groups" with distinguished authorities from academia to regale the audience with glowing reports about the documented benefits of drug treatment.

Perhaps the most insidious fact of all, however, is the care-ful management of medical thinking. This seems to be more obvious to those outside the field of medicine than to the doc-tors in the trenches. Most of the studies that are published in all the major medical journals are underwritten by the pharmaceu-tical industry. The average new drug coming to the market today has cost the company which owns its patent an average of a half-billion dol-lars to complete the necessary studies for full approval by the FDA.

So consider, are the pharmaceutical firms likely to fund any studies that may promote the thinking that there may be better treatment interventions than their drugs? Aren't they going to lavish funding on studies that will lead to the increased sales of their products?

So consider, are the pharmaceuti-cal firms likely to fund any studies that may promote the thinking that there may be better treatment inter-ventions than their drugs? Aren't they going to lavish funding on studies that will lead to the increased sales of their products? They are, after all, busi-nesspeople who know how to run a profitable enterprise.

Consider also that pharmaceutical representatives routinely sit on the boards of medical schools and hospitals, where their influence on the training and the thinking of physicians is exten-sive. They even sit on the boards of the private working groups at the Centers for Disease Control. Who is so naïve as to think these people are not concerned with their company's bottom line when far-reaching decisions are being made?

Can the scientists in the pharmaceutical industry speak out if they discover harmful practices? No, they are bound by exten-sive proprietary laws and non-disclosure agreements. Anyone who violates them is likely to face much more than professional suicide. Many saw a portrayal of the dilemma such scientists face in the movie *The Insider,* about the tobacco industry.

An example of how medical thinking is shaped with respect to the treatment of ADD is the near-exclusive emphasis on neurotransmitters, the brain's chemical messengers. Much is written on the neurotransmitters serotonin, norepinephrine, and dopamine. This is because there are a host of drugs that can increase the levels of these chemicals. We now also know there are many subtypes of these neurochemicals as well. New drugs will be developed that have more specific actions on these various subtypes. But this is only scratching the surface.

We do not yet have even an idea as to how many other neurotransmitters exist and what they do. Brain chemicals are the mother lode of the pharmaceutical industry, and there may be a multitude of neurotransmitters to yet be discovered.

The problem with this focus on neurotransmitters is that while these chemicals are essential, solutions lie in the *regulation* of the chemicals. The brain does not primarily regulate itself chemically, but electromagnetically. It is the frequency of the firing of our brain cells—that is, our brainwaves—that determines our brain functioning. It is no surprise to us that when we treat a child with neurofeedback for ADD, many other problems disappear. Through neurofeedback the brain learns to regulate itself better, which results in more optimal neurochemical levels and activity. This is most apparent in a patient with depression. Physicians state depression is the result of a "chemical imbalance" and prescribe drugs that increase brain chemicals such as serotonin. Patients with depression who do neurofeedback gain the same improvements as those who take drugs.

Tampering with chemical levels to achieve a desired physiological effect clearly has limits. It is like a general analyzing a battle by counting the numbers of corporals and captains and privates, and the like, on the winning side, then attempting to replicate those numbers on his side.

Surely it is the soldiers who wage the battle, but it is the organization and management of the troops that determines their effectiveness. The lack of success on the battlefield for General McClellan (a Union officer in the Civil War) was not due to the fact that he didn't have the correct ratio of sergeants to corporals, but because he lacked leadership ability. The brain of a child who has ADD does not need artificial boosts in the *number* of chemicals so much as better *self-regulation* of the brain's numerous activities.

Business forces will continue to dominate medical progress because, after all, medicine is a business—a very big business. Consequently, mainstream physicians will continue to think primarily about chemical manipulation of physiologic systems in an effort to decrease symptoms. But despite the powerful business forces influencing medicine, children will continue to have better treatment options for ADD from alternative medicine, which to be successful, will require parents to inform themselves and take a more active hand in making health decisions about their children. For your effort in doing this, we applaud you.

6

Neurofeedback—The Healing Potentials of Brainwave Biofeedback

Neurofeedback, often known as brainwave biofeedback or EEG biofeedback, is a sophisticated form of biofeedback. Biofeedback is one of these terms that most people have heard before but they do not necessarily understand what it actually means.

Biofeedback—Eavesdropping on Events inside Your Body

Biological systems in the human body are constantly sending us messages. We don't usually pay attention to them until they become so loud we can't avoid them. For example, if we run up three flights of stairs we notice we are breathing hard, sweating, and our hearts are pounding. We hear the message loud and clear, and we slow down, rest, and recover.

The internal messages are always there, but unless we exaggerate them or specifically go looking for them, they generally go unnoticed. When your doctor checks your pulse, he is listening in on biological information—hence, what he gets is biofeedback. If your doctor uses a stethoscope to listen to your heart and lungs, he is using a simple biofeedback instrument.

However, it is only in the past few decades that technology has provided us with machines sophisticated enough to detect, amplify, and record these biological signals. Being able to do this started a revolution in medicine. We soon learned that by getting feedback on internal processes, we could change internal activity.

Biofeedback is like eavesdropping on our body's own internal conversations. When these inside-the-skin events are detected and fed back to us through electrical signals using sight, sound, or touch, we can learn to use this information to change unwanted patterns that are contributing to poor physical and/or mental health. That's because our bodies are a sea of information and communication. Every organ is talking and listening to every other organ. This seems to be important if we are to remain healthy. We are a complexity of many organ systems and trillions of cells that are completely dependent on one another for life itself. If communication breaks down, or a system becomes dysregulated, it affects all other systems.

The idea that there is such a strong mind-body connection in healing has produced an entirely new field of medical study, psychoneuroimmunology (PNI). The term psychoneuroimmunology connects the mind (psycho), the nervous system (neuro), and the body's natural defenses (immuno). We know that these three systems carry on a constant dialogue, particularly the brain and nervous system, and this is where neurofeedback plays a major role.

Inside-the-skin events have often been ignored because they are subtle and often difficult to detect. Now, with the development of small, affordable computers, we are more capable than ever of listening in, amplifying, recording, and getting feedback information on biological events. This is revolutionizing the way we look at the whole body as a functioning system. The feedback may be in the form of sight, sound, or physical stimulation. With the latest advances in technology, the feedback can come in the form of sophisticated computer games. With practice, we can begin to change inside-the-body events to make us healthier.

The quieter messages that otherwise go unnoticed until we have a medical or emotional problem, are now available for study. With biofeedback, it is a relatively simple process to teach a person to change inside-the-skin activities. We can change things such as temperature, heart rate, blood pressure, muscle tension, chemical responses, even brainwaves.

To illustrate the effectiveness of biofeedback, we will share with you a wonderful story that Dr. Elmer Green tells. Dr. Green is one of the early pioneers in biofeedback and has contributed as much to the field as anyone in its history. Dr. Green would bring individuals with unusual talents for self-regulation to the Menninger Clinic in Topeka, Kansas, where they would be studied. On one of his trips to Menninger, Swami Rama demonstrated that he could create a ten-degree temperature differential on the palm of his hand just two inches apart. This, in anyone's opinion, would be extraordinary. Swami Rama said it took thirteen years to learn this. His biofeedback was the skin color of his hand. The swami would watch the palm of his hand to get his biological feedback. When a part of our body heats up, the area turns red. This is easily seen when a person is embarrassed and the skin flushes. The face, ears, and upper chest turn deep pink to bright red.

So Swami Rama would observe his own hand and would focus on making one spot red. When the one spot turned red, he knew that it was hotter than the surrounding area. This was obviously a result of changes in blood flow. A graduate student working with two temperature biofeedback machines was able to accomplish this task in two weeks. So with appropriate biofeedback technology, the graduate student was able to learn the task 300 times faster than Swami Rama. This reinforces the notion that we can change any organ system quickly if we provide it with appropriate information.

Biofeedback is simple and painless. The therapist attaches small sensory monitors to the scalp or skin, like placing tiny stethoscopes to listen to inside-the-skin events. The patient then sits back, usually in a comfortable chair, and begins to relax. The machines then show how a particular body system is functioning and feeds back information as the patient works to change that system. The patient may be trying to relax a group of muscles for back pain or increase skin temperature of a finger to help in Raynaud's disease. Raynaud's disease is a painful phenomenon in which the small arteries in the finger go into spasm, cutting off the blood flow. The fingers turn white and/or purple due to loss of blood flow.

As the patient becomes more proficient in the use of a biofeedback instrument, he becomes more aware of how a particular body system is functioning. This helps the patient bring that system under more voluntary control. Until recent decades, Western medicine believed that systems under the control of the autonomic nervous system functioned involuntarily, that we had no control over them. Yet, yogis in the East had demonstrated for millennia that they could control such processes. It was only through biofeedback that we were able to change the belief system of Western medicine.

Now, routinely in biofeedback practices all over the world, we train people to change those "involuntary" processes, bringing them under voluntary control. Once the patient learns to regulate a system, he no longer needs the biofeedback equipment. While training, he develops a sensory image. This is not a visual image, but a feeling that physical things are changing inside him. For example, he can sense when the hands are beginning to warm, the blood pressure is going down, the muscles are relaxing, and the brain is alert.

Imagine having voluntary control over your autonomic reflexes. A few decades ago physicians would have dismissed the idea as crazy. Now, informed physicians use and prescribe biofeedback daily to patients with disorders ranging from high blood pressure to urinary incontinence.

Neurofeedback—The Newest Innovation in Biofeedback

Neurofeedback is a sophisticated form of biofeedback that has been demonstrated to be highly effective in treating dozens of physical and psychological disorders. It has also been used for individuals who want to perform at peak efficiency. This is usually called "peak performance training."

Early in the history of neurofeedback it was used successfully to help individuals with uncontrollable epilepsy. This groundbreaking research was done by Barry Sterman and colleagues at the Sepulveda, California V. A. Medical Center Research Center.[16] There are many people who have seizure after seizure with little help from medication. By giving the patients feedback on their EEG rhythms, they were able to change the rhythms, thereby bringing the seizure activity under control.

Following closely on that work, Joel Lubar and his associates found EEG biofeedback to be a successful treatment for attention deficit disorder and hyperactivity.[7,8] EEG biofeedback's effectiveness was also demonstrated by Tansy and Bruen.[9] From there, the modality has demonstrated efficiency with disorders from alcoholism to depression, anxiety to migraines.

Neurofeedback is not a cure-all, end-all treatment. It is, however, an exciting treatment that offers hope to some of the hopeless by teaching them to regulate their own inside-the-skin events. The field is growing and changing rapidly, offering hope to larger and larger populations as research in neurofeedback continues in many universities and private settings.

Significant among the expanding fields of application is per-

Conditions Neurofeedback Can Help

Disorders that have been successfully treated with EEG biofeedback in clinical settings include:

- Attention deficit disorder (ADD)
- Attention deficit/hyperactive disorder (ADHD)
- Migraines
- Tension headaches
- PMS
- Alcohol and drug addiction
- Sleep disorders
- Depression
- Panic attacks
- Chronic pain
- Bruxism
- Mild closed head injury
- Oppositional and conduct disorders
- Epilepsy
- Chronic fatigue syndrome
- Stroke
- Multiple chemical sensitivities
- Autoimmune dysfunction
- Tinnitus
- Glucose metabolism dysregulation: Type II diabetes, hypoglycemia
- Specific learning disabilities/dyslexia
- Silicone related disease (breast implantation problems)

formance training. There is a growing interest in peak performance, so many practitioners of neurofeedback practice peak-performance training. Many governmental and industrial clients have their management teams go through neurofeedback training because it sharpens the brain, improves creativity, and enhances critical thinking. Japanese companies send management personnel to the United States for neurofeedback training because staying competitive is important and they know neurofeedback makes sharper, quicker thinkers.

The Neurofeedback Training Model

Most neurofeedback training clinics have their roots in client-centered psychotherapy and self-regulation, so there is a lot of personal attention when a patient receives neurofeedback. The neurofeedback therapist understands that a healthy brain has the ability and versatility to change states of arousal and attention. As each new situation in a person's life demands a specific level of arousal and awareness, the healthy brain can quickly move to the appropriate level of alertness.

In contrast, the unhealthy brain may be under-aroused and sluggish or over-aroused and anxious. Either way, the *dys-regulated* brain has a diminished ability to respond to specific demands. The immature, injured, or disordered brain lacks the normal elasticity of the healthy brain. Scientifically speaking, there appears to be discontinuity in the brain and nervous system processing or breakdowns in the way the brain and nervous system communicate. In other words, the brain is not processing information at the right speed. It is either too slow or too fast. Also, the brain is not communicating information correctly to itself, so it is out of sync with itself.

> *Neurofeedback is not a cure-all, end-all treatment. It is, however, an exciting treatment that offers hope to some of the hopeless by teaching them to regulate their own inside-the-skin events. The field is growing and changing rapidly, offering hope to larger and larger populations as research in neurofeedback continues in many universities and private settings.*

The disordered brain seems to be stuck or "parked" at the wrong place. It produces brainwaves that are inappropriate for the immediate situation. For example, the ADD brain tends to produce more daydreaming-type brainwaves than it does thinking, concentrating-type brainwaves.

Neurofeedback training teaches the person what specific brainwave states *feel* like and how to turn those states on voluntarily. The individual being trained can move their own brain to different physiological states, depending upon what the immediate situation requires.

We have been training people for many years to change their physiological state by altering their temperature or muscle tension. With neurofeedback, we are using a more sophisticated system that trains a more central process allowing direct access to the central processing system of the brain, rather than the peripheral systems of skin and muscle. Hence the new name—*neuro*feedback.

Neurofeedback makes the brain more flexible, and seems to have a generalizing effect on the full nervous system. The implications of this are profound. Training the brain to correct its dysregulated state seems to have a positive effect on neurological functioning as well as the cardiovascular, gastrointestinal, immune, and endocrine systems. Self-regulation not only enhances the brain's ability to improve cognitive/intellectual functioning, but it aids in the process of helping the body to heal itself.

Self-healing is what biofeedback is all about—it brings these involuntary processes under voluntary control. Self-regulation is exciting because it gives the patient some control over his own health and well-being. He is no longer at the mercy of a dysregulated brain and no longer completely dependent upon the pharmaceutical industry to provide him with the "magic pill."

What Is Neurofeedback Training?

A neurofeedback machine monitors the electrical activity produced by the brain, and the neurotherapist (neurofeedback professional) can correlate this activity with human behavior. The brain's electrical activity is measured in cycles per second, or hertz. A neurotherapist can examine the activity of a single frequency or a group of frequencies together, called a frequency band. By comparing behavior with the brainwave frequency, conclusions can be drawn about the relationship of the two. As a result of research in this area, we have been able to determine different subjective/ behavioral states and how they relate to rhythmic activity of the brain. In other words, we know what state of consciousness a person is in when the brain is producing a dominance of a single frequency or frequency band. (See table, pages 78-79)

By using feedback instruments, the therapist can feed back information to the patient on their level of consciousness at any given moment. The patient can subjectively evaluate what that conscious state feels like. With practice, the patient can begin to voluntarily approximate and reproduce that level of consciousness. Over time the patient will get closer and closer to that state until the desired rhythmic activity of the brain can be voluntarily produced. Once the patient has developed a level of sophistication in identifying the desired state, they no longer need the neurofeedback equipment to accomplish the task. They are now self-regulating.

Using the neurofeedback equipment to *train* voluntary control, patients are able to use this information on their own to relax, concentrate better, or feel calmer and be more focused. Therefore, the student shows fewer and fewer symptoms of attention deficit/ hyperactivity disorder. The businessman is much more efficient on the job, the migraine sufferer can dramatically reduce the frequency, duration, and intensity of her headaches. Neurofeedback uses this information about very subtle inside-the-brain events to change the levels of alertness and awareness. This is the fine and profound art of self-mastery. It makes the human much less dependent on any other person, drug, machine, or medical technology. It produces strong self-reliance, independence, self-esteem, and provides some control over one's physical and mental state of health.

The Neurofeedback Learning Process

All biofeedback, including neurofeedback, is a learning process. It involves physical learning and mental skills. It is a process of learning how to change your body by listening to its functioning. Soon the patient learns control and can change mental states. Like any other learning process, the more one learns, the more confidence one develops. So not only does the

Behavioral States and Brainwave Activity

Band Name	Frequency Band	Alertness Level
High Beta	19 Hz and above	Hyper-alert to intensely alert. Can range from fear, panic, rage, or anxiety to being super alert.
Beta	15 to 18 Hz	Active alert.
Sensory Motor Rhythm (SMR), Low Beta	12 to 15 Hz	Calm alert.
Alpha	8 to 12 Hz	Relaxed focus.
Theta	4 to 8 Hz	Drowsy, lethargic, dreamy.
Delta	1 to 4 Hz	Deep sleep.

Focusing Ability	When Appropriate	Efficiency
Can vary from super-focus to unfocused and confused. May be very intense to very scattered with fragmented thinking.	Appropriate for learning very difficult material when intensity is required. Inappropriate for normal daily activity.	Very efficient to very poor efficiency, depending on the situation.
Can focus very well and can respond quickly. Good selective attention; can shift focus easily; good anticipation.	Appropriate for learning, doing a task, staying focused. Inappropriate for relaxing.	Efficient for learning, working, reading difficult material, or being in school. Inefficient for leisure activity.
A calm focus. Ability to concentrate without a sense of urgency.	Appropriate for learning quietly without high intensity. Inappropriate for high-intensity learning.	Efficient for calm, focused learning. Good for reading light material.
Able to focus in a relaxed, meditative way.	Appropriate for relaxation and creativity. Inappropriate for intense learning.	Efficient for creative endeavors. Good for breaking away from obvious views. Inefficient for work or classroom learning.
Reduced awareness, poor focus, dreamlike, near sleep.	Appropriate for deep meditation, some creative work. Good for bedtime. Inappropriate for work or classroom.	Efficient for sleep preparation. Has some implications for creative inspiration. Very inefficient for work or classroom.
Loss of ability to focus. Loss of awareness.	Appropriate for deep sleep. Very inappropriate for thought processes.	No efficiency except sleep.

patient learn the neurofeedback skill, but her self-confidence improves.

Neurofeedback is not complicated. In our office practice we have four-, five-, and six-year-olds learn to change their brain-wave patterns. Anyone except the very mentally deficient can learn self-regulation, so neurofeedback is not just for the elite. It is for all humans who want self-control and self-determination. Although patients cannot explain what they have learned, they *know* they have changed.

For example, in temperature training, we have many patients who can quickly learn to take a seventy-nine-degree hand temperature and increase it to ninety-five degrees. They know they can do it, but they cannot tell you how they do it because the learning is at a subconscious level.

In neurofeedback, the brain learns what it needs to do to accomplish the task. You want it, you tell the brain to do it and it does it, leaving you never knowing exactly what you've learned. Truly, if there is any magic left in the world, it is the magic inside each of us.

Some biofeedback processes, like temperature training, may only take a few training sessions to achieve. The more complex the system, the longer training takes. Brainwave training takes longer than temperature training because you are dealing with a more complex system. In brainwave biofeedback, the patient learns the "feel" of a particular brainwave. The more training the patient has, the more easily he perfects the skill of producing a particular rhythmic state in the brain. Learning to modify a brainwave state in the direction of a desired mental state is a "discovery" process—a process of gaining more and more control over your thoughts, feelings, and behavior.

The Emerging Theory of Global Dysregulation

Because of the wide variety of disorders that have been helped with neurofeedback, the idea of a global dysregulation effect is emerging. This is a simple concept that means if the brain is dysregulated, it can have a global or body-wide effect. Seldom does a patient present to a health professional with a single symptom; usually the symptoms involve more than one body system.

For example, a patient may present with the chief complaint of depression, but after a thorough intake evaluation, they acknowledge trouble sleeping, poor attention span, irritable-bowel-type problems, low-back pain, sugar cravings, weight gain, alcohol use, irritability, and chronic anxiety. So the symptoms are not just in one system, they tend to be global or body-wide. Once neurofeedback treatment begins, symptoms from *several* systems begin to respond, and the response generally has lasting benefits.

It appears that once the brain becomes dysregulated, it may have a global effect on the body. After all, the rhythmic activity of the brain affects all functional systems of the body, and this rhythmic activity is central to all other systems. Therefore, to regulate the central rhythmic activity of the brain improves body-wide functioning. It appears that neurofeedback not only affects such problems as attention and concentration, but has a systemic effect. When we treat people for ADD with neurofeedback, other systems begin to improve because the brainwaves become regulated. For example, in treating ADD, not only does attention improve, but oppositional behavior, sleep, irritability, depression, anxiety, antisocial behavior, tics, and many other problems also improve.

> *It appears that neurofeedback not only affects such problems as attention and concentration, but has a systemic effect. When we treat people for ADD with neurofeedback, other systems begin to improve because the brainwaves become regulated.*

To give you an unusual example, several years ago we were treating a ten-year-old male for ADD, and during the treatment period, he started having visual problems. His mother took him to his ophthalmologist who told her, and us, that after years of following this child's visual problems, his "lazy eye" had suddenly got much better. We all concluded that focusing on the neurofeedback monitor must have helped train the eye to focus more normally.

Neurofeedback seems to have the ability to reduce or correct global dysregulation. The future implications of this are exciting; if such turns out to be the case, it could preclude taking multiple medications for different problems, or seeing several different specialists, each treating a different problem. Neurofeedback treats problems at the core—the brain—and when the functioning of the brain improves, it appears to produce global body-wide changes.

7

How Neurofeedback Works

When you make claims that a particular treatment is highly effective for a number of different diagnoses, professionals and laypersons alike tend to become suspicious. And we think they should. Snake-oil salesmen have long pervaded the arena of medical treatment. How many times have we all heard that this pill or that herb will heal, give you more energy, give you greater sexual prowess, or help you lose weight? Most products with broadly based claims just do not hold up to close inspection. They may help with one thing or reduce one symptom, but they seldom meet our expectations. When they don't, we find our optimism has turned sour.

Brainwave Researchers Take Advantage of Modern Computers

When we first ventured into the field of neurofeedback, we kept waiting for the bottom to fall out. After all, we remembered with vivid disappointment the "alpha craze" in the 1960s and 1970s. The promoters of alpha brainwaves promised that if we could make more alpha brainwaves through meditation, drugs, and primitive neurofeedback machines, we could achieve a life of bliss. In the 1960s, some people were turning on their TVs and adjusting the picture until it was a snowy fuzz. They sat staring at it because it was supposed to help them produce more alpha waves. Transcendental meditation was the craze, acid was the party drug, and companies made alpha machines. Those who promised nirvana could not deliver on the promise. The machines were too primitive and research too scarce. The alpha phenomena hurt the science of neurofeedback; it did not produce all the promises we were told to expect. In retrospect, there is nothing wrong with meditation, biofeedback, and learning to produce more alpha waves, but there were lots of reasons for the failures: the equipment was not as sophisticated; the science was too new to make such exaggerated claims; and it was too entangled with the metaphysics of the 1960s and 1970s.

Meanwhile, brain science has taken some curious turns over the past few decades. Medical science started out trying to understand the brain as a functional system. By looking at specific disorders, we hoped to see how the systems had failed. For example, when we first started looking at the ADD phenomena, we had the intuitive understanding that it was a functional problem, that it had to do with how the brain functions as a whole unit. This mindset is seen in the terminology of "Minimal Brain Dysfunction." Then, brain science went in a different direction.

Scientists began an attempt to understand the brain from a molecular level. They broke the brain down into the smallest bits, rather than seeing it as a whole, precluding the functional model of the brain.

Often our patients come in with normal CT scans, normal EEGs, and/or normal MRIs, but *functionally* they are a mess. So, structurally, and perhaps molecularly, they appear normal, but it is their routine brain function that seems disturbed. We frequently describe the patient's disorder to them by giving this example: "You are like a car with faulty timing. Your brain is okay—it just needs a tune-up."

By examining the brain at a molecular level, the issue of gross motor, gross thought, and gross emotional behavior is not the primary focus. Most of our patients are not concerned with their molecules, but they are concerned about balance and strength, quality and quantity of thought, and of being over-whelmed by their emotions. As a result, in the past few years, many brain scientists have returned to examining the brain as a functional system rather than as trillions of molecules. This has translated into practical therapeutic treatments for clusters of disorders. Not only are we concerned with the idea of global dys-regulation, where the brain causes body-wide problems, but we are concerned about clusters of disorders.

For example, accompanying depression, the person may also have tiredness, loss of interest, irritability, loss of sleep, or a decreased sense of humor. The cluster of symptoms relates to the same problem. Global symptoms may reflect problems from several systems. Therefore, a practical therapeutic approach focuses on a treatment such as neurofeedback that not only has a positive effect on clusters of symptoms, but also on global symptoms.

Let's consider the brain. The brain is a large, complex, self-organizing system. Occasionally the functioning of that system becomes dysregulated. As we explained earlier, it is likely a result of genetics or some type of injury. When the brain is dys-regulated for a period of time without restoration of its normal functioning, it interprets the new functioning as normal.

For example, if you smoke cigarettes long enough, the body begins to act as though they are as necessary to you as oxygen, water, or food. When you try to quit, the body rebels, making quitting very difficult. Brainwaves are much the same. If a brain receives a head injury during birth, it may produce the wrong brainwave for the task at hand. After long enough a time, the brain doesn't try to correct the dysfunction.

Neurofeedback works by challenging the dysfunction and nudging the brain's firing patterns in the direction of a healthier balance. This nudging seems to awaken the brain's self-regulating system. A process then begins to take place which appears to be the brain teaching itself to normalize. Because the brain is trying to maintain a balance, it pushes back, resisting a rapid change in one direction or another. This is why progress is not rapid with neurofeedback. This slow learning process insures that the brain does not rush to a new firing pattern that could be in a more dysfunctional, opposite direction. The fact is we can change any functional system of the body, including the brain and nervous system, if we give it appropriate feedback and enough time.

It took the newer, faster, more compact computers to make neurofeedback a practical therapeutic treatment that could be made available to the general public. If you are going to give the brain information about its own rhythmic activity, and give it fast enough for it to recognize and change the pattern, it has to be *fast*. It has only been in the past decade or so that we could even begin to formulate treatment protocols and to experiment on what types of disorders would respond positively to the training. We don't apologize for being a new science, but we still eagerly await the next research paper or treatment protocol for some disorder we have not previously worked with.

Neurofeedback offers hope to so many people who feel hopeless because it is able to provide the brain with information about its own rhythmic activity. Not only does it assist in regulating the dysrhythmic activity of ADD (when the brain's rhythms are not appropriate to the task), but also the dysrhythmic activity of epilepsy, chronic migraines, head injury, stroke, sleep disorders, PMS, depression, and anxiety.[1,2]

The brain communicates to all systems, including itself, through electrical activity. As odd as it may sound, it appears that the brain has generators that produce the brainwave activity, which are actually low-frequency electrical rhythms. It is this electrical activity that gives the information about what and how to do everything. This low-frequency rhythmic activity is central to life and the second-to-second functioning of every organ system in the body. If this rhythmic activity becomes dysregulated, it leads to dysfunction. We could end up sleeping rather than reading, anxious rather than calm, dull rather than alert.

We know now that the brain responds to many forms of intervention, including classical and operant conditioning, which we will discuss later. Neurofeedback directly affects the brain, so its impact is on the central processes of the entire person. Since the brain is intimately involved with every organ and system in the body, neurofeedback affects us at the core. You cannot change the brain without it having some effect on every functioning system. Because neurofeedback directly affects the brain, it has the opportunity to elicit a faster, more comprehensive, longer-lasting resolution to functional problems.

Adjusting the Brain's Rhythmic Activities—by Ourselves

To be more specific about how neurofeedback works, the brain controls our physiological state of arousal. This is done by the rhythmic activity of the brain, expressed through brainwaves. If our brainwaves become dysregulated for whatever reason, they may not return to a healthy functional state after the event has passed.

Earlier we discussed the notion that the brain may assume dysfunctional rhythmic activity to be normal and work to maintain it. When the brain is producing a steady state, regardless of the activity level, we say it is "parked," to use a term coined by brain researcher Dr. Michael Tansy. For example, if the brain is consistently showing a dominance of seven hertz, regardless of the human's functional activity, we say the brain is parked at seven hertz.

There are certain brainwaves that are characteristically seen as a result of a specific event. For example, when there is a problem, the brain will frequently emit a high burst of a single brainwave or a band of brainwaves. These are referred to as spikes. In closed head injuries, we may see spikes in the very low delta range (one to four hertz). In epilepsy, we see high spikes in the area of seven hertz. Frequently, these types of head injuries do not show up on conventional imaging such as MRIs or CT scans.

In other types of problems, such as ADD, we do not generally see spikes, but we see a single brainwave or band of brainwaves that are inappropriately dominant, expressed when they should not be. If sleep waves are dominant when one is trying to read, they are inappropriate, and he has a problem. Occasionally, we see ADD children who also have spikes in the one to four hertz range. We suspect these children have suffered some type of closed head injury: a fall, a sharp bang or hit, or some other trauma.

Dominance is an important term. Brains produce all of the various brainwaves all of the time, but depending on our level of arousal, a single brainwave or a band of several will be higher than others. That wave or band of waves will be dominant. To function at peak efficiency, we want the dominant wave to reflect the activity we are engaged in at the time. For example, if we are sleeping, we want slow "sleep" brainwaves; if we are doing a complicated math problem, we want the faster, "alerting" brainwaves to be dominant.

Children and adults who have attentional disorders demonstrate a dominance of low-frequency waves. In fact, both epileptics and boys with ADD show a dominance of slower EEG waves and a deficit of faster-frequency waves.[3] If the patient is asleep, it is appropriate to have a dominance of slow waves, but if he is producing excessive slow waves in math class, there is a problem. He would appear to be in a fog; short-term memory is compromised and lethargy is common (i.e., he probably has ADD).

A multitude of symptoms may be present when we see a dominance of low-frequency waves. If the brainwave states are not normalized, all other areas of the patient's life may be affected. If the rhythmic activity is normalized, normal functioning is restored. The normalization of the brain generally produces the following types of positive changes: improved executive functioning, restful sleep, improved memory, improved concentration, reduced hyperactivity, and elimination of depression and anxiety.

To better understand how brainwaves are related to functioning, let's look at some generalities. Think of brainwaves on a continuum from very slow to very frantic, in terms of what they mean about brainwave activity. Our behavioral functioning varies according to where we are dominant (or "parked") on the continuum.

In deep sleep, we are producing more of the very high-amplitude, low-frequency delta waves, less than four cycles per second (see figure 7-1), so delta is dominant. Moving along the continuum, next, we have theta waves. They are slightly lower in amplitude, and there is an increase in frequency. We will see four to eight cycles per second. In other words, they are not quite as "loud," but there are more of them. Theta is characterized by a drowsy, partial awareness or an unconscious state nearing sleep.

cps = cycles per second, or Hertz

DELTA Less than 4 cps	THETA 4–8 cps	ALPHA 8–12 cps	SMR 12–15 cps	BETA 15–18 cps	HIGH BETA more than 19 cps
Sleep	Drowsy	Relaxed Focus	Relaxed Thought	Active Thinking	Excited

Figure 7-1. The Range of Brainwaves in the Human Brain

The next frequency band on our continuum is alpha. They are lower in amplitude than theta, and, again, there are more of them. Their frequency increases and we see eight to twelve cycles per second. Alpha is characterized by a relaxed, focused awareness, somewhat like meditation or yoga.

Next, we find a low beta that was identified and named sensory motor rhythm (SMR) by the brain scientist, Barry Sterman, Ph.D.[4] Dr. Sterman first observed this process in physically relaxed cats. SMR is from twelve to fifteen hertz followed by the beta frequency band, which is a higher frequency band from fifteen to eighteen hertz. Beta is characterized by low-amplitude, higher frequency. It is very focused, but busier, and not as relaxed as the rhythm of alpha.

Last, we have a low-amplitude, very high frequency band labeled high beta or gamma. This high beta wave is characterized by an excited, super focused, anxious, fearful, or angry mental state, and ranges from more than nineteen hertz, up to or beyond forty hertz.

If the brain moves toward the slower frequency brainwaves, a person becomes decreasingly aroused, until they finally achieve sleep or an unconscious state. If the brain moves to higher and higher frequencies, the person becomes increasingly aroused until they are finally out of control due to excitation. Some people are able to sustain a state of super focus in the higher frequencies. There is some controversy about the exact labeling of such terms as alpha and theta, and about the exact frequencies that should be included in the bands, but we will leave such issues to academia. It is important, however (and generally agreed upon), that the lower the frequency, the more lethargic we become, and that the higher the frequency, the more agitated we become.

You can easily see how brainwaves affect our state of arousal. If we are underaroused, we don't function at full capacity because we are dull, lazy, or sleepy. It is okay to sleep in the low waves, but we don't want to be parked there all the time. It is okay to become excited over something, but no one would want to stay there. The normally functioning brain is very flexible, and can move easily up or down the frequency range, depending on the level of arousal needed for the task at hand. It is generally dominant in the mid-frequency range, focused but relaxed. Unfortunately, most people with ADD are parked in the lower frequencies, and we see dominant theta patterns in most individuals with ADD. They are often parked somewhere around seven hertz.

Neurofeedback treats the patient's central processing mechanisms, the brain. It doesn't merely chase one symptom with one drug and another symptom with a second or third drug. Neurofeedback treats the cause and not the symptoms, which is why it gets better results than stimulant medications overall.

It is surprising to most parents to find out that their wild, hyperactive child actually is in a state of under-arousal. The child is using hyper movement to wake up and stay focused in his surroundings. Otherwise, the child is in a dull, lethargic state. Hyper movement then becomes a very functional behavior for keeping the brain semi-awake. There are other children, primarily females, who do not use the hyper movement. They are the dull, listless, often irritable ones.

Another consequence of the slow rhythmic activity is sleep disturbance. A large number of individuals with ADD and other ADD-type problems also suffer from sleep problems. These may be delayed-onset insomnia, frequent awakening, early awakening, and/or restless sleep. This list would also include restless-leg syndrome, bed-wetting, encopresis (fecal incontinence), nightmares, and other nocturnal problems. Parents of ADD patients frequently tell us how their child's bed is torn apart every morning.

From a practical standpoint, it is hard to sleep at night if the brain has been semi-asleep all day. As practitioners, we often end up training the brain to wake up so that it will be able to sleep later.

When we treat ADD with neurofeedback, we see dramatic improvement in the other symptoms that manifest as a result of too much low-frequency brainwave activity. Low-frequency brainwave activity is directly or indirectly responsible for a host of problems. While neurofeedback cannot fix everything, it can improve dysfunctional rhythmic activity, which can alleviate many different symptoms. A treatment such as stimulant medications may make the child alert, but it also makes the collateral symptoms worse.

For example, parents often report school grades improve when the child is on Ritalin, but that their sleep is awful, their irritability more prevalent, and their tic behavior much worse. In contrast with stimulant medications, neurofeedback treats the patient's central processing mechanisms, the brain. It doesn't merely chase one symptom with one drug and another symptom with a second or third drug. Neurofeedback treats the cause and not the symptoms, which is why it gets better results than stimulant medications overall.

One technique to determine if the brain is functioning within "normal" parameters is to look at the ratio between the low frequencies and the mid-range frequencies. We generally

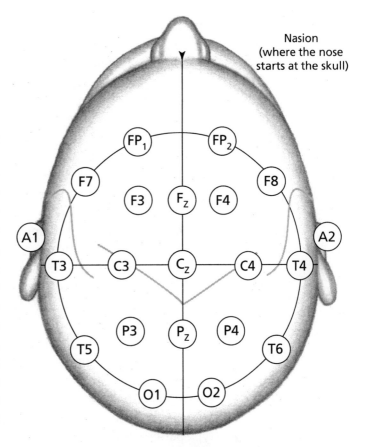

Figure 7-2. International Ten-Twenty System of Electrode Placement

The ten-twenty head chart is internationally recognized. It tells clinicians and researchers exactly where to place the sensors on the head. The *nasion* is located where the nose starts at the skull, and the *inion* is located at the two knots on either side of the back of the skull. A1 and A2 represent the left and right ears. Sensors are placed at the various sites on the head to record the EEG or to train the site with neurofeedback.

compare the ratio of theta averages to beta averages, measured with electrodes placed at different locations on the head.

To do this, neurotherapists use what is known as the international ten-twenty system of electrode placement. This system indicates the exact placement sites of the sensors (see figure 7-2). Research protocol and clinical treatments are standardized by placing the electrode sensors at specific head sites. Correct sensor placement is critical to success, so the neurotherapist takes great care to place the sensors at specific locations on the head. To train the wrong area could worsen existing problems.

The theta-to-beta ratio in adults generally ranges from one - to-one to one-and-a-half-to-one. With younger children, the ratio is somewhat higher, but we still want a ratio near that range. Frequently, the patient with ADD and the cluster of other disorders like depression, sleep dysfunction, tics, and head injury will have excessive ratios. We have seen two-, three-, four-, five-, and six-to-one ratios in severely dysregulated brains. This indicates that the patient is producing excessive low-frequency waves.

When treating patients with these high ratios, we do not always see the ratios change, but we almost always see the high elevations of theta come down. Individuals with anxiety usually have excessive high-frequency waves. They may even have a V-type pattern of elevated low-frequency waves, often indicative of a patient who is ADD with concomitant anxiety, and elevated high-frequency waves with deficits in the production of mid-range frequencies.

Operant Conditioning—
How to Train the Brain

The process of training the brain to make appropriate adjustments in rhythmic firing is as simple, in theory, as the way Dr. Ivan Pavlov conditioned his dogs to salivate at the sound of a bell. Dr. Pavlov's training paradigm is known as classical conditioning. Operant conditioning is about rewarding behavior that approximates a desired behavior. In education, we give an "A" to students who more closely approximate the learning behavior we want to see; we give "Bs" to those who are close, but not quite as close; and we give "Fs" to those who miss the mark.

An example of operant conditioning would be if we wanted a child to play in the sandbox, we would reward the child every time she would go to the sandbox and ignore her if she played elsewhere. Soon, she would play in the sandbox because it is the most rewarding place to be. Giving Fido a treat when he sits for us is also operant conditioning.

Brainwave training works the same way. If the brain is making too much low-frequency activity, we reward it with points or a tone each time it makes the more desirable, higher frequency brainwaves. Unfortunately, this is not as direct and as quick as training Fido to sit.

With neurofeedback we eavesdrop on complex inside-the-brain events, run the information through a computer, and feed back the information through the eyes, ears, and/or skin of the trainee. Each time the trainee improves his brainwaves, we reward him; if the brainwaves stay the same, there is no reward.

One of our standard techniques is a video game in which the patient directs a large dot along a path, eating smaller dots. If the brain is functioning better, the big dot eats more of the small dots faster, and the patient scores more points. There are a variety of games used to stimulate the brain to wake up, but they are specialized games programmed to reflect EEG functioning. Traditional video games lull the brain into producing the wrong brainwaves, which adds to the problems of ADD.

Moving toward Brainwave Balance

Figure 7-3 illustrates how the brainwaves normalized and the ratio balance was improved in the case of Otis, an eleven-year-old male with ADD and hyperactivity. The figure shows Otis' progress at his twenty-second neurofeedback session. During the first treatment, the theta-beta ratio was in the range of eight-to-one. This means that Otis was making eight times more slow sleep waves than the faster alert waves. By the time Otis completed twenty-two training sessions, his beta ratio was in the range of 4.6-to-one. Otis required many more sessions to normalize the dysregulation, but there were dramatic behavioral improvements at session number 22.

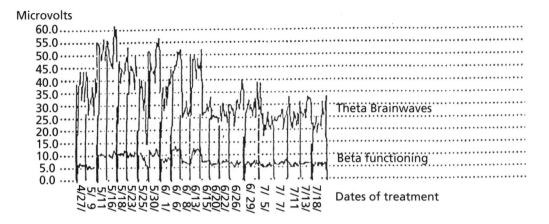

Figure 7-3. Neurofeedback Summary Chart

The numbers in the left-hand column are microvolts of electrical activity recorded from the brain. The top horizontal line that starts at approximately forty microvolts and wanders up and down ending the twenty-second session at approximately twenty-three microvolts is Otis' theta (4-8 Hz) brainwaves. The lower, less jagged line that starts at five microvolts is his beta (15-18 Hz) brainwaves. At session one, Otis' theta-to-beta ratio was slightly over eight-to-one. By the end of his twenty-second session, that ratio had dropped to slightly over 4.6-to-one and declining. The bottom line reflects the dates of training.

You will note in this figure that in treatment sessions one and two, the ratio looks better, due to the novelty effect. Otis is experiencing something new and exciting, so he is more awake. However, after a couple of sessions, the task becomes boring, as it usually does for ADD patients. For them, everything new is wonderful and everything old is boring.

For Otis, the twenty-two sessions improved his concentration, raised his school grades, and helped him feel "happier" as described by a parent. Otis made significant improvements, as do most ADD patients who are treated with neurofeedback. It took a total of forty training sessions before we discontinued Otis' treatment, and one year later his mother reported he was doing "great."

The proof that we can do this with neurofeedback has been established for over two decades. It has just taken a long time to get this sophisticated treatment to the general public, and it has taken us some time to understand what we are seeing and how to use it therapeutically to help individuals like Otis with these truly disruptive disorders of brain regulation.

It is quite possible that some day, the use of medications such as Ritalin for attentional and behavioral disorders will be a thing of the past. Human beings will then have easy access to neurofeedback for a wide variety of disorders. In the meantime, practitioners are becoming proficient at correcting disorders of brainwave dysregulation such as ADD and behavioral problems using neurofeedback. Why give any medication if the individual can self-correct a problem with neurofeedback training?

8

The Insider's View of a Typical Neurofeedback Session

Neurotherapy sessions are relatively similar, and usually last approximately thirty minutes. Sessions begin, continue, and end in the same way unless there are unusual circumstances. What is different from one session to the next, however, is the individualized feedback protocol based on the specific symptom patterns of the individual being treated. Patients present with different symptoms, so one individual may receive a completely different neurotherapy training protocol from another.

We tailor treatment for a patient to his particular symptom or symptoms. Our goal is to retrain brainwaves to overcome less useful or "bad" brainwave firing patterns. Not all people with ADD and not all aggressive individuals have the same behaviors. In addition, they may respond differently as we train a specific brainwave by varying the location of the electrodes on the skull. For example, when we train the same site on two individuals, it may make one person anxious while calming the other. Individual responses to specific training plays a major role in guiding the course of treatment. The neurotherapist must rely on good information reporting from the patient and his or her family, and they also need to be keen observers themselves.

To give you an idea of how the neurotherapy session works,

let's take you through a therapy session of a typical patient with ADD and moderately severe behavioral problems. Our example will be Newman, a twelve-year-old male in the seventh grade. His mother reported that he had had behavioral problems since "day one." He was tested by the school system and by independent psychologists several times, and this testing revealed a very bright young man with an IQ in the above-average to superior range. However, the testing also revealed a high variability in his performance. This usually indicates variability in the ability to pay attention—one minute he can concentrate well and the next minute he is off in his own world. As a matter of fact, his mother kept repeating, "Newman lives in his own little world."

The intake interview consists of an extensive medical and psychological history and review of all aspects of the patient's life. We interview the patient as well as any family members available, usually parents. When we did Newman's intake interview, it revealed that his symptoms ranged from moderate to severe and that there were a lot of them. Newman had moderate attentional problems and was hyperactive; in addition, he had a moderate level of tic behavior, which included throat clearing, sniffing, hiccups, head tossing, blinking, lip licking, and coughing.

Newman had many other symptoms including anxiety, depression, fearfulness at times, difficulty getting along with just about everybody, being difficult to manage, having temper outbursts, and accepting no responsibility for any of his behavior. Additional symptoms included poor school performance, not obeying rules, low self-esteem, tearfulness as a defense, social withdrawal, oppositional behavior, lying, taking things and denying it, fighting, and destruction of other people's property. We diagnosed Newman as having attention deficit disorder, oppositional defiant disorder, and Tourette's syndrome.

Oppositional defiant disorder is defined by a persistent and pervasive pattern of negative, defiant, disobedient, and hostile behavior, particularly toward authority figures. Tourette's syndrome is characterized by persistent motor and vocal tics, such as Newman's sniffing, head tossing, lip licking, and coughing.

Because it is impossible to work on all problems at once, we prioritized which symptoms to treat first. We decided to concentrate on the tic behavior first, knowing that protocol would also have an overall calming effect and would reduce Newman's hyperactivity and anxiety. The tics were a major concern for Newman's mother, but as is typical for someone with his symptom patterns, Newman denied he had any tics. As for the head tossing, he said he was just getting the hair out of his eyes. However, when his hair was cut short, the head tossing continued.

We usually see some improvement after four or five training sessions. Once one symptom is resolved, we move on to another symptom or groups of symptoms. Changing symptoms to be treated requires a protocol change; we place the EEG sensors in different locations on the head and vary the brainwave frequency to be trained. This allows us to train a different part of the brain at different frequencies and reward different brainwave activity.

When Newman came in with his mother for his tenth neurofeedback session he arrived on time. They had been late for all prior treatments. We observed that he was more relaxed and quieter in the waiting room. His tic behavior was still apparent, but the frequency was diminished by about half. When we greeted Newman and his mother, we asked them how things were. "Fine," he replied. We recognized by now that Newman only spoke when spoken to, and he used the fewest possible words to respond to us, unless he was angry. Then he was *very* verbal. Things were always "fine" and "good," or "okay" or "no problem" with Newman regardless of how difficult things actually were at home, at school, or with the authorities.

Newman's mother handed us the training report, a short form that is filled out after each neurotherapy session. Because neurotherapy is such a powerful tool, the patient will often feel differently or behave differently after each session. The training report (see table on page 101) helps us to know if we are using the correct training protocol on the correct location on the patient's head. Looking at the training report helps us to see if we're on the right path and are alleviating symptoms, keeping them the same, or making them worse.

The beauty of neurotherapy is the immediate information gained by the neurotherapist. This is not a therapy that uses the

"Let's see how you're doing in six months" philosophy. We want to know how the patient felt and behaved that same day after each therapy session. The training report indicates that the training was in the beta (15-18 Hz) or the SMR frequency range (12-14 Hz). These frequency ranges mean little or nothing to the patient but are very important to the therapist because they help to determine the treatment protocol.

To fill out the training report, the patient or family member simply observes any behavioral or mood changes that occur after the training session, and checks the corresponding change on the form. The training report is a simple A-B form: (A) the symptom got worse, (B) the symptom improved. For example, (A) sleep was worse, (B) sleep was better.

The information from Newman's training report form indicated that he was generally calmer, there was a reduction in his disruptive behavior, and there had been no angry outbursts. So, we felt it was appropriate to make no protocol changes. If the training report information or information obtained from Newman's mother had given us different information, we might have altered the protocol.

While still in the waiting room, we engaged Newman and his mother in general conversation. In this way, we were able to provide important modeling to Newman as to how to appropriately talk with his mother and other adults. It was also important to demonstrate to his mother how to talk to Newman. Because communication is usually a major problem with children suffering from the problems Newman was experiencing, we worked on this for a few minutes at every session. We generally do the modeling without telling the patient or family what we are actually doing. Occasionally, a parent wants a conference to discuss new events or how to handle a particular situation. We acknowledge their desire, then proceed with the neurotherapy, coming back later for the conference.

Newman was escorted to a neurotherapy room where he was able to discuss with us anything he wished without his mother being present. In Newman's case, he wished to discuss very little. Some of our youngsters are very verbal and often insightful, which can be extremely helpful in their treatment. We have learned a lot about children by listening carefully to so many of them. The secret is to really *listen*. Children know if you are listening or just pretending to listen.

Because Newman had great problems with trust, he was always very guarded and defensive. He did not trust us, or his parents, or the world. We had to be particularly careful about how we made suggestions to him. He generally viewed every suggestion as a criticism. His responses were very predictable. First he withdrew even more, then he might start crying and deny any wrongdoing. Some days, he would go into a violent temper outburst, kicking and throwing. We handled Newman very carefully.

Our neurotherapy rooms are specifically designed for biofeedback. They are approximately eleven-by-nine feet, and well insulated for soundproofing, so they offer the individual privacy and comfort. At one end of the room is a large desk-type surface that holds the neurofeedback equipment—two computer monitors, one that the patient watches and one that shows the patient's EEG brainwave activity.

The patient sits in a large comfortable recliner on wheels. Everything is designed to be adjustable for maximum comfort. Newman wanted to recline the chair to full extension, and we wanted him sitting up. It's too easy to fall asleep when the chair is fully reclined. A compromise was reached by elevating the footrest. Once Newman was seated and the chair was adjusted, we programmed the neurofeedback computer equipment for the placement of the three sensors on his head. These sensors are like little stethoscopes, listening to brainwaves and feeding this information into the biofeedback system. The reference sensor clip and ground sensor clip usually go on the earlobes, these provide no feedback but are necessary for a good signal.

The earlobes are used as a ground because there is little or no brainwave activity coming through the ears. The ears are prepared by gently rubbing the earlobes with a preparation solution on a small gauze pad. The prep solution cleans the surface of the skin of any body oils or other material so as to not impede conduction and allow a good contact between the skin and the ground clips. A conductive paste is then placed in a little cup on

Training Report—Beta/SMR Training

You may notice some of the following changes as a result of the training. Please check any noticeable changes OVER THE NEXT TWENTY-FOUR HOURS.

1.   Trouble sleeping   A. _____
       Slept better   B. _____

2.   Less energy   A. _____
       More energy   B. _____

3.   Anxious/Nervous   A. _____
       Calm/Relaxed   B. _____

4.   More hyper   A. _____
       Less hyper   B. _____

5.   Poor concentration   A. _____
       Better concentration   B. _____

6.   Sad or down   A. _____
       Happier/Feeling up   B. _____

7.   Got a headache   A. _____
       Reduction of headache   B. _____

8.   Too jazzed up   A. _____
       Moving in slow motion   B. _____

9.   More tic behavior   A. _____
       Reduction in tics   B. _____

10.   Spaciness/foggy   A. _____
       More awake/alert   B. _____

11.   Emotional discomfort   A. _____
       Feeling of well-being   B. _____

12.   Felt physically worse   A. _____
       Felt physically better   B. _____

13.   List any other changes   _____

_____

_____

NAME: _____ _____

DATE: _____

the ear clips. The conductive paste helps to transfer any electrical signal from the brain to the biofeedback system. Once the ear clips are in place, generally one sensor is placed on the head.

The individualized protocol directs us to a specific head location. Once the correct site is located, it is prepared the same way as the ears. The site is rubbed gently with the preparation solution to clean the area. The conductive paste is placed in the small sensor cup, and the sensor is pressed onto the selected location on the scalp. The conductive paste adheres the sensors to the scalp. We then place a one-inch-square clean gauze patch over the sensor to help hold everything in place. Now we are ready for the neurotherapy session.

Before starting the biofeedback, we spend a few minutes relaxing and focusing the patient. Our instructions are usually simple and consistent. We want them to put aside everything that is not in the room with them, to focus their attention on the monitor, and to sit back and relax. They are usually instructed to take a few deep breaths, and the biofeedback session is then started.

At first we watch them closely to make sure they are not chewing gum, singing, talking, or playing with something because this type of movement distorts the feedback. Once the trainee is quiet and focused on the monitor and the audio feedback, we begin adjusting the feedback to a certain level of reward. We generally want the trainee to be rewarded about 70 percent of the time. Rewards come in the form of beeps on the computer, a score on the task, or a visual cue to indicate a good performance.

So, if the task on the monitor is to have a big dot gobble smaller dots, we want it to do so about 70 percent of the time. If a task is to keep a ball going higher in the air, we want it to go higher 70 percent of the time. People generally learn a biofeedback task best if they succeed approximately 70 percent of the time. If they succeed at a higher rate, they lose interest and are not as motivated to succeed. If they succeed at a lower rate, they can become frustrated and give up.

Once we had Newman seated in a comfortable chair with his feet propped up, sensors were gently connected to his ears and head. There was no discomfort at all. In fact, it is usually pleasurable. Newman played a video game with his brain. If his brain generated the desired brainwaves, the game went well, and he had a high score on the game. He monitored his progress by the audio beeps produced by the video game: the more beeps, the higher the score. The volume of the beeps can be adjusted to suit the individual needs of the patient. If the patient gets bored, loses attention, or gets distracted, the game goes poorly and he scores low.

Newman was like most of the young people we work with; at first, neurofeedback was fun and exciting, then after a few sessions, it became boring. The trick is to keep working with them until they work through the boredom. Boredom is an essential feature of the ADD person. They often get in trouble at school or home because of boredom. So, when they complain of boredom, we acknowledge their complaint but encourage and reinforce their effort to keep working.

During the neurofeedback session, the lighting is usually dimmed so the most prominent feature in the room is the video screen. This helps the patient maintain focus. In Newman's case, after the initial excitement wore off, he became bored and had a tendency to drop off to sleep after about fifteen minutes. To avoid this problem, the lights were brightened, the sound was turned up, and we had more interaction with him. We moved the therapist's stool closer to him, encouraged him more, and verbally reinforced his efforts.

Sometimes if the trainee is very talkative, we leave the room in order to keep him focused on the task at hand. Sometimes our staying in the room is a distraction. There are some people who would talk through the entire session and no training would be accomplished. The point here is that good neurotherapy requires good observation. If the trainee needs the therapist to help keep them focused, the therapist is there. If they need to be left alone, the therapist leaves the room or sits quietly in the background. Once the neurofeedback session starts, the neurotherapist becomes only a part of the protocol.

The most important relationship is the trainee's relationship with the feedback. If the therapist plays too big a role in the process, the learning does not transfer outside the training room. In the case of Newman, we usually remained in the room, but only to keep him awake and focused on the task.

On this particular day, once Newman was engaged in the therapy, he was left alone in the training room so we could have a brief conference with his mother. She was a very concerned mother who had had to deal with a lot of difficulty. Our conferences with her were often just to let her talk about her fears and frustrations and to reassure her. On this day, we made specific suggestions for parenting Newman, then returned quickly to the neurofeedback room. Newman was doing well and was excited about scoring so highly.

We have a grading system on each session based on four criteria. If the trainee scores better on one criterion than was scored during the last training session, he gets to go to a "number one" prize box, which contains little toys. If, however, he scores better on the second, third, or fourth criteria, he gets to go to the number two, three, or four toy box. Each box contains a toy of a different quality level. The number four box contains some nice, though inexpensive, toys. Today Newman felt sure he would score a four, and this kept him focused and alert. We instituted the graded toy boxes as an added incentive to the children. We have even had adults go to the toy boxes for key chains or other items.

Because of Newman's many varying symptoms, we designed his protocol to include changing the sensor placement halfway through the session to bring more balance to his brainwaves. Fifteen minutes into the session, we interrupted the training and moved a sensor from the left side of his head to the right side of his head. This break was not only a balancing protocol, but it helped to keep Newman more awake and alert.

When the training session time was up, we turned the lights completely bright and discontinued the training. We removed the sensors from Newman's head and ears and cleaned the paste from those areas with alcohol. The computer gave us a complete report of how Newman's brain functioned during the training, and this information was saved to a disk. We evaluated how well he had done on the four criteria. In this particular session, Newman advanced on three of the four criteria and remained the same on the fourth. Because of the effort, we gave him a four. This was exciting and encouraging for him.

While removing the sensors and cleaning the sites where they were located, Newman was asked a number of questions about how he was feeling, how he felt the session went, and how easy it was to concentrate. The response was typical of Newman: "It was okay"; he felt "fine"; there were no problems. Initially treating Newman was frustrating. We knew he was struggling, but we could not get him to open up. Fortunately, he finally began to trust us and to talk a little about how he was feeling. A few times, he even filled out the treatment report form without his mother's input.

Once the session was completed and Newman had been debriefed, we took him out to rejoin his mother. We reviewed the session with her and gave her a treatment report form to return to us at the next session. Newman got his toy from the number four box, his mother checked out at the front desk, made a new appointment, and they left the office. After the training session was complete and Newman and his mother had left the clinic, the staff discussed his progress and shared their observations.

We have had many young people come back to us and say that they would have never made it through high school, college, or even graduate school had it not been for neurofeedback. A forty-five- to fifty-minute visit for a training session two to three times a week for twenty weeks or so is a small price to pay for the quality of results we have seen. The sessions are quick, noninvasive, affordable, and can even be entertaining.

Almost all treatment sessions go the same way. They may vary slightly due to specific problems, but the overall program is relatively standard. Some patients require only twenty to thirty training sessions, while an occasional patient may go over a hundred. The average is forty to fifty, depending on how firmly entrenched the problem is, how dysfunctional the person is, and even how difficult the home or school environment is. In Newman's case, we had to do more than fifty sessions to calm his aggressive behavior. The tics started to disappear between ten and twenty sessions. When we discontinued treatment, there were no tics, the violent temper outbursts were gone, and there was a significant improvement in the remaining symptoms.

Newman remained moderately oppositional, but he is no longer hostile. He and his parents are doing a much better job of communicating with each other and they are optimistic about the future.

Neurotherapy is not magic, but we accomplished in twenty-five or so weeks what may take years to accomplish in traditional talk therapies; and may never be accomplished at all. We do so at a fraction of the cost of traditional therapies. Traditional talk therapy for the same number of treatment sessions will generally cost $4,000 to $6,000. Neurofeedback for ADD at our office usually costs between $2,000 and $2,500. Newman's course of neurotherapy cost his parents less than what a set of braces would have cost, and, like braces, the benefits are usually long lasting.

We have had many young people come back to us and say that they would have never made it through high school, college, or even graduate school had it not been for neurofeedback. We have also seen patients who were headed for serious legal troubles turn their lives around. A forty-five- to fifty-minute visit for a training session two to three times a week for twenty weeks or so is a small price to pay for the quality of results we have seen. The sessions are quick, noninvasive, affordable, and can even be entertaining. Even Newman thanked us when we finished his training.

9

Nutrition: Another Powerful Tool for Enhancing Brain Activity

In this world of Ritalin, Prozac, and neurofeedback, why include a discussion about nutrition? This book is not as much about decreasing symptoms as it is about optimizing brain functioning. As we have stated, neurofeedback is a powerful tool for enhancing brain activity, and nutrition is another powerful tool. It plays a crucial role in how effectively your child accesses her brain's potential, regardless of whether she has ADD or not.

Nutrition includes everything we eat and drink—protein, carbohydrates, fats, vitamins, minerals, fiber, and everything that goes along for the ride, such as sweeteners, preservatives, fillers, colors, flavors, and binders. The goal of good nutrition is to take in substances that promote good health and avoid taking in harmful substances. The results of good nutrition are often profound.

Without good nutrition, the behavior of any child with ADD may well worsen, and the child who does not have ADD may act as though he does, as the case of Michael shows.

Michael, a burly eighth-grader, had been diagnosed with ADD and placed on Ritalin. His teachers noted a marked improvement in his behavior and his attention at school. However, his mother reported that Michael continued to be aggressive and impulsive after school and on weekends. His pediatrician increased his dose of Ritalin, but without any improvements. In fact, he seemed somewhat more sullen at school.

When we evaluated Michael, we noted that he had a very poor diet. We recommended neurofeedback as well as ways to improve his diet. His parents worked patiently to gradually decrease and then eliminate a variety of bad foods and snacks, including soft drinks, candy, cereals, and fast foods. They gradually introduced more nutritious, energy-producing foods, often in the form of "health drinks." His behavior at home became calmer, and he was more purposeful in his activities. He was able to decrease the Ritalin to a quarter of his previous dose. His parents reported to us that his football coach said that Michael was finally playing up to his potential. Still burly, but with much less body fat, Michael came to associate his "star" status with his ritual of health drinks, and to an extent, so did we.

Foods Beneficial to the ADD Child

What we eat serves both as the raw material for building our tissues and as fuel for energy production. Every cell in our bodies is both a factory and a power plant. One does not have to be a biochemist to realize that the quality of what goes into a cell will, in large part, determine the quality of the energy and materials that that cell produces.

The beneficial foods we are referring to include macronutrients, such as carbohydrates, fats, proteins, minerals, and fiber, and micronutrients, including vitamins, trace minerals, and enzymes. The following are considerations for any parent of an ADD or ADD-like child.

Carbohydrates: Otherwise known as starches, carbohydrates include all fruits, vegetables, and grains. All carbohydrates are broken down into simple sugars in the digestive tract to provide glucose, the essential fuel for each cell. The glucose produced is the same whether it comes from candy, table sugar, broccoli, or rice, so why bother to avoid sweets? The problem is not the body metabolizing carbohydrates into sugar; it is the speed with which this process occurs.

A sudden increase in blood sugar triggers a sharp increase in insulin secretion, rapidly lowering the sugar level in the blood. The more rapid the rise in the blood sugar level, the more rapid the body's response with insulin to lower the level. A gentle rise in sugar levels leads to a leisurely response in the release of insulin and a more gradual lowering of the sugar level over a longer period of time.

There are two potential problems created by eating foods that are rapidly broken down into sugar. The first is that the high sugar level can itself be activating and can trigger hyperactive behavior. The second is that the quick release of insulin may then lead to a low-sugar level. A low sugar level worsens the low brain arousal level of the ADD child and aggravates behavioral problems. A low blood sugar level can also trigger food cravings—especially for sweet or rich foods. It's simple: glucose is fuel, and when levels are low, the brain sends out urgent messages to refuel, but the next snack may send the sugar level through another too-high/too-low cycle.

The best carbohydrates for a child with ADD or ADD-like behavior to consume are those which are slowly broken down into glucose. Which foods are these? Conveniently, this is easily determined by checking a list showing the glycemic index of foods.

The glycemic index of a food indicates the speed with which the body converts that food to glucose. The higher the glycemic index, the faster the rise in blood glucose levels. These high-glycemic index foods are the ones to avoid. Foods with a glycemic index of 80 or above are generally unfavorable, while those 60 or below are highly favorable. A list of the glycemic index of many foods is found in appendix G.

Many people are surprised to find several foods that are otherwise nutritious have an unfavorably high glycemic index. These include potatoes and virtually all the grains—bread, rice, cereal, pasta, and corn. There are some rice and pastas that have a favorable glycemic index, but like other grains, they are extremely carbohydrate-dense. For example, a mere one fifth of a cup of cooked rice or pasta has the same carbohydrate content as in one juicy peach, three cups of broccoli, or ten cups of chopped spinach. Does this mean your child should not eat these foods? Of course not, but they should be eaten in modest quantities and in combination with foods with low glycemic indexes.

Note that a high glycemic index does not necessarily mean sugar is added to these foods. The problem is that the digestive tract rapidly breaks these foods down into glucose. Consider the tasteless, sugar-free, fat-free rice cake. It has virtually the same glycemic index as glucose (glucose 138, puffed rice 132). Interestingly, the glycemic index of table sugar (sucrose) is 92. So the rate of increase in the blood glucose level of a child munching on a rice cake will be faster than that of a child nibbling table sugar. Go figure. The point is that foods with a high glycemic index need to be treated the same as cookies and candy because their effect on blood sugar is similar.[1]

Adding sugar to carbohydrates with a high glycemic index only adds fuel to the fire: you get a more rapid sugar level increase. Although it seems contrary to accepted belief, the typical bowl of cold cereal for breakfast can be a particularly unfavorable food. Not only is it a high-glycemic-index carbohydrate on its own, most cereals have a substantial amount of sugar added to them by the manufacturer, to say nothing of the sugar that is usually added at the table.

Most diets recommend a person eat complex carbohydrates and avoid simple sugars. "Complex" refers to the molecular structure of the carbohydrate, and the assumption is that if the structure of a carbohydrate is complex, the rate of its breakdown to sugars will be slow. This seems sensible but it does not always correspond with established scientific data.

Cereal or rice cakes are complex carbohydrates, but do not be lulled into thinking that a complex carbohydrate is necessarily a low glycemic index food. Many are high. On the other hand, most fruits, ripe and sweet as they may be, have a low glycemic index. The sugar in fruit (fructose) tastes sweet, but the body is not able to metabolize that chemical form of sugar quickly. It is carried to the liver where it undergoes several conversions before it becomes glucose and is released back into the blood.

Another consideration is that in addition to the glycemic index, the quantity of carbohydrates consumed should be considered. Overloading the system with carbohydrates of whatever glycemic index will produce the same roller coaster blood sugar level effect. Science has finally caught up to our grandmothers who advise us to eat modest portions of food.

Fats: We are all aware that dietary fats play a role in heart disease and cancer, but the parent of an ADD child needs to be aware of the importance of dietary fats on brain functioning, and that effect is probably not what you would expect.

The brain is largely composed of fatty tissue, and the majority of these fats are found in the membranes of the cells. These membranes provide the outer layer for each cell and protect the carefully regulated environment inside the cell. The health of the cell's membrane is essential to its proper functioning.

There are two important points to note about how dietary fats affect brain functioning. The first is that dietary fats are used as-is—the fats you eat are the fats that will become important structures in your brain. They are not broken down and reassembled for specific uses like proteins and carbohydrates are. The quality of the fats in the diet will directly affect the quality of the cell membranes in the brain.

The second point is that the cells in our brain and nervous system are not likely to regenerate. What we have is what we have. Taking special care to nourish the brain cells you have includes eating those fats needed for the cell membranes to function best, and avoiding those fats that lead to poor functioning.

To understand which fats are best for cell membrane health, it is useful to know a bit about the essential fats. There are two essential fats our bodies require but cannot manufacture; they must be obtained through our diets. These fats are called omega-6 and omega-3. Most of our tissues have more omega-6 fats than omega-3. The ratio is often about four-to-one, the brain being a distinct exception where the ratio of omega-6 to omega-3 fats in brain tissue is one-to-one.

Fats in the typical diet are chiefly omega-6. In fact, the average American diet provides twenty times more omega-6 than omega-3 fats. Most of us do not take in an optimal amount of omega-3 fats unless we eat fish regularly. Omega-3 fats are quite flexible and are ideally suited for cell membranes. We find these fats in fish, and to a lesser extent in vegetables, sprouts, nuts, and soybeans. They are also easily supplemented by using the right kind of fish oils, flax oil, and borage oil.

The fats to avoid are the highly processed fats, hydrogenated fats, and fats that are heated to high temperatures in processing or in frying. These fats have a structural rigidity that is most undesirable for use in brain cell membranes. They also promote free radical damage of cell membranes.

Free radicals are unstable molecules that are produced from the metabolism of food during energy production by each of the body's cells. Free radicals cause damage to the cell until they are neutralized by antioxidants, such as glutathione or vitamins E or C. The protective outer layer of each cell, the cell membrane, is particularly susceptible to free radical damage. Such damage to the membrane allows substances to enter the cell that should remain on the outside of the cell, and also causes the loss of substances that should remain inside the cell. A cell damaged in this manner has difficulty performing its necessary functions of energy production, replication, and detoxification.

In general, the raw, monounsaturated oils are the better fat choices—olive oil, peanut oil, and nut oils. These fats will contribute to more supple brain cell membranes. Although well-marketed, canola oil is an exception. Even though it is a monounsaturated fat, it is unstable and has components that are toxic. Look for oils that have been cold-pressed in low-light environments, and are protected from becoming rancid with antioxidants (such as vitamin E) and refrigeration. A health foods store will no doubt have a selection of such fats and oils, but few, if any, corporate chain grocery stores will.

Butter, primarily a saturated fat, is acceptable if not cooked to very high temperatures and if eaten in relatively small quantities. However, avoid using any margarine at all. Keep in mind that margarine does not melt at body temperature. Even if you do not know anything about biochemistry, that should tell you something about its potential harm. Think of margarine more as a plastic than as a food. Try to avoid foods that include "partially hydrogenated" oils in their list of ingredients. Hydrogenation of fats simply means adding hydrogen to the molecules. It is a process used solely to prolong the shelf life of oils, but it causes them to become rigid molecules.

Take peanut butter, an otherwise excellent nutritional fat, as an example of what happens as a result of this process. The hydrogenation changes its fats from thin, flexible, high-quality structures to thickened, rigid structures that have very poor characteristics for use by the body, both structurally and metabolically. Fortunately, there are peanut butters available that are not subjected to hydrogenation. The ingredient list on the peanut butter we prefer is simply "peanuts."

Do not be misled into thinking the fats are only hydrogenated a little bit if they are listed as "partially hydrogenated." These oils are hydrogenated well above 90 percent, which is as much as is technically feasible for the costs. If labeling were fair and honest, these fats would be listed as "almost completely hydrogenated." The only reason they are not 100 percent hydrogenated is that it would be too costly to do so. By the way, just because margarine has "no cholesterol" does not mean it is wise to eat it. Zero-cholesterol, partially hydrogenated fats increase total cholesterol and LDL cholesterol (bad cholesterol, carried from the liver to the tissues, a risk factor for heart disease) and decrease HDL cholesterol (good cholesterol, the form of cholesterol that is carried from the body to the liver for excretion in the bile.).[2]

While the above recommendations can be broadly applied to any child, ADD or not, there is a subset of children with hyperactive behavior who require a specific supplementation of fatty acids.[3] The essential fats omega-6 and omega-3 are converted in the body to important derivative fatty acids, such as EPA, DHA, and GLA, essential for healthy brain development and functioning. Some children, however, are unable to adequately convert dietary fats into these important fatty acids.

Children who have this fatty-acid deficiency may exhibit hyperactive behavior, dry skin, excessive thirst, clumsiness, and/or learning disorders.[4] Their dry skin and thirst are due to inadequate waterproofing by their cell membranes.

Certainly, not all hyperactive children have this fatty-acid deficiency, but for those who do, Ritalin is not the answer. The need is for simple dietary improvements and supplementation of the fatty acids. Adequate intake of these fatty acids can make a significant difference.

This type of fatty-acid deficiency can be confirmed by a blood test, but that is usually not necessary because the deficiency itself is often clear from the clinical history. The following case was such an instance and was most instructive to us.

Tonya was an unruly, hyperactive six-year-old who was in danger of repeating first grade. She had few girlfriends and was seldom invited to birthday parties. In the year prior to coming to our clinic, she had been on unsuccessful trials of Ritalin, Dextroamphetamine, and Cylert, and was currently on Prozac drops. Upon evaluation, it quickly became evident she had classic signs of a fatty-acid deficiency. She had had a history of chronic cradle cap (seborrheic dermatitis, a scaly rash on the scalp) as an infant. Her mother reported that she made Kool-Aid by the gallon, even in winter, for Tonya's insatiable thirst, and that everyone said she was like a bull in a china shop. She had exceptionally dry skin, especially on her hands and the backs of her arms, and her nails were split. The sugar and dye in the Kool-Aid probably did not help either.

We made numerous dietary recommendations, including supplementation with fish oils and evening primrose oil. We also discontinued the Prozac. On follow-up however, it appeared that the only dietary recommendation Tonya's mother consistently followed was the supplementation of oils. Nonetheless, within three weeks Tonya's behavior began to dramatically improve. Eventually, her excessive thirst and dry skin also resolved. Tonya is the only child we have found in our clinic to have had such a significant fatty-acid deficiency.

However, there is one large group of children that is deficient in converting essential fats into the derivative fatty acids— *all* infants. Infants do not develop the capacity to adequately convert the essential fats to the derivative fatty acids for several months after they are born. Not surprisingly, breast milk is replete with high concentrations of these fatty-acid derivatives that are so important for healthy brain development.[5] The Japanese have long added these fatty acid derivatives to their infant formulas, but not so in the United States, as there is no outcry to have them added.

In light of these facts, we believe all pregnant women and all nursing mothers should supplement their diets with essential omega-3 fatty acids. The mother is able to convert the omega-3 fatty acids to the derivative fatty acids for delivery to the baby through the placental blood and later through breast milk. All bottle-fed babies should have the derivative fatty acids, especially DHA, added to their formulas because they are unable to break down the omega-3 fats on their own.[6] Further recommendations are provided in appendix F.

Proteins: Proteins provide the necessary building blocks for tissue growth, healing, making enzymes, and numerous other activities. Every cell in the body, except fat cells, requires protein for daily maintenance and repair. Children, in particular, require high-quality protein for growth and development.[7] Since protein is not stored, an adequate intake is necessary each day.

Adequate protein in the diet is crucial for optimal brain functioning. The brain's chemical messengers, neurotransmitters, are produced from amino acids, the building blocks of protein. Another crucially important function that requires adequate protein intake is detoxification—the processes that rid our bodies of toxins. Estimates of daily protein requirements are provided in appendix F.

Vitamins and Minerals: Due to the processing of foods and the depletion of minerals in the soil, it is virtually impossible to obtain an optimal intake of vitamins and minerals from the diet alone. Supplementation is necessary if *optimal* health is the goal.

Vitamin-mineral supplementation has been demonstrated to improve the academic performance and behavior of school children. Although this is a simple statement, its implications are profound. Significant improvements have been documented in numerous scientific studies, several of which were carefully controlled, randomized, triple-blind studies. In these, neither the students nor the teachers nor the researchers knew who was getting supplementation or placebo until after the study was completed and the code was broken. (We list examples of the supplements used in appendix F.) Among the findings are the following:

Increased IQ.[8] While the overall gain in the supplemented group is usually modest (two to four points), subgroups as large as one-third of the supplemented group have shown increases of ten points. Ten points on an IQ test may be the difference between mild mental retardation and a normal IQ, or between a normal IQ and an IQ in the upper five percent of the population. The reason for the remarkable increase in the subgroups appears to be that a significant percentage of school-age children have an unrecognizable clinical deficiency state that impairs cognitive performance.

Decreased violent and delinquent behavior.[9] The rates of decreased antisocial behavior measured in these studies approached 50 percent. Several studies noted that the differences were largely seen in "habitual offenders" or "hard core rule-breakers." After one study in a juvenile correction facility in Oklahoma, the state employees chipped in to buy the children supplements while the bureaucracy contemplated the matter.

Improvements in learning disabilities.[10] Academic improvements were noted within weeks to months and continued for four years. Some children improved their reading comprehension by three to five years within the first year of supplementation. Those who discontinued supplementation showed a decline in academic performance in the first year and had lower grades in the following year.

Other studies have shown connections between nutrition and behavior:

Zinc deficiency was shown to correlate with hyperactivity, episodic violence, and conduct disorder.[11]

Magnesium deficiency was shown to correlate with hyperactivity and disruptive behavior.[12]

Elevated zinc-copper ratios were shown to correlate with delinquent and assaultive behavior.[13]

It is difficult to overestimate the importance of proper nutrition, as this next case shows.

Jason was a seventeen-year-old eleventh grader who came to our clinic for a course of neurofeedback. He had been diagnosed with ADD and had exhibited modest improvement on Cylert. His liver function tests, however, indicated he needed to discontinue this medication. He had subsequently received trials of Ritalin, Zoloft, Prozac, Wellbutrin, and Dextroamphetamine, each with either unacceptable side effects or treatment failure.

We prescribed DMAE (dimethylaminoethanol), a naturally occurring brain nutrient that is a mild stimulant (which we discuss in chapter 10) and started neurofeedback. Jason appeared to be improving gradually, but it eventually became evident that his hyperactivity and impulsivity were still present and disruptive. A hair analysis was obtained to determine the amount of various minerals in his hair, giving an estimate of the amounts of the minerals in the tissues. The analysis revealed a zinc-to-copper ratio of one-to-twenty. His copper excess was quickly traced to his family's well water. A blood test confirmed he was not toxic, only out of balance. The simple addition of bottled water and mineral supplementation, including zinc and manganese, proved to be sufficient to stabilize his behavior.

A hair analysis can be a useful screening test for the zinc-copper ratio and for deficiencies of other essential trace minerals. It may also help uncover toxic levels of harmful metals, which will be discussed in chapter 10.

Fiber: As with fats, many people are aware of the beneficial role fiber intake plays in avoiding the development of heart disease and cancer. The importance of adequate fiber in the diet of the ADD or ADD-like child is due to its effects on carbohydrate metabolism. Fiber in the gut slows the absorption of sugars into the bloodstream and stabilizes the glucose/insulin effects we discussed earlier. It also enhances the proliferation of beneficial bacteria in the gut, which helps prevent yeast overgrowth, discussed in chapter 10.

Other Nutrients: *Ginkgo biloba* extract stands head and shoulders above the array of nutrients beneficial for enhancing brain function. It is an excellent antioxidant that penetrates tissues quite well. It crosses the blood-brain barrier and exerts its antioxidant activity directly on brain tissue where it neutralizes free radical molecules that damage tissue. In addition to acting as an antioxidant and decreasing damage from free radical activity, it has other important effects on brain tissue. Ginkgo increases both the uptake of glucose and the energy production by brain cells and improves nerve transmission in the brain. Basically, it boosts normal brain activity, which is desirable for anyone, but especially for someone with ADD.[14]

Pycnogenol is another antioxidant that has received a great deal of attention. It is an excellent antioxidant, but, in our opinion, is expensive compared to other, comparable antioxidants.

Foods that Are Harmful to the ADD Child

There are a number of foods and additives that can produce a worsening or mimicking of ADD behavior. Problems stem from these substances being either toxic in and of themselves, or allergens which trigger an undesirable immune response.

The likely reason ADD children are so much more hindered by quickly absorbed sugars is that they are more susceptible to anything that interferes with brain functioning. The brain uses the lion's share of the body's energy production. The solution is to limit carbohydrate intake and eat primarily low glycemic index carbohydrates to maintain stable blood sugar levels.

Sugar: There are several factors that play a role in the varied food susceptibilities associated with ADD. The one most people already know about is sugar-driven hyperactivity. Interestingly, whether sugar causes hyperactive behavior is technically a controversy. But the studies that suggest that sugar does not cause ADD-like behavior are flawed by the use of high-glycemic-index carbohydrates in the control group.

That is, both groups were getting a sugar effect, whether they consumed refined sugar products or "complex carbohydrates." The reality is that one does not need to wait for conclusive scientific evidence to determine if sugar plays a role in ADD behavior. Just look in the back seat of the car after your children have consumed sodas, either caffeinated or caffeine-free.

The likely reason ADD children are so much more hindered by quickly absorbed sugars is that they are more susceptible to anything that interferes with brain functioning. The brain uses the lion's share of the body's energy production. As described in the section on carbohydrates, the solution is to limit carbohydrate intake and eat primarily low glycemic index carbohydrates to maintain stable blood sugar levels.

Food labels list ingredients in descending order (from most to least) according to amounts. If the first or second ingredient is a sweetener, consider that food a candy, even if the box it came in has a robust athlete pictured on the front. A tactic the food industry uses to disguise how much sugar is in many foods is to use smaller amounts of numerous sweeteners so that the more nutritious ingredients appear at the top of the list. Some of these sweeteners may be honey, invert sugar, corn sweeteners, molasses, maltose, corn syrup, galactose, glucose, dextrose, fruit juice concentrate, and maltodextrin.

If necessary, food can be sweetened with stevia. Stevia is a potent sweetener that is naturally occurring but does not cause a rise in blood sugar levels. A very small amount (approximately one-sixteenth of a teaspoon) is equivalent to one teaspoon of table sugar. Using too much stevia makes foods taste bitter.

If you purchase stevia, make certain that it is a pure product. Maltodextrin is sometimes added to the lower-priced stevia products, but maltodextrin and maltose are the two carbohydrates that have the highest glycemic index of all: 150. It is a better idea to pay a little more for the pure stevia.

Additives: Over the past two decades numerous studies have documented the adverse effects on behavior triggered by food additives.[15] Behaviors commonly seen include hyperactivity, irritability, and sleep disturbances, and behavior is not the only thing affected. A study done in 1980 on hyperactive children demonstrated that the group subjected to food dyes had a significant decrease in learning performance when compared to the group of hyperactive children that did not receive the dyes.

The late allergist and pediatrician, Ben Feingold, M.D., long championed the use of diets eliminating additives and avoiding certain food products. He was of course attacked and ridiculed by mainstream medicine. We do not believe that food additive exposure is *the* cause of ADD, but there is a significant percentage of children in whom food additives are detrimental and can produce a range of problems that may mimic or worsen ADD. The numerous non-profit Feingold-based organizations and parent support groups that robustly continue to propound his ideas give one indication of the usefulness his approach has had in the lives of many children.

Dr. Feingold believed that in addition to removing synthetic colors and flavors, and the preservatives BHA, BHT, and TBHQ, that foods containing a high amount of salicylates should be avoided, at least temporarily. These preservatives have been demonstrated to produce a significant decrease in neurotransmitters, including serotonin. Not surprisingly, the animals used in studies on additives exhibited problems with sleep and increased aggression.

We agree with Dr. Feingold that food additives should be avoided as much as possible, but attaining complete elimination is difficult for most people. Fortunately, we have found that reading food labels carefully and selecting foods with no (or minimal) preservatives is sufficient for most children. Avoiding artificially colored foods is a good place to start. Some additives are not named on the label, so scrupulous attention as to how these substances are concealed under terms such as "colorings" or "flavorings" may be necessary. The Feingold Association provides a list of such foods; see appendix D for details.

Feingold's recommendation to avoid foods with high salicylate levels was based on his observations over time. Since many high-salicylate foods are otherwise highly nutritionally desirable, e.g., oranges, apples, strawberries, and apricots, we recommend that elimination of these foods be considered if other interventions are not working adequately and that they be reintroduced after a period of time. As with the need for complete elimination of additives, our clinical experience suggests the need to eliminate salicylate-rich foods is rare if the other initial interventions discussed in this book are instituted.

Aspartame: The artificial sweetener aspartame, found in most diet drinks, many foods, and in Equal, NutraSweet, and Spoonful, is another substance that would be banned from use if science and public health concerns were more powerful than business concerns.[16,17]

Aspartame is composed of three substances—two amino acids and methanol.[18] Methanol, or wood alcohol, is a known neurotoxin that damages nerve cells. It takes approximately six times longer to metabolize methanol as it does ethanol (the alcohol in liquor, beer, and wine) so even moderate but regular intake of aspartame will result in accumulation of methanol in the tissues. Methanol is broken down to formaldehyde, another potent neurotoxin. The formaldehyde is further broken down to formic acid, yet another neurotoxin.

Thus, a daily intake of aspartame will lead to an accumulation of not only methanol, but its toxic byproducts as well. Numerous neurological problems have been traced back to aspartame use, including seizures, headaches, dizziness, memory loss, anxiety, depression, vertigo, tremors, slurred speech, hearing loss, and vision loss. Also of concern is the fact that there is an increase in the incidence of brain tumors in animals that are fed aspartame.

The two amino acids in aspartame—aspartic acid and phenylalanine—while essential to normal brain functioning, are toxic in excessive amounts, and can also cause hyperactivity and aggressive behavior. In excess, these amino acids cause rapid, uncontrolled firing of brain cells that may lead to cell damage or death. Substances that produce these effects are called excitotoxins, and should be avoided by ADD children.

We had successfully treated Antione for ADD while he was a tenth-grader. He had had no history of head trauma and no medical problems at the time. Later, he returned to our clinic after he had been medically discharged from the Army for a seizure disorder. While stationed at Fort Benning, he had three seizures in a two-month period. The Army had performed an extensive medical work-up, including serial EEGs and a CAT scan, and found a persistent seizure focus in the right parietal lobe (an area on the right side of his brain, near the back), but no underlying cause. They even did unannounced urine tests because they suspected alcohol could be a factor, but Antione was a fitness enthusiast who would drink alcohol only on occasion.

We learned that Antoine had been drinking four to eight diet sodas per day due to the grueling Georgia heat, and he was still drinking two or three per day after his military discharge. We counseled him on the potential central nervous system toxicity of aspartame-sweetened sodas and its byproducts. He just shook his head in disbelief. He had been purposely drinking diet soda in an effort to avoid sugar, thinking it was a harmless, although a non-nutritional, drink. After removing aspartame from his diet, he has been seizure-free for over ten months. A repeat EEG done recently showed that the abnormality in the previous EEGs had reverted to normal.

We have no way of proving that the aspartame caused Antione's seizures or if discontinuing it led to his apparent recovery, but it is at least as likely as any other scenario food additive apologists may propound. Antoine is the third patient we have encountered over an eight-year period with the same history— no prior seizures, liberal use of aspartame, the sudden onset of seizures with no explainable cause, and the remission of the seizures after aspartame consumption was discontinued.

Monosodium Glutamate (MSG): This flavor enhancer contains glutamate, a substance that can cause behavioral problems and brain symptoms. Glutamate is related to glutamic acid, an amino acid essential to normal brain functioning, but it is an excitotoxin when taken in excessive amounts.[19] MSG is found in a wide range of foods, sometimes hidden under other names. Watch out for these ingredients: hydrolyzed vegetable protein, yeast extract, autolyzed yeast protein, or even "natural flavorings." A more extensive list may be found in appendix B.

Caffeine: Caffeine can insidiously work its way into the diet of the ADD child and bring along with it a host of other troublesome substances, such as sugar, aspartame, or additives. In the ADD child, caffeine's stimulant effect can provide a temporary boost in arousal levels that may be experienced as desirable.[20] But since sodas are the most common caffeine drink children consume, they are also taking in a considerable quantity of sugar or a neurotoxic artificial sweetener, plus a collection of synthetics.

The high phosphate content in sodas can interfere with the absorption of calcium and magnesium. The diuretic effect can contribute to a salt/water imbalance. This is a horrendous mixture for an ADD child, who, seeking another boost from caffeine, may well drink sodas nonstop.

The non-ADD child who frequently drinks sodas may behave like an ADD child. The stimulant effects from the caffeine, sugar, etc., can destabilize the behavior of any child. How many children, pumped up on the various substances in sodas, run wildly through the halls at the doctor's office while their genuinely concerned pediatricians are writing out prescriptions for Ritalin?

We realize the consumption of sodas is practically considered a patriotic duty by masses of people, and parents regularly use sodas as a reward. But the compelling reality is that the parent of a child with *any* behavioral problem would do well to wean him off of sodas.

The Role of Food Hypersensitivities and Allergies

Many children with ADD are intolerant of certain foods that normally have no bad effects, such as green beans, bread, and many chemicals.[21] A common denominator in those with food hypersensitivities is that they have been exposed to foods and medications that harm the lining of the bowel.

Caffeine, alcohol, the byproducts from the metabolism of hydrogenated fats, and highly refined sweets and starches, and some of the synthetic additives to food, may harm the protective mucous lining of the bowel. Medications that may also harm the bowel lining cells include antibiotics, prednisone, aspirin, and the nonsteroidal anti-inflammatories.

These lining cells provide a barrier that limits what is absorbed into the bloodstream from the gut. When damage occurs to these lining cells, it results in a hyperpermeable state in which the lining becomes excessively porous and substances that have no business entering the bloodstream are readily allowed access. This is known as "leaky gut syndrome."

An example of a food substance that may leak into the bloodstream is a protein that is normally broken down into its component amino acids before it is allowed into the bloodstream. The immune system recognizes this substance as foreign, and mobilizes to defend itself against this intruder. Antibodies are produced to attack the substance invading the bloodstream. The next time that food is eaten and a similar

> *Many children with ADD are intolerant of certain foods that normally have no bad effects, such as green beans, bread, and many chemicals. A common denominator in those with food hypersensitivities is that they have been exposed to foods and medications that harm the lining of the bowel.*

protein particle is again absorbed through the leaky gut, it will trigger an immune response.

Those with food sensitivities display a range of responses that may include malaise, nasal and other upper respiratory tract symptoms, skin rashes, gastric discomfort and bowel disturbances, irritability, moodiness, and restlessness. A child with food sensitivities is likely to have poor attention and concentration, and may be quite restless or withdrawn.

The first order of business if there appears to be food sensitivities, is to ensure that healthy bowel functioning is regained. Regaining a healthy bowel lining will restore its proper permeability, and the particles the body has become sensitized to will not find their way into the bloodstream. They will remain in the bowel for further metabolic breakdown and absorption or pass through in the feces.

To regain bowel health, offending foods and drugs should be avoided whenever possible. This certainly includes antibiotics, dispensed in a knee-jerk response at any sign of a bad cold or sinus infection.

A useful guideline we use regarding taking antibiotics is to limit their use to bacterial infections that present a significant risk if not treated, such as strep throat or pneumonia. A sinus infection should not be treated with antibiotics unless the symptoms are not diminishing by the second week. This severity of infection that would require antibiotics is not likely to occur in more than 90 percent of cases of acute sinusitis. Viruses cause most colds and the flu. Antibiotics do not kill viruses or reduce cold or flu symptoms, and in fact are likely to contribute to symptoms by killing the beneficial bacteria and promoting an overgrowth of undesirable organisms.

When people, young and old, begin to consume a high quality-diet and an intelligent combination of nutritional supplements, the numbers of infections invariably plummet.

After bowel-unfriendly foods and drugs are reduced and eliminated, a nutritional regimen to regain and optimize bowel functioning should be instituted. In addition to the daily basic vitamin, and mineral, nutrient intake, additional nutrients are beneficial. L-glutamine, deglycyrrhized licorice (DGL), and N-acetyl-glucosamine (NAG) particularly benefit the bowel lining cells. L-glutamine serves as the main source of energy for the cells when there is any increased stress to the bowel, such as irritation from the foods and drugs discussed above. DGL speeds the growth and promotes the longevity of the cells that line the gut. NAG improves the production of the critical protective mucous layer that is secreted by the lining cells.

To ensure that an optimum balance of organisms is reestablished in the bowel, it is also useful to add capsules of beneficial bacteria. These should include *Lactobacillus acidophilus,* which takes up long-term residence in the small intestine, and *Lactobacillus bifidum,* that reside in the large intestine. After an imbalance, it takes approximately three weeks to completely recolonize the bowel with desirable organisms.

Once the integrity of the bowel lining cells is regained, no further steps may be necessary as food allergens no longer find their way into the bloodstream through leaky areas in the gut. Previously offending foods may be gradually reintroduced. If there continue to be food sensitivities, treatment may be indicated.

The safest and most effective treatment of multiple food sensitivities, and many other types of allergic reactions, is enzyme potentiation desensitization, or EPD. Unlike the weekly allergy shots with which most people are familiar, treatment with EPD is brief and safe. Information about EPD may be obtained at www.dma.org/~rohers/allergy/epd_faq.htm. Pending FDA approval for EPD, you may meanwhile receive EPD in Canada.

To summarize, here are the nutrition basics for ADD:

- Use corn, potato, and grain products sparingly, as you do highly sweetened foods.

- Avoid soft drinks, sports drinks, and fruit drinks.

- Avoid artificial sweeteners. Use stevia instead.

- Use the monounsaturated fats, such as olive oil or the nut oils. Small amounts of butter are acceptable.

- Avoid margarine, canola oil, and all partially hydrogenated oils.

- Get adequate protein at each meal.

- Supplement with vitamins and minerals, and consider additional antioxidants like *Ginkgo biloba*.

- Avoid monosodium glutamate (MSG), also labeled as hydrolyzed soy, vegetable, or plant protein, autolyzed yeast, textured protein, sodium or calcium caseinate, soy or whey isolate.

- Avoid synthetic additives such as colors, flavors, enhancers, stabilizers, and binders.

- Avoid products containing caffeine.

A final word about nutrition: The parents we work with in our clinic who make the effort, and undergo the inconveniences of improving their children's nutrition are almost always rewarded tenfold. Not only does good nutrition significantly contribute to improved behavior and a marked decrease in the minor medical problems that appear to plague so many children—ear aches, colds, skin problems, bowel problems, and sleep problems—but it adds to the robustness of health that is our children's birthright.

10

How Toxic Substances Can Contribute to ADD

Toxic substances can produce the *entire* range of behaviors seen in ADD, learning disabilities, and even autism. They can cause attention problems, restlessness, learning problems, impulsivity, anxiety, depression, listlessness, and many more problems.

There are no estimates of how many children are diagnosed with these psychiatric conditions when they are actually affected by toxic substances. Since only a relatively small percentage of children are actually diagnosed with toxic problems each year, most physicians believe these problems are rare. On the other hand, the extraordinary increase in the numbers and types of synthetic chemicals and environmental pollutants over the past sixty years directly corresponds to the increased incidence of chronic and disabling diseases in the United States.

Rachel Carson warned us eloquently in *Silent Spring* forty years ago about the dangers to our natural world from the accumulating array of harmful chemicals being discharged into the environment. But the numbers and varieties of these chemicals continue to increase. When we consider the long-term exposure, beginning in utero, of our brains to these chemicals, are we really surprised that our children appear to be struggling with more puzzling health and behavioral problems than previous generations?

Hazardous Substances

The top ten on the Priority List of Hazardous Substances listed by the Agency for Toxic Substances and Disease Registry/Environmental Protection Agency are as follows:

Arsenic	Polychlorinated	hydrocarbons
Lead	biphenyls (PCBs)	Benzo(b)fluoranthene
Mercury	Cadmium	
Vinyl chloride	Benzo(a)pyrene	
Benzene	Polycyclic aromatic	

For example, consider lead. The American Medical Association estimates 1.6 million children under the age of six (practically ten percent of that age group) have elevated lead levels. The academic, neurological, and social consequences of exposure to lead should in and of themselves be cause for rightful action to correct the problem. Then consider the other toxic metals, pesticide residues, petrochemicals, chlorinated solvents, and a multitude of other poisons that we are all exposed to every day. Sadly, even as the situation worsens, few physicians are aware of the degree of the problem.

One can hardly blame physicians for their lack of knowledge on this subject. After all, they depend upon information supplied to them by their medical schools and the major medical journals. As we implied earlier, powerful business forces determine the brunt of the prevailing attitudes in medicine.

We have learned in our practices the need to actively consider toxic substances as a possible cause of any behavioral or academic problem. While our mainstream colleagues may dismiss this as you-find-what-you-look-for thinking, we believe that if you do not look for it, you certainly will not see it, even if it is right under your nose. The reality for us has been that when we treat apparently toxin-related problems, our patients often experience clear clinical improvements.

Heavy Metal Toxicity and Yeast

There are two common toxic substances that we consider first when we are faced with behavioral or academic problems—heavy metals and yeast overgrowth. Although there are a multitude of toxic substances in our environment due to the enormous increase in the use of hormones and metabolism-disrupting chemicals since the 1930s, these two are common and are detectable and treatable. Unfortunately, avoidance of the substances and enhancing the immune system and overall health are often the only reasonable interventions for many toxic substances, such as pesticide residues in foods.

Heavy metals, such as lead, mercury, and arsenic have become a continually increasing part of our environment and they are unavoidable. Each one of us, including newborns, has detectable levels of several toxic metals. Yeast *(Candida albicans)* is also present in each of us, predominantly in our bowels. Commonly used medications can lead to a detrimental proliferation of this yeast. Anyone who has taken antibiotics may have an imbalance of organisms in his gastrointestinal tract and an overgrowth of this yeast.

Neither heavy metal toxicity nor yeast overgrowth is given much thought by mainstream physicians when considering how to treat behavioral, attention, and learning problems. For patients, the same holds true in this situation as it does for neurofeedback and nutrition—parents must inform themselves and make the best decisions they can for their children.

Since heavy metals and yeast are present in every one of us, why do some people have problems with toxicity and others not? The factors that determine whether we are being poisoned by their presence are the amounts in our bodies, the tissues in which they accumulate, and the individual's immune response to them. A relatively large accumulation in one person may not produce clinical symptoms, while a fraction of that amount may disable another person. Although either heavy metal toxicity or yeast overgrowth can be a major problem in and of themselves, they may also interact with each other and magnify problems.

The Damage Heavy Metal Toxicity Can Produce

Each one of us is at risk. Due to the ever-increasing pace of industrialization, the amounts of heavy metals in our air, water, and food are at an all-time high, and they continue to increase every year. The Agency for Toxic Substances and Diseases

Registry and the Environmental Protection Agency prioritize the list of the most toxic substances in the environment. The list contains heavy metals, chlorinated hydrocarbons, pesticides, and solvents. In 1999, the top three in the environment were the heavy metals arsenic, lead, and mercury.[1]

Heavy metals are large atoms that bind to our tissues and cause damage. Most heavy metals have little or no use in humans. A few heavy metals, such as nickel, are essential to us in minute quantities, but, even so, they are commonly toxic because they are too often present in excessive quantities.

There are many metals that are highly toxic to human physiology[2] such as lead, mercury, cadmium, and arsenic. They tend to accumulate in specific organs—brain, kidney, liver, bone—depending upon the metal involved. Because of their extremely slow excretion rates, they continue to be toxic until they are cleared from the body. The half-life of the heavy metals—in this sense, the length of time it takes the body to clear half of the initial quantity that was taken in—is estimated to be between forty and sixty years. That means, for example, that half of the mercury a person may have absorbed at age ten is still in her body at age fifty, not taking into consideration any further accumulation in the intervening years.

Distressingly, the rate at which we are being exposed to toxic metals is escalating hand-in-hand with advancing technology. These metals may be inhaled, ingested, or absorbed. Sources include tap water, well water, foods (including breast milk and infant formula), the air we breathe, medicines, exhaust fumes, dental amalgams, cosmetics, paints, electronic devices, dyes, dust, tobacco smoke, insecticide residues—and on and on. The list is long. Unfortunately, exposure begins very early during human development with the placental blood from our mothers.

Children are much more vulnerable than adults to environmental toxins.[3] Their small size and high absorption rates make them particularly susceptible to heavy metal toxicity. Because they are growing rapidly, children absorb minerals such as calcium to build bones at a high rate through their gastrointestinal tracts. However, this mechanism also promotes a higher rate of heavy metal absorption. A toddler absorbs five times the amount of lead an adult does, and children put things into their mouths and travel much closer to the ground, where atmospheric metals settle.

For the first three years of life, children's brains are even more vulnerable to toxic exposure because their blood-brain barriers have not yet fully developed. The blood-brain barrier is the barrier between the blood and the cerebrospinal fluid, which bathes our brains and spinal cords. Until the blood-brain barrier is fully developed, chemicals in the blood will more readily gain access to the child's brain.

Consider also that the developing brain grows at an exponential rate through the first year of extra-uterine life. It is even more vulnerable during that period of time. The rapid growth means higher nutritional requirements and greater susceptibility to damaging processes.

The problems that result from heavy metal toxicity may *mimic* ADD, learning disabilities, or autism, or they may worsen those conditions if they are already present. We'll now review the heavy metals of most concern.

Lead: Lead is everywhere. There is a veneer of lead over our entire environment. Every time lead levels are measured in the oceans, lakes, soils, polar ice caps, and atmosphere, they have increased. Worldwide in 1995, 5.4 billion pounds of lead were used in the production of paint, construction materials, electronics, and ceramics. In addition to industrial processes, lead is discharged into the atmosphere from auto exhausts and waste incineration. There has been a considerable reduction in lead from auto exhaust in the United States, but still the world's lead output is rising. Lead is now also less widely used for solder, but the amounts already present in the home and workplace are still significant.[4]

In addition to air and water, we may take lead in from newsprint, ink, hair dyes, soldered tin cans, improperly glazed

> *Children are much more vulnerable than adults to environmental toxins. Their small size and high absorption rates make them particularly susceptible to heavy metal toxicity. Consider also that the developing brain grows at an exponential rate through the first year of extra-uterine life. It is even more vulnerable during that period of time. The rapid growth means higher nutritional requirements and greater susceptibility to damaging processes.*

plates and cups, bone meal supplements, lead pipes in old plumbing, lead batteries, ammunition, and lead-based paints. There is no way to avoid lead. There are measurable amounts of lead on vegetables even from a spring-fed, organically raised garden that is 500 miles from the nearest smelter. In less than 150 years, bone lead levels in humans have increased 500-fold.

Lead is used as a stabilizer for PVC plastics, including children's toys. Lead may impart a sweetish taste to materials, which is why some children eat paint chips. Since children absorb lead so much more quickly than adults do, children are at highest risk. Low calcium intake can make matters worse, because when calcium levels are low, the body's uptake of lead increases. Decades of studies demonstrate that lead's harmful effects are directly correlated to the concentrations present in the tissues. Body systems most likely to be harmed are the central nervous system, immune system, kidneys, and the blood.

Problem behaviors resulting from excessive lead may include hyperactivity, impulsivity, distractibility, and daydreaming. Skills that lead impairs include organizational ability, ability to stay on task, ability to work alone, ability to follow directions, and frustration tolerance. There is no estimate as to how many children with excessive lead levels are being diagnosed with ADD and prescribed Ritalin or some other equally inappropriate drug.

Studies have documented significant improvements in symptoms after excessive lead was removed from the tissues of children with a chelating agent. "Chelation" is a chemical term that specifies a type of chemical bond formed between a chelating agent and a metal. When a chelating agent is administered, it binds with the heavy metals which are then excreted in the urine or feces. The improvements made were observed in every area of concern in a child with ADD. There were behavioral improvements such as less disruptive and aggressive behavior; scores on IQ and achievement testing were higher; and academic performances increased and continued at an elevated level. Consider the case of Bryan.

Bryan, a nineteen-year-old who had worked as a truck driver since flunking out of college his freshman year, came to our clinic to see if neurofeedback would help his headaches. His girlfriend had had a complete resolution of her migraine headaches after a course of neurofeedback, and Bryan was hopeful he could be helped. His history included intermittent abdominal pain for which he had been evaluated multiple times. The medical findings did not reveal any obvious source of the pain. He was prescribed an acid-blocker, but he continued to have sharp abdominal pains at times. Though intelligent, he reported he had always tested poorly in high school, and had difficulty maintaining his concentration when reading. He had been tested for a learning disability and was found to have visual and perceptual deficiencies, but no recommendations had been made to his parents following the testing.

His father had actually asked Bryan's physician about the possibility of lead exposure because of the family's ceramic business, but he was told that because Bryan did not have the anemia lead exposure causes, it was not necessary to look further.

A heavy metal analysis on Bryan revealed moderately elevated levels of both lead and cadmium. We prescribed a course of chelation treatment with the chelating agent dimercaptosuccinic acid, or DMSA, to bind and remove these metals from his tissues. This drug is approved by the FDA for lead toxicity, and is preferable to many other chelating agents because it crosses the blood-brain barrier and chelates lead, mercury, and arsenic from brain tissue as well as other organs. Most of the other chelating agents do not have this property of removing accumulations from the brain. DMPS, for example, does not cross the blood-brain barrier, so does not remove lead or mercury from brain tissue. It gets pushed by some clinicians because it is more lucrative to do a series of hundred-dollar treatments than to hand someone a prescription for DMSA. They say DMSA is too toxic; DMPS is, in fact, somewhat more potentially toxic.

Bryan's headaches and abdominal pains resolved completely. He also reported that he was reading and remembering with less effort. He is currently taking six hours of college courses at night, and is on target to graduate soon.

Bryan was fortunate. Damage from heavy metals can become irreversible. We do not fault Bryan's physician; his approach to Bryan's problem was quite consistent with his training. However, maybe now the training ought to include something about the toxic effects of heavy metals in the body and their possible role in ADD. Approximately 3 to 5 percent of our population has ADD; more than 4 percent of preschool aged children have lead levels that are above the Environmental Protection Agency's maximum acceptable level—makes you wonder. How many children diagnosed with ADD and treated with Ritalin would be better served by removing the lead from their brains with chelation?

Mercury: Mercury is even more toxic than lead. Mercury toxicity can mimic and cause many neurological, endocrine, or immune diseases, and it can damage DNA. It accumulates in the kidneys, liver, and the most toxic forms of mercury accumulate in the brain. The distribution in the brain is not random, as higher concentrations are found in the hypothalamus and the pituitary, two crucial regulatory centers.[5]

While we could discuss the role mercury plays in suicidal depression, autoimmune diseases, medication-resistant infections, hypothyroidism, chronic neurological diseases, and other serious health problems, we will restrict ourselves to those problems that mimic or worsen ADD, learning disabilities, and autism.

Like lead, mercury toxicity may produce symptoms at both ends of the ADD spectrum—irritability, excitability, restlessness, aggression, and anxiety on the one hand, and memory and learning problems, fatigue, lethargy, and depression on the other. If you then include allergies and headaches, you see that mercury *alone* may produce *any* ADD-like symptoms a pediatrician is likely to see.

Mercury is also in the air, the water, and on the soil. It is found on grains treated with methyl mercury fungicides, in seafood, cosmetics, medications—especially in over-the-counter topical ointments, sprays, and drops. It was used as a preservative in immunizations given to infants from the 1930's until 2001. It is in a wide range of household products, including mildew and corrosion resistant paints, and it is used in numerous industrial processes. Many electronic products contain mercury, and small amounts are released when they are turned on. Fluorescent lights or booting up a computer are only two examples. Mercury is in the small disc batteries in so many devices such as watches and cameras. It is in polyurethane, which is pervasive.

Not only is mercury in various products, but the mercury in these products frequently finds its way into the atmosphere for further distribution after the products are discarded. In many parts of the country, coal-burning or trash incineration distributes mercury vapors for more than a hundred miles.

For millions of people, the source of the greatest amount of mercury is from their dental fillings. Although these fillings release tiny amounts of mercury, they are released steadily, day after day, decade after decade.

Dental fillings, also called "silver" fillings or amalgams, are composed of approximately 50 percent mercury and only around 20 percent silver. A debate is raging over whether these mercury-laden fillings are toxic or not. Dental authorities state that the more than 180 years of mercury-amalgam use demonstrates it is not toxic. On the other side, the research accumulating over the past two decades suggests otherwise.

Mercury amalgams placed in the mouth have been scientifically demonstrated to produce a wide-ranging list of actions. These include mercury absorption through the gums and mercury vapors in the mouth increasing after chewing. These vapors are being inhaled into the lungs, where mercury is then carried to the brain. Autopsy studies show that the amount of mercury in a person's brain is directly proportional to the number of amalgam surfaces in that person's mouth.

Your dentist may not be able to provide you with much help. The political maneuvering surrounding this debate is such that the American Dental Association has decided it is *unethical* for a dentist to tell you or agree with you that your mercury amalgams are harmful. Many believe this is a tactical move in anticipation of a class action suit against dental associations due to the mountain of information that is accumulating about the health dangers from mercury fillings. There are dental practitioners who specialize in the safe removal of mercury amalgams.

Mercury may be safely removed from the tissues with proper chelation. The agent we prefer for mercury chelation is DMSA.

Cadmium: Cadmium is approximately ten times more toxic than lead. It commonly travels with lead and is often airborne, settling on bodies of water and soils. Consequently, like lead, most of us get cadmium by simply breathing and eating. There are many sources—smoking and second hand smoke, paints and coatings, farm and garden products, and a number of industrial processes. Cadmium is used mainly in the production of nickel-cadmium batteries, and it is another heavy metal used as a stabilizer in plastics.[6]

Cadmium is particularly toxic to kidneys and can cause anything from high blood pressure to kidney failure. It is also implicated in lung and prostate cancers. Our specific concern with cadmium is that it may produce dyslexia and other learning disabilities, low IQ scores, especially verbal IQ, and low academic achievement. Every child who has any type of learning difficulties should routinely be screened by the school system for cadmium toxicity as well as other heavy metal toxicity. But this is not likely to be the case. Parents must be the active forces in getting their children properly evaluated.

Cadmium may also be readily removed from the tissues by chelating agents.

Aluminum: Aluminum, a smaller atom than the heavy metals discussed above, nonetheless has many of the same harmful effects in the body that heavy metals do. Many people are aware that aluminum is found in brain lesions associated with Alzheimer's disease. Less well known is the fact that increased aluminum tissue levels are associated with learning and memory deficits at *any* age.[7]

There are two known effects of aluminum on the brain that are liable to be harmful to anyone. One is that aluminum increases the permeability of the blood-brain barrier. This means that substances in the blood, including aluminum itself, which should not be permitted to cross into the cerebrospinal fluid, are able to do so.

The other effect is that aluminum chemically interferes with the production of neurotransmitters—the brain's chemical messengers. Children with ADD have been noted to have decreased dopamine functioning in their frontal lobes. Dopamine is one of the brain's most important neurotransmitters. There is also evidence to suggest that aluminum toxicity impairs certain vision functions.

We take in aluminum by breathing and eating. It is in baking powders, food additives, creamers, cans, and cookware and containers. If you have ever cooked an acidic food, like tomatoes, in an aluminum pot and noticed how shiny the surface was afterwards, it is because the acid removed aluminum from the surface like a polish shines silver. Of course, it means the aluminum removed is in the spaghetti sauce. It is not a good idea to cook acidic foods in aluminum cookware. Infant formulas are, relatively speaking, loaded with aluminum, as are several antacids. It is also in antiperspirant deodorants.

Tissue levels of aluminum may be decreased with chelating agents.

Arsenic: We all know arsenic is a poison. It damages any of a number of organs by blocking energy production at the cellular level. In addition to fatigue and headaches, arsenic toxicity commonly causes nerve damage and leads to intellectual, motor, or sensory defects. Learning problems occur, especially with language. It is a known carcinogen.[8]

Arsenic is produced and distributed over the earth in great quantities because it is effective against insects, fungi, weeds, rodents—you get the picture, against *living* things. In addition to spraying it on crops and adding it to animal feed, it is used to preserve wood and is added to paints, wallpaper, and ceramics to make them more "durable."

Arsenic may also be chelated out of our bodies.

Nickel: Though nickel appears to be necessary to our DNA in minute quantities, deficiencies of this metal are not the problem. Most of us take in far more than we need. Inhaled nickel compounds lead to nerve cell damage of the brain and of peripheral nerves. Fortunately, we do not absorb much nickel through our gastrointestinal tracts, but we do inhale it from tobacco and industrial smoke.[9] Nickel may also be chelated from the tissues.

An Important Note to Prospective Parents: The heavy metals we have discussed in this section are passed from mother to child in the placental blood and from breast milk. This is a particular problem for lead, as it is stored primarily in bone. These lead stores enter the blood when bones demineralize. Unfortunately, two life events that are characterized by a heightened rate of bone demineralization are pregnancy and lactation.

Throughout pregnancy, the placental blood will have more lead than the mother's blood usually has due to the demineralization of her bone, especially during the second half of pregnancy. Also, there will be more than usual lead in the mother's milk for the same reason. For some metals, like mercury, the blood going to the fetus actually has a greater concentration than the mother's blood.

By the way, this is *not* an argument against breastfeeding. Infant formulas also contain heavy metals. The point is simply that the mother's lead blood level will rise somewhat during pregnancy and breastfeeding, and more lead will enter her placental blood and her milk. Supplementing calcium can reduce these elevations in lead.

Any woman planning to become pregnant can have her own tissue levels tested for heavy metals, and she can choose to undergo chelation prior to pregnancy to reduce the burden her child will encounter.

Why Heavy Metals Testing Is Recommended for ADD Children

Although we have discussed these toxic metals separately, they are present in each of us in combination. Certain combinations, such as lead and aluminum, have been demonstrated to work synergistically. This means that they magnify the effects of one another. The synergistic damage caused by two is greater than adding the amount caused by each separately. In other words, two plus two does not equal four, but eight, sixteen, or thirty-two. Not much is known about the extent of such synergistic damage because toxins are almost never studied in combinations, only individually.

The Environmental Protection Agency (EPA) recommends that all children be screened for lead toxicity annually, especially children under six years of age. We agree, but add that other toxic metals should be screened for as well. It is not that lead is so toxic when compared to the others. The EPA's attention to the problem is more of a historical circumstance. Lead has been studied for the longest time, and the precautions and restrictions pertaining to lead were in place prior to the current mechanisms for identifying and restricting the use of toxic substances that are so favorable to industry.

Just because a substance is found to cause cancer or neurological damage to laboratory animals and to people exposed to that substance does not mean that the substance will be removed and prohibited from extensive use. In general, chemicals produced for industry enjoy a free ride unless the evidence they are toxic is overwhelming, and the alternative is affordable to industry.

Our recommendation for toxic metal testing is divided into two groups. The first group includes a screening test for all children. These screening tests should be performed on children whether or not they have behavioral or medical symptoms. Early detection of an elevated level of a metal toxin can lead to interventions that can *prevent* a lifetime of physical or mental problems.

The minimum screening test to consider is a blood lead level done by one year of age, and repeated at least every few years. Our opinion is that other metals should also be screened, at least once during toddlerhood. The blood levels for the other metals are not as well worked out, however, so a simple blood test at the time it is done for lead will not suffice. As we shall discuss, blood levels are useful for detecting an acute or recent exposure, but the purpose of screening is to find out if there is an accumulation that has built up over months or years.

Hair analysis can be a useful screening test for several of the other metals, including cadmium, arsenic, and mercury. There are several important caveats about hair analysis, however. Although hair can reflect the uptake of metals into the body, metals can also bind to hair externally, and a laboratory cannot determine how the metals got there. This means that exposure to hair products or any other substances that come into contact with hair can cause false results.

Further, since hair grows slowly (about an inch every two months), different sections of hair will reflect metal exposure only during the period of time that length of hair was growing. This kind of metal elevation will be detected if there has been a persistent low-grade exposure, such as through drinking water. But the hair of a boy with a crewcut who, three years ago, sucked on plastic toys that were stabilized with cadmium will not show that he has cadmium in his tissues. The hair with the cadmium was cut off long ago. Also, hair analysis is a difficult procedure to perform accurately, so labs must be painstaking in their methods.

Just like an X-ray, the interpretation of the resulting hair analysis requires knowledge and experience. It is not simply a matter of reading the bar graph in the laboratory report. Many of the complaints by mainstream clinicians about the unscientific use of hair analysis are legitimate. There are numerous instances of people being shepherded around a health food store by a well-meaning "nutritionist," hair analysis report in hand, picking this product up because it is "low" and that one because "it removes the one that is high." Using a hair analysis in this manner can promote or cause metabolic problems.

Any abnormal results from hair analysis must be confirmed by more accurate testing before a diagnosis is established or a treatment is initiated. The limitations, potential sources of error, and the interactive metabolism of metals in the body must be taken into account for a clinician to use a hair analysis properly. Understanding trace element/mineral physiology is important since hair analysis usually includes the levels of essential nutritional minerals as well as levels of toxic metals.

For example, a low zinc level on hair analysis does not mean a child should be given zinc. Other factors must be taken into consideration. The discussion of these factors is beyond the scope of this book, but it is essential to keep in mind that a hair analysis is for screening only and must *never* be used to make a diagnosis. Despite these limitations, the Environmental Protection Agency, among other agencies, has found hair analysis to be one of the tests useful for screening for heavy metal exposure.

The second group in which testing for toxic metals is needed includes any child who has learning or behavioral problems. These problems include learning disability, dyslexia, autism, hyperactivity, aggressive behavior, poor academic performance, excessive shyness or avoidant behavior, unexplained fatigue or listlessness. Any child with neurological problems, including vision or hearing problems, should also be considered for testing. Every child with any type of developmental arrest is certainly included, and we also include children who have chronic bowel symptoms, including colic, nausea, loss of appetite, diarrhea.

This is not to say that if a child is responding well to current interventions, e.g., Ritalin for supposed ADD, that she should not be tested. The reason for the testing in this case is to attempt to uncover a possible underlying cause or an exacerbating factor to her condition that can be treated. Testing for toxic metals does not preclude other medical evaluation. For example, if a child develops diarrhea, first look into other, more obvious causes. But if a child has chronic problems with loose stools and the medical workup has not pointed to adequate treatments, think about having her screened for heavy metals.

Testing for chronic heavy metal toxicity begins with a detailed history and a careful evaluation of the child's problems. Depending on the history and the problems present, hair, urine and/or blood samples may be analyzed.

The second group in which testing for toxic metals is needed includes any child who has learning or behavioral problems. These problems include learning disability, dyslexia, autism, hyperactivity, aggressive behavior, poor academic performance, excessive shyness or avoidant behavior, unexplained fatigue or listlessness.

Heavy metals that are ingested or breathed in are absorbed into the blood. Consequently, most physicians assume that a blood test is the best way to determine either adequate levels of the nutritional minerals or the presence of heavy metal toxicity. This is true for an acute or very recent exposure, but a blood test may in fact be the least useful method for determining accumulation from a chronic exposure.

The primary reason that blood levels do not necessarily reflect the amount of metals or minerals in the tissues is that blood components are controlled so carefully by the body. Heavy metals present in the blood are quickly removed and deposited in the tissues. Consequently, tissues may be burdened with toxic metals, or deficient in desirable trace minerals, and the blood levels may be "perfectly normal." The disparity between blood levels and the levels in specific organs was documented more than twenty years ago.

Acute heavy metal toxicity is, of course, a serious problem, but we need not concern ourselves with this in a discussion of learning and behavioral problems. A child with acute heavy metal toxicity will have severe medical problems. It is the *chronic* heavy metal toxicity from a gradual accumulation over a period of time that is more likely to be implicated in the problems we are addressing in this book.

That said, we agree with screening children's blood levels for lead toxicity. Lead has been the heavy metal studied the longest and most intensively, and has become so pervasive in our environment, and consequently in our tissues, that even blood levels tend to reflect steady-state tissue levels. The current acceptable level determined by the EPA is ten µg/Dl (micrograms per deciliter). Actually, there is strong evidence this value should be reduced, but it is at least a starting point.

How is a toxic level determined? Basically, levels are obtained from people who appear to be healthy and their levels are averaged. A "normal" range is obtained from this average. It may not be immediately apparent, but this does not mean that these levels are actually safe or non-toxic. The assumption is that these levels do not appear to be causing problems in most people.

One would think that these "normal" ranges would at least be fairly consistent, but this is not the case. There is a continual redefinition of what amounts of heavy metals are considered to be acceptable. The acceptable range of some metals understandably decreases as more clinical data accumulates evidence of toxic effects at low levels. For example, the acceptable blood lead level was sixty µg/Dl until 1970, when it was reduced to forty, then to thirty in 1978, twenty-five in 1983, and to ten in 1991.

But some so-called acceptable ranges increase despite evidence to the contrary, simply because everyone's levels are increased due to widespread environmental contamination. The difference may well depend on financial considerations. For example, if the acceptable level of lead were lowered to the level that scientific studies now indicate is toxic, too great a percentage of school age children would be deemed as having toxic levels, and this would, in reality, bankrupt Medicaid and other third-party health care payors. So, we accept a higher lead blood level than scientific data suggest is safe.

The test we find most useful for determining tissue levels of most of the toxic metals is a urine test called DMSA challenge test. The patient is given a capsule of DMSA and then she collects her urine for six hours. The urine sample is analyzed for the presence of several heavy metals.

DMSA was developed as an alternative to EDTA (ethylenediaminetetraacetate) for the treatment of lead toxicity. EDTA is usually administered intravenously, though it can be given with an intramuscular injection, but it is extremely painful when given in this manner. DMSA may be taken orally so it is more suitable for children. The majority of the research done on DMSA was carried out in the former Soviet Union and in China in the 1950s through the 1980s, and studies indicate that DMSA has a low potential for toxicity when administered correctly.

DMSA attaches to heavy metals in the tissues, literally pulls them from the tissues, and carries them to the kidneys for excretion in the urine. The reason it is used prior to collecting a urine sample is because the heavy metals are not readily excreted from the body.

Removing Heavy Metals from the Body

If a person is found to have elevated levels of one or more toxic metals, the treatment to remove the metals from the body is called chelation. As we said before, chelation is a chemical term that specifies a type of chemical bond formed between a chelating agent and a metal.

The chelating medication we use preferentially for decreasing metal toxicity is DMSA, the same agent used in the test discussed above. It is taken orally, and it very avidly binds mercury and lead. An important feature of DMSA is that it crosses the blood-brain barrier, which is essential if it is to be able to remove toxic metals from brain and spinal cord tissues. DMSA also promotes the excretion of other heavy metals including arsenic. The dose of DMSA is determined by the patient's age and weight, and by the level of the metal. A patient undergoing chelation treatment must supplement nutritional minerals since DMSA will also increase the excretion rates of these. A rapid detoxification should be avoided to reduce the likelihood of gastrointestinal or kidney toxicity.

There are several other chelating medications, including EDTA and DMPS. EDTA is poorly absorbed from the gastrointestinal tract however, and must be taken intravenously or intramuscularly. Intramuscular administration is quite painful. DMPS is also an intravenous treatment, but it does not cross the blood-brain-barrier.

The Role of *Candida Albicans* and ADD

Yeast is a form of fungus, and *Candida albicans* is the most common yeast that inhabits our bodies. Although everyone has yeast growing in multiple sites—bowels, skin, mucous membranes—it does not usually cause problems unless it proliferates and disturbs the healthy balance of microorganisms. Yeast overgrowth is a common occurrence and may cause significant health problems. The organ systems yeast is most likely to disturb are the gastrointestinal tract, the central nervous system, the endocrine system, the immune system, and the skin. Yeast problems result from both the reduction of beneficial organisms and from the wide range of toxins yeast produce, called mycotoxins.

Sean was an eleven-year-old boy from Washington, D.C. His parents were desperate to obtain neurofeedback for him and arranged for one of them to stay with Sean in a motel near our clinic for a month during the summer so he could have two neurofeedback treatments daily.

Sean had a history of hyperactivity dating back to preschool. His behavior was so disruptive that his parents had to hire an adult baby-sitter to supervise him one-on-one throughout the day, or the exclusive preschool he attended would have refused to allow him to remain as a student. He also had a history as a colicky baby and had recurrent severe rashes. Following treatment for pneumonia, he then had recurrent ear infections and developed multiple allergies and asthmatic symptoms. His performance at school was low, especially considering his high I. Q. The headmaster at his school had recommended to Sean's parents that he repeat the fifth grade, hoping that an extra year of maturity might help.

A significant number of children we see in our clinic have a history of treatment for numerous ear and respiratory infections or acne with antibiotics. This is not coincidental. Antibiotics are the main cause of yeast-related problems, and prednisone, acid-blocking drugs, and the presence of mercury worsen these problems. Although problems from yeast do not necessarily resemble ADD, in some instances they do mimic it. Even if a child with yeast problems doesn't have hyperactivity, lethargy, or inattention, the symptoms he does have from yeast—headaches, stuffed sinuses, abdominal discomfort, and skin irritations—are likely to interfere with academic work.[10,11]

In addition to those children who have had several courses of antibiotic treatment, we also think about the possibility of yeast in those with a history of seborrheic dermatitis (cradle cap) or other skin conditions, asthma or allergies, or autistic behavior. Further, there is evidence that some children diagnosed with autism have toxic levels of yeast byproducts in their urine, which indicate high levels of yeast in the tissues.[12] In some cases, treatment of yeast in these children has produced a number of behavioral improvements.[13]

The adults we see in our clinic who have had yeast overgrowth problems for years typically have primary complaints of chronic fatigue. Many have anxiety or depression, and many are on antidepressants or have complaints labeled by their family physicians as psychosomatic. Women frequently have recurrent vaginal yeast infections.

So what is the problem with yeast, specifically *Candida albicans?* Yeast is a fungus that inhabits our skin, mucous membranes, respiratory tracts, and intestines. Yeasts are parasitic in nature and have no known beneficial effects in humans. By far the largest population of yeast resides in our intestinal tracts. A healthy bowel has a much larger number of beneficial bacteria than yeast, so a small population of yeast in our bowels is not usually a problem.

Problems can arise when the yeast multiply to excessive numbers. Not only are there then fewer beneficial bacteria to resist the yeast, but the yeast itself is toxic. The yeast most commonly found in our bowel, *Candida albicans,* is capable of producing a number of enzymes and at least eighty different toxic substances. These enzymes and toxins can adversely affect health. In addition, yeast attaches to the lining cells of our bowels and can cause or contribute to the "leaky gut" problems previously discussed.

The toxins produced by the yeast can cause a wide range of symptoms. They may produce generalized symptoms, such as fatigue, lethargy, or irritability, or symptoms may be more localized, such as headaches, gastrointestinal disturbances, or sinus problems.

Antibiotics kill the desirable bacteria in our bowels and inadvertently support an overgrowth of yeast. Most traditional physicians assume that after the antibiotics are discontinued, the proper bacterial balance in the bowel is regained. This has not yet been demonstrated to be the case, and the percentage of people who never reestablish a proper balance is unknown. It is clear, however, that the more courses of antibiotics a person has, the less likely she is to reestablish the proper balance of organisms in her bowel without assistance, such as with *Lactobacillus acidophilus* and the like.

Other medications contribute to yeast overgrowth. Immune-suppressing drugs, such as prednisone, and antacids or acid-blockers, such as Tagamet or Zantac, create a favorable environment for the yeast to proliferate. A diet high in sugar or high-glycemic-index carbohydrates also enhances the proliferation of yeast.

After evaluating Sean, in addition to neurofeedback, we recommended a course of nystatin oral powder, nutrients that promote a healthy bowel, and a diet free of sugars and high-glycemic-index carbohydrates.

In the confines of the motel room for that month, it actually proved to be easier to carefully control Sean's diet and monitor any changes in his behavior than it would have been at his home. His improvements were dramatic. Within two weeks, his behavior had stabilized and he had a significant decrease in his allergy symptoms. He also no longer required the usual dose of his asthma inhaler after playing.

The child that emerged before our eyes was a charming, engaging, and ebullient boy. In a follow-up note to us from his father, we learned that Sean was able to focus his boundless energy on his schoolwork, and the progress he was making was astounding his teachers. He had become the class computer wiz, no small accomplishment in a class of bright, talented children.

The diagnosis for a yeast overgrowth is largely based on the clinical history. Ironically, this is one of the main reasons that many conventionally-minded physicians do not believe this syndrome even exists. Why? Because no laboratory test is available to confirm or rule out the presence of a yeast overgrowth. There are tests that support the likelihood of its presence, but the clinical history remains the most important diagnostic instrument. In today's technology-reliant medical atmosphere, the clinical history is often regarded lightly.

The treatment of a yeast overgrowth is based on the severity and duration of the symptoms. Dietary changes and nutrient supplementation may be adequate for some, especially children, while others may require an aggressive regimen of antifungal medications. The most important dietary measure for a person with yeast overgrowth is to avoid sugar and high-glycemic-index foods, as discussed in chapter 9. Sugar feeds the yeast and activates them.

Some nutritional interventions for reducing yeast include inoculating the bowel with beneficial bacteria. These should include *Lactobacillus acidophilus* and *Lactobacillus bifidum* species. Many people are familiar with *acidophilus*, but this bacteria takes up long-term residence in the small intestine only. Bifidobacteria are needed, as they prefer the large intestine. The *bulgaricus* species found in yogurt are also highly beneficial, but since they do not form part of the permanent bowel inhabitants, acidophilus and bifidobacteria should be added.

Another naturally occurring nutrient that is helpful to reduce yeast growth is a nontoxic fatty acid found in coconut oil and in milk fat, caprylic acid. It works primarily in the intestinal tract where it inhibits yeast propagation while not interfering with the beneficial organisms. A dose of one hundred to eight hundred milligrams per day is easily tolerated by most children and adults.

Naturally occurring antifungals that help reduce yeast include olive leaf extract, citrus seed extract, and oil of oregano. Each of these has specific activity against yeast, and, by the way, they all have anti-viral activity as well. Be warned, oregano oil has a potent odor and a person may reek of it for several days after one dose.

These three antifungal agents can produce a Herxheimer, or die-off, reaction. When a person with excessive yeast takes one of these, or takes a prescription antifungal, they may experience flu-like symptoms for several hours. This reaction is the result of killing large numbers of yeast. The toxins the yeast produce are released from their fragmenting bodies. Until the toxins are detoxified and removed from the body, a person may feel achy, listless, nauseous, and fatigued. It is not a harmful condition, and is actually a positive sign of impending improvements.

Garlic is a highly useful nutrient with numerous health benefits, one of which is yeast reduction. Other metabolic activity of garlic produces immune system and cardiovascular benefits. The odorless supplement variety is useful for decreasing yeast, as are regular garlic products.

Some cases of yeast overgrowth require prescription antifungal medication. These include nystatin powder and amphotericin-B (Fungizone). Other medications are available for adolescents and adults, including Sporanox and Diflucan; their use in children should be restricted to exceptional circumstances, since safety studies with children are limited. Nystatin and amphotericin-B are not absorbed from the intestinal tract, so they do not enter to the blood. Consequently, they are very safe medications. At first, this may seem to prevent any benefit if they are not absorbed, but recall that the bulk of yeast in our bodies is in the gastrointestinal tract where these medications have their entire activity.

Amphotericin-B is not generally available from pharmacies in the oral form, except in combination with the antibiotic tetracycline—the cure with the poison. It is generally believed that taking antifungals while taking an antibiotic will create yeasts which are resistant to treatment. The pure form may be obtained from compounding pharmacies or from overseas suppliers; in France, Squibb makes a very high quality product.

Most American physicians are not aware of the benefits and safety of oral amphotericin-B. In the United States, amphotericin-B is used intravenously to treat life-threatening fungal illness, but it is potentially extremely toxic to the liver. Unfortunately, most physicians assume the oral form must be liver toxic as well, and will advise against taking it. This is unfortunate because amphotericin-B has a much wider range of antimicrobial activity than nystatin, and the combination of the two is highly effective.

The consequences of exposure to toxins and yeast overgrowth can range from subtle to dramatic. Understanding and treating these exposures can range from relatively simple to extremely complicated. Advice should be sought from a competent health care practitioner who is experienced in the treatment of these conditions.

11

Television—An Unsuspected Behavioral Influence

This chapter will cover a topic that we feel is very important in a discussion of problems with children and families in this modern age—television, that enigmatic box that sits in virtually every living room in America.

Televisions are finding their way into our bedrooms, kitchens, and even bathrooms. With so many of them, you would think we should know more about how they affect us, but we know surprisingly little about how television affects us psychologically or biochemically. Does it, for example, affect our endocrine systems, our neuromuscular or sensory systems, or even our central nervous systems?

This lack of information stems from the fact that research money goes into learning how to keep us watching and buying more of the products advertised on TV. Precious little has been spent on understanding how television affects us intellectually, socially, and physically.

The research that has been done, however, is unnerving. We can say with confidence that excessive television viewing, particularly in young children, causes neurological damage. TV watching causes the brain to slow down, producing a constant pattern of low-frequency brainwaves consistent with ADD behavior. This low-frequency theta (four to eight hertz) reduces the brain's capacity for higher thought processes. Excessive television viewing by small children causes the brain to miss some of the early development stage, resulting in less-than-adequate brain functioning. The brain becomes limited in creative ability as well as higher levels of abstract thinking.

Television lulls the brain into a dull, barely conscious state resembling hypnosis. Television viewing may be one of the culprits in the cause of ADD, and we know that children's attentional problems are made worse by television and video games. Television viewing gets in the way of the brain developing the plasticity or flexibility necessary for a successful adult life.

In this chapter, we will discuss how television viewing affects intelligence and attention, how it makes worse such problems as ADD and hyperactivity, and how it contributes to the loss of creativity. We will also look at how TV contributes to other problems, such as violence and aggression, physical underdevelopment, personality changes, visual and language problems, and underdevelopment of social skills.

The latest figure that we can find from TV research suggests that a child sees approximately 5,000 hours of TV by the age of five.[22] This not only has a negative effect on the brain, reducing high-level thinking processes and creativity, but it has an influence on social behavior.

> *We can say with confidence that excessive television viewing, particularly in young children, causes neurological damage. TV watching causes the brain to slow down, producing a constant pattern of low-frequency brainwaves consistent with ADD behavior. Television viewing may be one of the culprits in the cause of ADD.*

Since the beginning of time, parents and families have been the models for children's behavior, but all of that began to change when television catapulted sight and sound into our living space. It first happened in the United States, then spread throughout the industrialized nations. Now television reaches every nook and cranny of the planet. For example, 32 percent of homes in Beijing, China, had televisions in 1980. By the end of the 1980s, that figure had soared to 95 percent.[1] Today there are well over a billion TV sets in homes around the world. In the early 1990s, CNN was broadcasting to 150 countries and MTV videos were seen all over the world.[2]

American television programs are broadcast to every country on the globe, from Russia to Australia, the Pacific islands to India, and everywhere in between. A problem arises for all viewers though, in that television does not reflect an accurate representation of any culture. During the period of time between the 1980s and the early 1990s, only about one-third of the TV characters were female, fewer than 3 percent were older individuals, 1 percent were Hispanic, Blacks were poorly represented, and only one in ten characters were married.[3] Even though network programmers have made attempts to correct these social misrepresentations, television today has failed to adequately represent who we are as a people.

In addition to the social inequities, in 1993, network programs had three violent acts per hour when adults were the primary viewers, and eighteen violent acts during children's Saturday morning programs.[4] This trend has continued through the 1990s. During the twenty-year period from the early 1970s to the early 1990s, the average child viewing television saw approximately 8,000 murders and 100,000 other violent acts before they even finished elementary school.[5] The violence does not accurately represent our U.S. culture, but reflects the desire of media to increase viewership and revenues.

If television were the only medium pouring violence and social misrepresentation into our homes, it would be bad enough. It gets worse with the proliferation of video rentals and the now-booming industry of video games. Our children are flooded with violence, sex, social stereotypes, and brain-numbing programming.

In 1939, a *New York Times* writer characterized the future of television in the following statement: "The problem with television is that the people must sit and keep their eyes glued to a screen: the average American family hasn't time for it. Therefore the showmen are convinced that . . . television will never be a serious competitor of broadcasting."

Broadcasting until then had been the exclusive dominion of radio—a wonderful medium that gave us news, information, music, and stories that were illuminated and played out in our minds. You could listen to radio and continue to work, as the vivid pictures danced in your head involving almost all of the higher functions of the brain. Little did the *Times* writer realize how wrong his prediction could be. Today, television has all but reduced radio to a five-minute news report on the hour and the remainder filled with music and shallow chatter. Gone forever are the wonderful storytelling, the great sound effects, and the "movies" in our minds.

Television is perhaps one of the greatest advancements in human technological progress, but its misuse may turn out to be very destructive. Television gives each of us immediate and personal access to events occurring around the world, provides unlimited educational possibilities, and along with computers, it may provide an unparalleled opportunity for interactive communication between peoples and their governments.

However, television has been allowed to sink to the level of mindless sitcoms that require a fourth grade education to understand, and tragically, television has become the global babysitter. Social commentators generally agree that television overall has done more harm that good. Marvin Minsky once said, "Imagine what it would be like if TV were actually good. It would be the end of everything we know." Perhaps it is a good thing that television programming is so poorly done; if it were good, more people would be habituated to, and thus be potentially damaged by, its effects.

Over the course of our medical practices we have seen what we believed to be the negative results of television played out in the everyday lives of our patients. Nowhere is it more observable than in the children who we treat for attentional and behavioral problems. Scarcely a day goes by that TV wrestling, or some other violent act as seen on TV, isn't acted out in our waiting room.

Recently we were taken aback when we encountered a family dealing with a relationship dispute. The family consisted of elderly parents and six adult children, four male and two female. The oldest child was a fifty-four-year-old male and the youngest a forty-year-old male. All of the children except the youngest were thin, highly motivated, and attentive. The youngest male was obese, unmotivated, and had a very short attention span. He was so different we concluded he was adopted.

When we questioned the two older children if he was adopted, the oldest answered, "No, he's not adopted; he's just different. We call him the TV baby. We grew up on a farm and did not get a TV until he was born. The rest of us never got interested in TV but that's all he did. So, we call him the TV baby. I think that's why he's the way he is."

If this is in fact the case then parents and professionals must respond to the looming crisis. It stands to reason that children who grow up receiving a significant amount of their social input from television are bound to be different from children getting these social instructions from family and friends.

Even in the most loving and attentive families, television, like the car keys, becomes a convenience for parents. Busy parents do not have time to drive older children to all of their activities, so it becomes a convenience to parents to pass the car keys to sixteen-year-olds, handing over the keys of a dangerous vehicle to someone whose brain is not fully developed. Likewise, busy or exhausted parents hand over the remote control to children far too young and immature to be able to discriminate between what is good or bad for them.

Television, for all its potential, is likely to be very harmful, particularly to young viewers. There are eight major areas of concern that parents and professionals need to be mindful of. The areas that offer the most potential for harm are:

- Cognitive-attentional problems
- Neurological damage
- Violence and aggressiveness
- Physical underdevelopment
- Gullibility
- Passive-dependent behavior
- Visual and language problems
- Social problems

Let's address each one of these separately.

Cognitive and Attentional Problems: If a child spends more time in front of a television than he does in a classroom, it stands to reason that the intelligence level will be less than that of the child who reads rather than watching TV. Even if he is watching PBS, television viewing causes neurological changes that lessen arousal levels. Television has replaced reading for fun; many young people only read when they are forced to. We contend that the more exposure to television children have, the lower the arousal level and the more difficult it is to read. Reading encourages the brain to build better internal connections and operate at a higher level, whereas television allows the brain to operate at the lowest level of functioning.

Efficient learning takes place when the brain is in a state of active alertness, not when the brain is in a deep state of relaxation. When the brain is producing alert brainwaves in the beta range, it is open and receptive to information. It can integrate bits of information into a whole picture. In the slower brainwave states, the brain is less alert, less awake.

When children sit in front of a television, their brains begin to slow down, moving toward the slower, less alert brainwaves. Reasoning, logic, and higher thought processes are absent in the lower frequencies. These frequencies approximate a state of hypnosis in which you appear dazed and follow instructions of the hypnotist. This is why children and even adults often appear in a daze when they sit in front of a television. They are in what is known as "ocular lock," or dazed staring.

This is also why it is difficult to get their attention; they are hypnotically locked onto the TV. One study indicated that children who watch TV six hours or more a day are more likely to have lower IQs than children who watch two hours or less.[11] Unfortunately, children who come from lower socioeconomic homes tend to be more at risk because of longer exposure to television viewing.

It is generally accepted that watching TV makes the brain slow down. To verify this, on several occasions, we have placed children in front of a TV and attached EEG sensors to the scalp in appropriate locations. Within a very short period of time the brain begins to exhibit low-frequency dominance. The brain slows down and higher thought processes stop.

In 1988, two researchers published an article stating that television inhibits the growth of reading and may inhibit intellectual problem solving.[15] A second study suggests there were three negative effects on learning for young children: television has the ability to manipulate the brain to pay attention to it; television induces neural passivity; and television may be hypnotic and possibly neurologically addictive.[16]

Television presents constant action, high drama, and dramatic effects, and this puts parents and teachers at a disadvantage. They cannot compete with television and video games. A teacher standing sedately in front of a blackboard is no comparison to the constant movement in television. She would have to create a circus-type atmosphere to be competitive.

Hence, children raised on TV easily become bored and disinterested. The child with ADD cannot sustain attention in most normal situations, but television or video games lock him in. Yet there is a paradoxical effect here: the television grabs his attention, then lulls him into hypnosis. This child who cannot pay attention is now transfixed and very difficult to disturb. For these children, commercials are even more captivating than the regular program.

Long hours of television watching make children behave like zombies and after television viewing, they may also be more hyper. One research article suggests there is a proportional increase in attentional disorders with time spent viewing television.[17] Our clinical findings would suggest that this is indeed correct. We have noted that the more time a child spends watching television, the less he reads, the less effort he makes on homework, the more trouble he has sustaining attention, the lower his grades are, and frequently, the higher the incidence of behavioral problems.

Neurological Damage: In terms of the effects of television on the brains and nervous systems of small children, we appear to be where we were with the knowledge of cigarette smoking and health in the 1960s. We know there is a danger, but we do not know the full extent of it. It would be ironic if thirty years from now we witness class action lawsuits against broadcasting companies for injuring young brains.

As dangerous as the possible impact of television content is to children, the neurological damage may be far worse than anyone expected. Television viewing may be causing a significant form of brain damage because of the way the brain reacts to it. The ancient art of storytelling carried on by parents and family, then by radio, had a profound impact on the way our brains formed and built neural connections. Television viewing, as opposed to storytelling, causes the brain to function very differently.

Research indicates that our brains operate by activating small clusters of neurons or brain cells. They in turn interact with other clusters of brain cells known as neural fields.[21] A single brain cell is connected to an average of 10,000 other neurons, and clusters of these neurons are organized into fields of neurons containing approximately a million brain cells each.[22] Brain cells communicate with one another through the use of chemical messengers called neurotransmitters. The brain is an amazing network of single brain cells communicating with other single cells of clusters of brain cells interacting with other clusters and of entire neural fields talking to other neural fields.

When the brain is involved in some low-level activity, not requiring a lot of thought, perhaps only a single field of neurons will be activated. This is exactly what happens in television viewing. It requires a very low level of brain activity. When complex thought is engaged during a behavior like problem solving or seeing a story in the mind, many neural fields are interacting with each other. The brain is a buzz of activity when this happens. Efficient brains are capable of speeding up for problem solving or slowing down for relaxation. When brains are busily engaged in problem solving or creative activity, all kinds of information is being passed back and forth between neurons and neural fields.

Violence and Aggressiveness: Violence and aggressiveness are the most researched area of potential harm from television. Television has a great capacity for manipulating our emotions. We can watch TV and feel sad, excited, frightened, or happy. Small children have difficulty distinguishing reality from fantasy, and when exposed to certain scenes on TV, they may feel frightened or threatened. When our emotions are directly linked to fear, our expressions may come out as an explosive reaction, or we may go underground in depression. Our brain stems and central nervous systems react to scenes on TV and in movies, and in younger children the reaction may be a violent reaction, giving rise to aggressive tendencies.

Perhaps the statement that says it all was made by psychologist Leonard Berkowitz in 1973.[6] In concluding his research, he said, "Violence ultimately produces more violence." Children who view violence are likely to have more aggressive behaviors than those who do not view violence.

In 1963, social learning theorist Albert Bandora and his colleagues demonstrated that children exposed to aggressive action on television tended to replicate those aggressive acts.[7] The general idea that viewing more aggression makes us more aggressive is widely accepted, but we do little to change this. Politicians are reluctant to seriously take on the entertainment industry because the industry wields a two-edged sword—powerful lobbyists and a means to get their message to the public. Parents acquiesce to the TV as baby-sitter, leaving their children at the mercy of programmers who choose violence to keep their ratings up.

American pre-school children ages two to five watch approximately twenty-seven hours of television a week.[8] If our society ever recognizes the social impact of seeing one violent act after another, perhaps we will do more to protect our children and our society. Amazingly, 24 percent of American households keep a TV in the children's bedroom.[9] Television should never be in anyone's bedroom, most particularly a child's room. Television could be a medium used to stimulate family interaction by discussing what has just been viewed; however, it tends to be a medium that isolates family members from each other.

In examining television viewing as a risk factor for violence, B.S. Canterwall discovered a very unsettling correlation in the United States between the years 1957 and 1974. A doubling of the homicide rates coincides with the introduction and spread of television into regions of our country that were new to TV. As other regions of the globe acquired television, they showed corresponding jumps in homicides.[10] Television teaches children that aggression is an appropriate way to resolve conflicts.[11] Research on violence in the media and its effects on our children has been accumulating for the past thirty years. There is scarcely a health professional who does not accept the idea that violence in the media encourages violence in our children.

Perhaps the most convincing argument for limiting these violent programs came in July of 2000. The American Medical Association, American Psychological Association, American Academy of Pediatrics, and the Academy of Child and Adolescent Psychiatry joined together to issue a statement to Washington lawmakers. These professional organizations urged legislators to take action curbing violent programming in television, music, video games, and movies. These organizations declared, "Its effects are measurable and long-lasting. Moreover, prolonged viewing of media violence can lead to emotional desensitization toward violence in real life."

The most powerful condemnation in the communication stated, "The conclusion of the public health community based on thirty years of research is that viewing entertainment violence can lead to increases in aggressive attitudes, values, and behaviors, particularly in children."

The three major points in the joint communication submitted to lawmakers were:

- Children who see a lot of violence are more likely to view violence as an effective way of settling conflicts, and are more likely to assume that acts of violence are acceptable behavior.

- Viewing violence can lead to emotional desensitization toward violence in real life. It can decrease the likelihood that one will take action on behalf of a victim when violence occurs.

- Viewing violence can lead to real-life violence. Children exposed to violent programming at a young age have a higher tendency for violent and aggressive behavior later in life than children who are not so exposed.

The only way that children will learn to deal with conflict and emotion appropriately is to have good models. If we want our children to deal with their feelings in healthy ways, we must demonstrate healthy ways over and over until good patterns are formed. Even if a child has a propensity toward aggressiveness and impulsivity, good parenting can alter the course of that predisposition.

Physical Underdevelopment: Another major area of concern is the physical development of our children. Obesity is a problem with our children today. It is not uncommon to read medical reports attesting to the presence of coronary artery disease in a growing number of young children. So, why is this happening?

It is logical to assume that if you spend more time in front of the television than you do in classroom activity, it will take its toll on your physical well being. In addition to the sedentary lifestyle of TV viewing, there is the propensity to snack while viewing. Not only are snack foods loaded with calories and fats, they are a firestorm of free radicals. Free radicals are the molecular agents many scientists view as the cause of heart disease, some cancers, and premature aging.

It seems that the "age of play" is over and has been replaced by the "age of TV." Kids are no longer building forts and riding broomstick horses. They are riding the couch and circling the refrigerator. Inactivity is the daily routine. Parents of yesterday could not get their children to interrupt their play long enough to come in the house for supper. Parents of today cannot get them to go outside.

Children are becoming like the elderly, their lifestyles do not include exercise and activity. A sedentary lifestyle leads to loss of bone mass and muscle development. In addition, there is less mental activity while watching TV, which leads to less plasticity or flexibility of the brain. The quality and quantity of thought diminishes and the body loses its energy. Without physical outlets for natural childhood energy, children are likely to develop a low frustration tolerance, anger and irritability, and purposeless movements or hyperactivity. This happens because television stimulates emotional and physical reactions with no suitable outlet for them.[11,12]

Mental and physical movement are vital for good health. In a Canadian study, 500 children spent an extra hour in the gym each day, and they scored significantly better on exams than children who were less physically active. Researchers also found that men and women in their fifties and sixties who were put on a four-month aerobic exercise program scored ten percent higher on mental tests.[13] The mind-body connection is critical in the development of the whole person. Children need to be off the couch and engaged in physical and mental play, and their play must not only be physical, but creative as well.

Today most play is team or league play, in which children participate in organized sports. On the surface this looks like a good idea, but upon close examination we find children are asked to play by adult rules and are closely supervised. They are asked to perform to adult expectations. Much like college and professional athletics, the children are playing for the coaches and the spectators rather than for the fun of it.

Children need to play sports, but at least for a time they need to make the rules; they need to set the times and boundaries. They need to evaluate the quality of their play. They need to be completely free of overzealous adults living their lives vicariously through children. Sandlot ball and kickball in the park are important foundations in the building of a vibrant child who grows into an intelligent, creative adult.

Gullibility: Television seems like a cheap baby-sitter, but the price we are paying may be horrendous. Not only do small children have an inability to distinguish reality from fantasy, they accept everything uncritically. This makes them easy prey for marketeers who want to sell everything imaginable to children.

Saturday morning cartoons are neatly spliced with product commercials designed to stimulate childhood desires. Small children are unable to realize that commercials are designed to sell products. Instead they see them as entertainment, a wish fulfillment, something that, if they had, they could have fun. Children do not realize that commercials are not the whole truth. They are completely accepting of whatever they see. Companies try to sell children toys that do not replicate the fun they exhibit in commercials and sugar-filled drinks, cereals, and snacks. It is imperative that parents and adult caregivers be an integral part of any TV viewing, to demystify commercial messages and to set boundaries between reality and fantasy.

Most of the research money that has been spent to assess the effects of television has been spent by advertisers, concerned with the value of their advertising dollar. They want to be sure that their commercial message grabs and holds the brain's attention long enough to sell you their products. There has been very limited funding to find out how TV programs and commercial messages affect such human activities as learning and social behavior.

Passive-Dependent Behavior: Not only does television create a sedentary lifestyle, but it fosters a state of passivity by actually changing the way brainwaves fire. The younger the child, the more vulnerable to being lulled into passivity, because their brains are more susceptible to change. Viewing television is an easy activity. It requires no physical or mental effort—just sit passively and be lulled into a hypnotic state. If the program looses your interest, hit the remote and go to another mindless channel.

We contend this passive attitude dramatically reduces sustained attention. Children particularly give up too easily if they are used to being completely entertained by television. Learning is an active process that involves effort, often trial and retrial. It requires that one push through frustration, failure, and boredom. If we are trained to hit the remote when we are bored, we lose that necessary mechanism to try again.

As a generalization, up until forty years ago children were not bored, or certainly not like they are today. Today boredom is a chronic complaint of young people, particularly children with attentional problems. Until the 1940s and 1950s, children had chores and few toys, but in a way they had everything. An ordinary stick had the possibilities of being such things as a horse, a spear, or a magical sword. Trees and hills offered ideal spots for forts and hideaways. There was adventure at every turn.

It was this ability to see something from nothing that led us to our current place in human evolution. This creative spark produced what humans have today. When plastic is molded into an exact replica of something, it has one use—what it looks like.

Our children are losing their creative geniuses because TV is the prime source of their adventure. For many children, their after-school activity involves hitting the remote and walking to the refrigerator. They are left to be deprived of real-world activities and appropriate human emotional expressions. Jane Healy, in her excellent book, *Endangered Minds,* refers to these children as "touched starved." They are "touched starved," but if they are left with TV alone, they are physically starved, intellectually starved, creatively starved, emotionally starved, and nutritionally starved. They can develop a number of unwanted characteristics such as passivity and unmotivated or undirected behavior.

What is worse than this is the fact that television viewing, particularly for young children, can actually change the way the brain functions. As the brain slows down due to television viewing, we can see a wide variety of psychological problems, including ADD, hyperactivity, depression, and anxiety. The implications of television viewing are not just social but neurological.

Visual and Language Problems:
There is very little research in this area, but it appears there is a negative relationship between watching TV and visual and language problems. From a logical perspective, it would appear that long hours of watching TV would impair visual development.

To understand this, we need to explain a few facts about the eye. The eye contains two types of light receptors, rods and cones. Rods outnumber cones 95 percent to 5 percent. Cones are generally concentrated in the central part of the eye and require bright light. They generally come into play for such two-dimensional activities as reading, television, or looking at a computer screen. Visual development requires taking in the whole world, not an excess of two-dimensional patterns. Therefore, we have another important reason to limit the exposure of small children to television, video games, and computer screens. Not only are their brains developing, but also their ocular systems.

Language is an expressive skill that is enhanced by speaking and listening to other individuals speak. Without language, humans would not have developed abstract, categorical thinking.[18] So, language fosters intellectual growth. Language poorly understood and poorly spoken reflects on the intelligence of an individual. The problem with television is that language is spoken too quickly. Children often pick up words and phrases that make them sound more intelligent, but they lack the ability to integrate these words or phrases into proper context. Language development takes time; children need to play with words, roll them around in their heads and put them in an integrated context.

> *Television viewing, particularly for young children, can actually change the way the brain functions. As the brain slows down due to television viewing, we can see a wide variety of psychological problems, including ADD, hyperactivity, depression, and anxiety.*

Children often become pseudo-sophisticated watching television. They not only use adult words but also adult gestures. Television fosters this type of expression. This type of behavior may appear cute to adults, but it may get the child in trouble. The child may outwardly appear older and more mature, which may result in their being taken advantage of. Not all adults recognize good boundaries between themselves and children.

When our language models are TV sitcoms, we lose the sense that speech is special. Many shows exhibit incomplete speech patterns, slang, colloquial grunts and idioms that reflect the poorest quality of language. Our young children and teens pick up these expressions because they are easy and require no thought; expressions that do not convey a complete thought: "Like," "for real," "you know?" These expressions do not convey meaning, and therefore increased use leads to incomplete thought and lower cortical processing.

In 1928, a study was done estimating that our daily communications involved 45 percent of our time listening, 30 percent speaking, 16 percent reading, and 9 percent writing.[19] In 1993, it was estimated we spend 38 percent of our time watching TV and less than 10 percent of our time reading.[20] The less we read, the poorer our reading skills. The less we talk, the poorer our communication skills, and the less we read and communicate, the lower our intelligence levels.

Social Problems: Socialization occurs through social contact and good social modeling. When a child spends more time watching TV than going to school, the social influence of television is strong. Since television does not accurately reflect our society, the influence may be an undesirable one. The same is true for video games, Internet, and home video. Anything that inhibits social interaction with real, live humans can have a detrimental effect on socialization.

Children need appropriate gender role identification and good adult role models. Perhaps one of the reasons males exhibit hyperactivity approximately four times more often than females is the gender role portrayed on TV. Look how often our male role models on TV are fighting, shooting, risk-taking. This may also account for risk-taking behavior exhibited by ADD males. If they see high adventure on television, they are likely to imitate the behavior. Professional wrestling on TV has become a favorite show for many young people, and even though much of it is staged, not all children realize this. Violent behavior, mistreatment of women, disrespect for authority, and drug and alcohol abuse are portrayed daily on TV. A favorite expression in our office is that no child ever got changed by a lecture; they get changed by example. We do not believe that television gives proper examples.

Our suggestions are always the same for children: limit TV viewing; don't tell your child how to behave, *show* your child how to behave; and send your child to school (do not home school). Children need the daily interaction with other children from diverse backgrounds; then they need to process the day with their parents to get a more mature perspective of events in their lives.

Let them do most of the talking, but help them set rules, guidelines, and boundaries. All too often parents just issue rulings without any input from children. Socialization is how one interacts with society, not how well one takes orders. Teach children to listen, to express their feelings appropriately, and to negotiate social contracts with others.

Television has replaced the family conversation. Many families eat with the TV on and so the family scarcely talks or interacts except with phrases like, "be quiet," "we'll talk when this is over," or, "this is my favorite program, leave me alone." Perhaps the biggest social tragedy of all is that the TV has become the surrogate parent. Television has replaced the parents in that it baby-sits, tells the children how to dress, how to act, how to talk, and what to buy. We are amazed how often parents get angry when children behave or talk like children on TV. After all, the parents gave them television instead of time.

The Importance of Developing the Brain's Functions

Brainwave activity is an important measure of the transmission of information. Brainwave activity relates to the vibrational quality of the neurons. For example, a sleepy brain is vibrating more slowly than a brain that is problem solving. A brain that is afraid or experiencing a panic attack is vibrating much more quickly than a brain that is listening to a story or reading a book. The efficient brain speeds up or slows down its vibrations to match the task at hand.

The problem with attention deficit disorder is that the brain stays turned down. The dominant brainwave of ADD is a low-frequency brainwave generally in the area of seven Hz. A problem-solving brain may be operating in the fifteen- to eighteen-Hz range with intense bursts up to forty Hz. Children with ADD cannot speed up the brain when they need to; their brains remain parked in the low frequencies.

For higher thought processes like problem-solving or creative projects, it is important that our minds form images. This is why storytelling and family conversations are important. They allow, and even encourage, the brain to make images. Television gives both the stimulus (talk) and the response (picture), so our brains do not need to make them. When young children are exposed to television, they do not learn to make the images the way non-TV viewers do.

Television makes brainwork too easy. It gives us everything we need and we do not develop fully. It is for this reason that television lulls the mind into low-frequency or low-vibrational states. Even the most exciting television programs require so little brainwork that it eventually leads the mind to a dull state of thinking. Television is like the hypnotist, talking and doing all the work until the patient is eventually lulled into hypnosis.

In higher thinking processes, neural fields are firing and interacting with each other with lightning speed. The brain adjusts to television quickly because it does all the work. The brain very quickly stops all of that intricate communicating with itself; it slows down, and the activity of TV watching can be handled by a single field of neurons.[23] This is called single-field firing.

Since television requires so little energy and no response from the viewer, it is habit-forming. The viewer becomes so habituated to the lack of effort that it is difficult to turn the TV off, even if we do not like the program.[24] So not only do we become like hypnotism subjects whose brain is lured into a very low state of activity, this state becomes a habit that is difficult to break. Some experts think that it may be addictive to the nervous system.

We need to get back to family conversations where family members tell their histories. These stories are important. When a child listens to a story told by a parent, his brain becomes very active. The child soon learns to experience the "story in his mind." He sees the action, lights, colors, and sounds in the brain. The words of the storyteller become bigger than life as the story vividly unfolds in the brain. This can only take place if many neural fields in the brain are firing and interacting with each other. The brain is like a sophisticated computer talking and interacting with itself.

The same thing takes place when the child plays make-believe. As we said before, broomsticks become horses, bushes become animals, and the child is caught up in a symphony of internal brain play and external make-believe. The bush moves in the wind and immediately the child responds by shooting at "the bad guy," then jumping on the broomstick horse and riding to the top of the mountains. The child has conversations with imaginary people, fights imaginary battles, lives in imaginary castles, and the brain busily allows it all to unfold.

Television, on the other hand, gives the brain everything it needs without the child ever getting off the couch. No wooden swords or homemade bows and arrows, no sword fights, no evil men need to be invented in the brain. So, the brain does not need to develop itself fully. If a body never walked, jumped, and climbed, it would never become strong, versatile, and flexible. Similarly, a brain must be exercised to develop.

For example, the human mind is capable of abstract and symbolic thinking. We see symbols and know what they mean. We use metaphor and allegory to teach, but if these abilities are poorly developed, we think in very concrete terms, and we are incapable of being truly creative and intelligent.

Television gives both the stimulus and the response. In other words, it does everything for you. The brain just has to sit there with no response. The child doesn't have to think what to do, just to wait and see what will be done. This creates a lazy brain that doesn't see the need to respond, to answer questions, or to do homework. TV may take away the initiative to make decisions and develop response patterns the brain should be making for itself. In the TV-fed brain, the neural relationship between the brain and the environment is not as well developed. The brain needs metaphoric images and higher cortical responses if the person is to be creative, energetic and socially developed, but television does not provide this.

Let's take a deeper look at the nature of the brain. Human beings have three "brains." The first brain is basically the base of the spinal column, and is often called the reptilian or primitive brain. The function of this part of the brain is reaction. If something tries to hurt you, you move or run or jump. Without this brain your survival would be in question. It allows you to eat when hungry, run when chased, and sleep when tired.

The "second brain" is called the limbic brain. This is the seat of the emotional you. You cry when sad and laugh when happy. It allows you to describe how you feel. The development of the limbic brain affords an opportunity to do more than just eat when you're hungry and sleep when you're tired.

The cerebral cortex is the big gray cap we all recognize as "the brain." It developed so late in evolution that we often call it the neocortex or "new" cortex. This is the "hot shot" of brains. The neocortex allows us to think and reason, read and write, and be creative. We can make movies, fly planes, build ships and trains, write books, paint pictures, and enjoy symphonies because of the cerebral cortex. Without it we are just reacting to the environment.

The well-developed brain integrates all the systems making our lives more complete. If, however, you have the TV screen and blaring speakers flooding a child's brain with visual images and sound at a time when the brain is ordinarily learning to make the internal images, connections don't get fully completed.

If we fail to allow a child to develop the ability to image, conceptualize, be creative, and learn, we have failed as parents and teachers. We have also failed the species by not allowing our young brains to develop.

The reptilian brain and the limbic brain are very good at dealing with concrete information. Once they learn a response it becomes a habit very quickly. These two brains do not like change or novelty and avoid both. Instead, they seek out old, comfortable and familiar situations and experiences. Once something becomes comfortable these two brains don't want to let go. This is why the TV is hard to turn off.[12,23]

The neocortex, on the other hand, likes novelty. That is where most of the new learning takes place. For example, if you tell a child a new story, the complete brain gets involved, engaging many neural fields. All three systems get tied up in an integrated flow of creative imagery. Everything works together. But with TV giving us everything, the reptilian brain and the limbic system get locked into a pattern where very little of the brain is firing and the cortex zones out. So we sit in front of the TV like zombies, with no creative energy at work.

People with attentional problems are already making too much low-frequency brainwave activity. What is even more frightening, television may actually be training children to be ADD. When we place very young children in front of the TV, we may be training their brains to lock in these low-frequency patterns.

To summarize the most important point, watching TV puts the brain in a low frequency state; it slows down the brain. This is a level of very low consciousness or one just below consciousness. TV drives us into an unconscious state. We sit benumbed in front of the box. This is precisely what we do *not* want with our patients suffering with ADD. People with attentional problems are already making too much low-frequency brainwave activity. What is even more frightening, television may actually be training children to be ADD. When we place very young children in front of the TV, we may be training their brains to lock in these low-frequency patterns.

While we confess that we do not know what the critical period is for brain development (because no one is willing to fund research of this nature), we do offer several suggestions:

- No television viewing at all until after age five.

- The television is never to be watched without a parent present until age ten.

- Limit television viewing for any child to one hour a day up to age twelve, and two hours a day up to ninety-nine years of age (and that is probably too much), except for special occasions or exceptional programming.

- Let television become a privilege and a treat, not a right.

- Carefully govern the viewing of any violent and socially questionable programming.

- Do not be afraid to cut a show off in the middle if it is non-educational or becomes violent or socially questionable.

Television has become a very important part of everyday life. It offers enormous potential for future learning and interactive communications, but parents and professionals must deal with the negative impact on our society, especially on our young children. We have outlined the potential dangers explored by social scientists. We ask you, as parents, to put aside all the scientific studies and use common sense: Do you want your child exposed to violence every day? If there were not one single scientific study reporting that violence leads to violence, is this what you want your child to watch?

If you are having trouble answering that question, remember that our brains are like computers—garbage in, garbage out. Where does a child learn to cuss? He hears it. Where does a child learn to be violent? He sees it.

Limit your child's viewing to nonviolent shows. No small child should watch TV without a parent watching it with him. The parent needs to be there to direct what is learned and to answer questions. *Sesame Street,* one of the best shows on TV for children, is reported to have been designed for viewing with the parent. TV can be a wonderful catalyst for learning, but never let a TV executive in New York or Los Angeles have the exclusive power to determine what goes into your child's brain.

12

Violence, Aggression, and ADD

If you take an adolescent with a dysregulated brain—who cannot sit still, who is impulsive, who makes poor decisions, and who cannot see the consequences of his or her behavior—you have a management problem. Then, if you add the wrong crowd or the wrong environment, inadequate parental guidance, and alcohol or drugs, you have a prescription for trouble. You cannot pick up the paper or turn on the nightly news without being faced with the ugliness of violence. All too often, that violence involves juvenile offenders. It would be conjecture for us to say that a disproportionate number of these offenders are ADD, but we think that is probably the case.

In the previous chapter, we discussed the relationship of television to ADD, violence, and developmental issues; but that is not the complete picture. There is a relationship between violence, aggression, alcohol, and drugs, and ADD that goes beyond the effects of television. The relationship between aggression and ADD is often direct and observable, but sometimes it is subtle and difficult to see, and sometimes there does not seem to be a relationship. So, to tell this story we may seem to wander off course at times, but we think the story is worth telling.

We have seen the relationships in our clinical work so often that we intuitively look for early behaviors that can lead to serious behavioral problems like oppositional defiant disorder or conduct disorder. If we see oppositional behavior or conduct disorder, we look for signs of ADD. If we see any of these disorders, we are on the alert for substance abuse problems.

All of these disorders are likely to have undesirable companions because they have the probability of brainwave dysregulation at their core. The one bright spot in an otherwise gloomy picture is that neurofeedback has been shown to be an effective treatment for all of them.

In this chapter, we will take you through aggressive behavior, violence, dealing with frustration, and drug and alcohol abuse. We will try to show you the direct and indirect association of these problems to the dysregulated brain, and how neurofeedback can bring about changes in problem behaviors.

Individuals with violent and aggressive tendencies, drug and alcohol abuse problems, and ADD live dysregulated lives. The more serious problems that we discuss in this chapter start out as ADD. However, over time, problems such as alcohol abuse and antisocial behavior become so prominent that the ADD is overlooked or seems insignificant by comparison. It is significant that ADD-type symptoms may be our first observable clue to the brain dysregulation that leads to greater problems in the future.

Is the Escalation of Social Violence ADD-Driven?

In 1998, there were 616,000 serious violent crimes in the United States involving youths ages twelve to seventeen. These crimes included homicide, aggravated assault, rape, and robbery.[1] In 1999, 4.9 percent of our juveniles admitted to carrying a gun, and of that number, 6.9 percent carried a weapon on school property, 35.7 percent were involved in physical fights, and 19.3 percent had seriously considered suicide. In addition, 31.5 percent acknowledged episodic heavy drinking, and 47.5 percent acknowledged some marijuana use in their lifetimes.[2]

In spite of a recent decline in violent crime rates, surveys indicate that our youth are more fearful than ever. The young people of America are afraid to travel to school, afraid to stay at school, and afraid to leave to go home. Large numbers of students report feeling unsafe at school, avoiding certain areas of the school and grounds. They are fearful of what is taking place there and what could happen to them if they go through or into these areas. From 1989 to 1995, that fear quotient bounced from six percent to nine percent.

During that same general time period, there was a dramatic rise in gang-related activity at schools. Gang activity jumped from 15 percent in 1984 to an astounding 28 percent in 1995.[3] It is currently estimated that as many as 50 percent of adolescents use alcohol, 4.9 percent of them use alcohol, and 7.2 percent use marijuana while on school property. With the high use of illegal substances and the dramatic increase in gang activity, it is no wonder that 7.7 percent of our school-age population reports that they have been threatened with a weapon or injured while on school property.[2]

ADD is more than an inability to sit in class and pay attention. It is a disorder that includes poor impulse control, acting before thinking things through, and unpredictable behavior. We speculate that a high percentage of aggressive acts are committed by people with ADD. We also hypothesize that our prisons are filled with ADD inmates.

We made several calls to prison psychologists to get their opinions. In general they said it was impossible to tell because the screening of prisoners at intake facilities does not specifically look for ADD. Most of these psychologists were quick to point out that by the time they saw an inmate, ADD would be the least of the institution's concerns. A high percentage of this population has florid antisocial personality disorder. One of the psychologists, who had an interest in ADD, pointed out that most of the people he had seen in the prison population probably started out with ADD symptoms, but by the time they reached him, the ADD was concealed by many other problems. Nevertheless, we still contend that brain dysregulation causes ADD and its sometime-companions, aggressive and violent behaviors, and drug and alcohol abuse problems. A dysregulated life often starts early and is not restricted to city slums.

Crimes involving juvenile offenders do not take place only in Detroit, New York, Los Angeles, or Atlanta. They take place all over this country from the smallest hamlet to the largest metropolis. It appears that the potential for violence waits just under the surface of society. How many people were familiar with Littleton, Colorado, before Dylan Klebold and Eric Harris rocked the nation with the heinous murder of their fellow students and a teacher? Fort Gibson, Oklahoma, was certainly not well known until the cherub-faced, thirteen-year-old Seth Trickey opened fire on students at school.

Both small-town and big-city violence leave indelible imprints on the minds of students and concerned adults. So far, however, these violent tragedies have done little more than heighten awareness of how real the problem is, and they produce more insecurity and fear in our children. Our governmental, societal, and legal solutions have only refurbished ideas from the past that didn't work then and will not work now. As a society, we must take a serious look at other options that show new promise.

We contend that neurofeedback is the option that shows the most promise. Not only does it treat ADD symptoms, but it has been demonstrated to be a successful treatment for violent juvenile offenders. The implications of this are profound. Since ADD and aggressive behavior are often companions, to treat one is to address the other. If we can successfully treat these populations quickly and cost-effectively, we have not only helped the individual, but benefited society at large.

It's easy to sit back and label aggression and violence a direct result of poor parenting, a breakdown of the family or society, some deep character flaw, or not having prayer in school, but that is too easy. Besides, nothing we have tried to correct these problems as a society has worked. We just keep spending more and more tax dollars, building more and more prisons, and adding more and more uniformed officers in an attempt to keep up with the growing number of criminals.

What we need to do is start early, with the first signs of ADD and oppositional behavior. We need to *change the criminal mind,* producing fewer and fewer criminals. This change would reduce our need for more police and more prisons. The *only* way to change the upward trajectory toward societal chaos is to treat what we feel to be the root cause of the problem—a dysregulated brain, which shows up most notably in the symptoms labeled ADD.

If we corrected the dysregulated firing patterns of the brain, we would end up with a person who is much more resistant to the negative influences of bad parenting and poor environment. The well-regulated brain is not as vulnerable to undesirable social influences and is not as impulsive. We need to stop ignoring solid evidence that implicates the dysregulated brain as the single most important factor in ADD and aggressive behavior.

In a December 1999 *TIME* magazine article, Dr. James Garbarino, professor of human development at Cornell University, makes an interesting point. Dr. Garbarino states that boys commit 85 percent of all youth homicides. Out of that group of males, he contends 90 percent of them come from bad environments with poor parenting. However, the remaining ten percent come from good environments with good homes.[4]

If the problem of violent behavior were exclusively a problem of environment and parenting, then no child from a good home would commit homicide. This is not the case; youths from all levels of society commit violent acts, so there must be an underlying cause. We contend that it is the dysregulated brain. We also propose that children from bad environments who receive poor quality parenting are much more likely to suffer head injury from lack of supervision, much more likely to be beaten and slapped around, and much more likely to suffer from genetic injury. Their mothers, in all probability, received poor prenatal care, and the children received less physician overview, poorer nutrition, and poorer child care in general. This leaves them more vulnerable to brain injury from many sources, and injury is the primary cause of brain dysregulation.

We strongly contend that parenting and environment are important factors in the matrix. The psychological literature gives us good evidence that parents can affect outcomes in their children's lives. They can lessen or intensify the tendency to be violent, depending on what they reinforce and how they direct their children. The dysregulated brain, however, seems to be a much more important factor in the mix. There are many children who come from horrible situations who have no aggressive tendencies, and in fact do quite well in society. It is likely that they have well regulated brains; this has certainly been our clinical observation. Brain dysregulation seems to be the common denominator for both environmental groups. However, brain dysregulation seems to be more prevalent in children from bad environments with poor parenting. With this group of children, we often conclude that we are dealing with second, third, or fourth generation problems. This offers some support for the idea of genetic injury. We feel that genetics play a role in both ADD and aggressive behavior.

Interactions of Parents and the ADD Child

The child with ADD generally has an ADD family history and, to a lesser extent, this is true of aggressive behavior. During our extensive intake interview we can usually spot the parent or parents with ADD symptoms. A family history frequently discloses grandparents, uncles, cousins, and other relatives who exhibit ADD and/or aggressive behavior. Unfortunately, there are genetic components to many brain-related disorders. If you see a violent parent with a violent child, it is more likely a genetic injury that gets reinforced by poor parenting, rather than simply a learned behavior.

ADD children are more prone to aggressive behavior than non-ADD children, but this certainly does not mean that all ADD children will be aggressive or get into legal trouble. The overwhelming majority of these children will never commit a crime, but the possibility is there to a greater degree than in the non-ADD person. The concerned parent should be aware of this and make the extra effort required to help this child. The ADD child must be guided to an appropriate life direction with adequate social and coping skills. A good environment and positive parental guidance can help the ADD child to avoid a disastrous lifestyle.

Some aggressive behavior is a natural part of childhood development. At some point in his development, practically every child will demonstrate some aggressive behavior. He takes a toy or pushes another child or sasses the parent. This usually occurs first in the pre-school era when children are learning to deal with integrating themselves into society. It usually happens again when they are in their teens and begin to experiment with independence.

Most children grow through these aggressive stages, but some children seem to get "parked" in bad brainwave states and remain ADD and/or aggressive the rest of their lives. This is where neurofeedback can help: it nudges the brain out of "park," making it more flexible and adaptable to change.

If a brain is "parked" in low frequency brainwaves, it lacks the flexibility necessary for normal life functioning. Such skills as sharing, communicating, negotiating, and getting along with others are dependent upon being flexible. Children with ADD, violent tendencies, and oppositional behavior lack flexibility. They lack the ability to deal with daily frustrations and feelings of aggression, which are normal for children and adults. However, it is how we deal with these feelings that makes the difference. If our brains lack the necessary flexibility to deal with different situations, we are likely to respond inappropriately to those situations. If there is dysregulation when it comes to dealing with impulses of aggression, a person is likely to lash out violently because the dysregulated brain lacks the control to deal with impulsivity and hostility.

If a brain is "parked" in low frequency brainwaves, it lacks the flexibility necessary for normal life functioning. Such skills as sharing, communicating, negotiating, and getting along with others are dependent upon being flexible. Children with ADD, violent tendencies, and oppositional behavior lack flexibility.

If you put a child with a dysregulated brain into an environment where physical aggression is valued and reinforced, he is likely to develop into a highly explosive adult. On the other hand, if you put that same child in an environment where violence is looked down upon, he is likely to develop some control, yet may still be vulnerable to impulsive acts.

Parenting a child who has aggressive tendencies is never an easy job. It is very easy to give mixed messages that only end up confusing the child. How do you teach the difference between standing up for one's rights and not being aggressive? Understanding these often subtle differences requires a lot of time, clear explanations, and above all, good modeling. But if these lessons are not learned early, they become increasingly difficult to teach as a person ages. The issues become more complex with age, and without a good foundation, they just confuse and frustrate a person even more.

We strongly recommend psychotherapy along with neurofeedback when treating an older child or an adult. By using both modalities, you not only change the dysfunctional brainwaves that preclude effective problem solving, but you can also teach appropriate responses to social situations.

Understanding the "Ritalin Rebound"

One major cause of aggression is that previous aggression was reinforced. This often occurs in families that value aggression, but it also occurs in other situations. For example, many children on Ritalin experience what is termed "Ritalin Rebound." This is a phenomenon that occurs in late afternoon. The child has been on Ritalin all day, and when the effects wear off the child becomes tired, irritable, angry, and at times very difficult to manage. He may even exhibit episodes of uncontrolled rage. Sometimes, parents have no idea what to do with such violent episodes.

The "Ritalin Rebound" occurs, and the parent reinforces this bad behavior by ignoring it, giving in to the child's demands, pampering the child, or by being afraid of the child. Thus, the aggressiveness gets reinforced.

Imagine the power some children must sense when they see their parents afraid of them. At the very least, the child learns that he can get away with inappropriate behavior. Unfortunately, this behavior tends to escalate over time until you have a late adolescent that is completely out of control.

Aggressive behavior, rage, and violence must always be dealt with for the good of the child, the family, and society in general. The parent or teacher who is frozen by fear or incapability is only setting up a more severe scenario for the future. All aggressive behavior, Ritalin Rebound or not, must be addressed in an appropriate and timely manner. If parents, school authorities, or another agency feels unsure of what to do, they should call in professional help. Individuals with ADD, with or without aggressive tendencies, are not easy to manage under the best of circumstances. They are rambunctious and impulsive. If you let their behavior escalate they can become completely out of control. When we work with these children, we are aware that we are not only modeling behavior for the child, but we are also modeling for the overwhelmed parent or teacher in the situation.

Fix the Brainwaves or Life Gets Worse over Time

No matter how loving, kind, and caring the parents are, there are some children who do not respond to appropriate treatment. Their brains and/or previous conditioning will not let them incorporate normal societal rules and behavior. They act inappropriately in social situations, are aggressive, and are risk-takers. Often these children take risks that threaten life and limb with no thought of the consequences. Violent behavior leads to more violent behavior; risky behavior usually leads to more risk. If not treated, this can become a way of life.

Our prisons are full of people who have life-long histories of aggression and risky behavior. Many of these offenders meet the criteria for a diagnosis of ADD. They are the risk-takers who took greater and greater risks. They are the poor decision-makers who made worse and worse decisions. Some are violent offenders whose aggressive acts continue to escalate. They are individuals who were not able to predict the consequences of their behavior.

The low frustration tolerance of people with ADD often leads to aggression that gets them into trouble. The child or adult with ADD usually feels powerless to change things through normal measures, so they resort to desperate measures. Frustration leads to aggression. If things do not go their way, they overreact. People with ADD frequently feel unworthy, unwanted, unloved, and overwhelmed. When they become overstimulated by life's ordinary demands, like cornered animals, they fight back. They yell, stomp off, throw things, break things, threaten, and even become physically violent.

For those individuals who take this explosive nature into adulthood, they destroy relationships, lose jobs, get into physical fights, become violent, and often find themselves involved with the criminal justice system. These people often "explode" for no obvious reason. Although they may show a great deal of remorse later, it is usually too late.

Individuals with ADD are self-defeating, tending to "shoot themselves in the foot." Just when it looks like they are gaining some self-control, they "explode" and are in trouble again. It is not easy seeing yourself as being "alone against the world." This is why the ADD sufferer often fights back like it is necessary for their very survival. It is this type of intensity that gets noticed. Unfortunately, people get hurt and laws get broken when the intensity reaches a certain level.

The Explosive Mix of Addictive Substances and ADD

As if it is not enough to deal with attentional problems and impulsivity, if you throw in mind-altering drugs like alcohol and street drugs, the picture can get much darker. This is what happens all too often for people with ADD. Sometimes the only thing that seems to offer relief from the stresses of life for these people is alcohol and drugs. They already have compromised decision-making ability and impulsivity; add addictive substances and things are much worse.

We have seen many adolescents and adults alike who have tried to "fix" things with drugs and alcohol, only to end up in serious trouble with the law. In all our years of practice, we have never seen alcohol or other drugs solve a problem, and they always make problems even more severe for the ADD individual. You do not add a problem to fix a problem.

Significantly more children with ADD develop problems with drugs and alcohol than do children without ADD.[5] If you are looking for a place to hide, forget, or escape, and you have impaired decision-making abilities, alcohol or drugs certainly can look or feel like the answer.

Dr. Gabrielle Weiss and Dr. Lily Hechtman of Montreal Children's Hospital performed one of the best follow-up studies about these adults that we have found. They published a fifteen-year follow-up on 104 hyperactive children.[6] Approximately 12 percent of ADD adults are likely to be diagnosed with some type of substance abuse disorder.[7,8] Keep in mind that these figures do not include the people who drink, take drugs, and act in dysfunctional ways who refuse to acknowledge a problem, and never come to the attention of mental health professionals.

Violence, aggression, and criminal behavior tend to increase when adolescent boys with ADD turn to drugs and alcohol. Substances that alter the mind inevitably alter behavior. Shy boys become loud, angry boys act out their anger. These substances give people a false sense of courage. A major reason that ADD juveniles turn to drugs and alcohol is that these substances seem to offer relief from the chronic feeling of inadequacy and unworthiness. ADD is a life-long disorder if not treated, and dealing with it day after day, year after year, wears the ADD person down. They are searching for relief. Drugs and alcohol make them feel a sense of happiness, relaxation, and invulnerability. They think they are ten feet tall and bulletproof. A little drink or smoke can boost their courage and give them a false sense of superiority.

Soon they are addicted and find themselves acting out their impulses. At this point they have often crossed the line and are in trouble with the law. After they have a few minor brushes with the legal system tucked under their belts, their confidence grows along with their aggressive behavior. When the body is full of alcohol and/or other drugs, years of pent-up frustration, anger, and a sense of failure are unleashed. It's like mixing gasoline and matches.

The telltale signs of aggression are usually there, but families often miss them, chose to ignore them, or forgive them as isolated events. Most people with ADD who have aggressive tendencies present to the healthcare professional with consistent patterns. Often when we are meeting with parents we can almost see light bulbs going on as we ask certain questions, and they begin to see the patterns of aggressive behavior emerge.

Interestingly, we have had parents express fear of their children while denying that there are any real problems. We have had a few families who have worked very hard to keep their child's violent behaviors a secret. This type of family secret usually prevents the child or adult from receiving help until it is too late. Fortunately most of the parents we work with are not afraid *of* their children; they are afraid *for* their children. Good parenting and appropriate treatment have turned many difficult situations around.

Aggression should not be overlooked, kept secret, or ignored. When someone willfully hurts someone or something, it is time to take steps to get appropriate treatment. When we do our intake interview, we want to know about histories of hitting, biting, pushing, throwing, lying, stealing, and stabbing. We want to know about attacks against family, neighbors, or friends. We want to know about cruelty to animals, destruction of property, or self-aggression.

Assessing ADD is not just looking at attentional problems and hyperactivity. We want to know about all behavioral patterns, then we want to see what the brainwave patterns look like. There have been times after looking at the brainwave patterns we have gone back to parents and asked, "Are you sure there is no aggression or no seizure-type activity?" Often that is when more of the story unfolds and we are able to get a much clearer picture of what is going on. Parents are sometimes reluctant to disclose certain behaviors, so we do not always get a complete picture at first.

The Prevalence of Conflict for the ADD Child

Conflict is a big issue with ADD. People with ADD are frequently in conflict with the world, with teachers, parents, friends, siblings, school peers, coworkers, even the law. They do not manage conflict well. They have poor negotiating and compromising skills, they tend to escalate rather than negotiate, they are too inflexible. Overreaction is commonplace, and a minor conflict can quickly escalate into a major catastrophe.

The ADD individual will impulsively drop out of school or quit her job over minor events. She may drop out of school because the principal "is a jerk." In worst case scenarios, she punches or hurts someone. We have all heard stories about someone being hurt or killed over something as small as ten dollars, or over where a fence post was placed, or over who won a sporting event. This is the type of impulsive behavior that can be exhibited by the individual with ADD.

Individuals with ADD are not only in conflict with others but also with themselves. It doesn't usually take too long before this pattern of behavior leads them to dislike themselves. They are usually "parked" only a short distance from being out of control; and when they do lose control, the aggression may be directed toward others or toward themselves.

Self-aggression takes different forms. You may hear the negative self-talk or even see self-hitting: "I hate myself." "I'm so stupid." "What is wrong with me?" "I'm going to kill myself." It's easy for the ADD sufferer to lose control. They lose it at school, on the job, with ideas, alcohol, money, relationships, at sporting events or concerts, in the car, or just about anywhere. There is very little contentment and a lot of frustration in the life of the person with ADD.

If the ADD individual also has hyperactivity, then their life is operating at a faster level than normal. They are bouncing from one thing to another. They appear to be racing. In order for any one thing to stand out, it must be very loud, exciting, dangerous, or high-emotion in some way. When behaviors or emotions reach that high level, the ADD individual stands out. Others notice their anger, impulsivity, or risky behavior. That is usually when patients come to the attention of professionals.

Disruptive, frenetic, impulsive behavior wakes them up. It alerts them, lets them know they are awake and alive. The things that wake them up would make most of us keyed up or anxious. It is not easy experiencing everything at once, yet that is often what it's like for the ADD person. It is not always true that they cannot pay attention; often they pay too much attention.

Often they are paying attention to everything at once, so nothing stands out. They are in a state of perpetual overload and feel like they have no control over anything and can't put the brakes on. These feelings can lead to a state of anger toward everything and everybody. This anger usually manifests itself as a general state of irritability, grumpiness, and discontentment.

We have worked with some very difficult cases, not all of which were treated to a satisfactory conclusion. People suffering with ADD, oppositional disorders, conduct disorders, and antisocial behavior frequently drop out of treatment before they can be helped. They generally do not think they have a problem—everyone else has the problem. We have also seen parents and spouses give in and allow the patient to drop out if they become too difficult to deal with at home.

For example, it's almost impossible to take an adolescent to treatment twice a week if they are fighting you every step of the way. Over the years, we have seen dropouts from treatment quit school, destroy relationships, get into trouble with the law, go to jail, and even get killed because of their risk-taking behavior. Fortunately, we have seen many more turn their lives around.

We have seen angry, disruptive children become model students, brawlers become calm and less reactive, chaotic relationships settle down, risk-takers give up dangerous activities, and law-breakers stop getting in trouble. We have also been very pleased to see families and friends become able to stop worrying all the time and finally relax.

ADD and Oppositional Defiant Disorder

As we said before, a large number of people with ADD carry a second diagnosis of oppositional defiant disorder (ODD). Some experts suggest that as many as 50 percent of males with ADD meet the criteria for ODD. You see oppositional defiant disorders in the youngsters who demonstrate a recurrent pattern of oppositional, defiant, disobedient, and hostile behavior toward authority figures. We have all seen this type of child: if you say the sky is blue, they will argue it is green. They are almost impossible to please. The oppositional-defiant child is rarely in serious trouble, but they do tend to cause a lot of trouble for others. They get suspended, get sent to the principal's office, fail their classes, and stay perpetually grounded, but they seldom end up in front of a judge.

ADD and Conduct Disorder

A smaller group of children is given the diagnoses of ADD and conduct disorder. This is where matters become more serious. Members of this group often do end up in front of a judge. They demonstrate a flagrant disregard for the rights of others. Aggression toward other people, animals, and property is commonplace. People with conduct disorders engage in fighting, threatening, cruelty, stealing, lying, fire setting, and cheating. They may use a weapon to gain what they want or to commit a burglary.

Unlike the oppositional child, the conduct disorder child is more likely to commit a crime and come to the attention of legal authorities. The person with conduct disorder usually has their first brush with the law in adolescence; then he is "in the system." Subsequent run-ins with the law may become increasingly serious and the criminal sentencing usually becomes stiffer.

Females who have ADD—even those with a secondary conduct disorder diagnosis—tend to be less violent, although they can be just as self-destructive as their male counterparts. They tend to be impulsive, make poor decisions, and they are also not able to predict consequences any better than the males. Like the males, they tend to develop poor self-esteem, which leads them to do things they might not ordinarily do. Because they tend to be more promiscuous than non-ADD females, they have more unwanted pregnancies. They, too, do not see the consequences of their behaviors.

ADD females tend to feel unsuccessful, undesirable, and unlovable, so they may end up trading their bodies for attention and affection. Of course, their love relationships are generally superficial and short-lived. They go from relationship to relationship, each time with a new burst of enthusiasm and renewed hope. Although the ADD female with a conduct disorder is generally not as violent, she may still engage in criminal behavior.

If the conduct disorder is not resolved before a teenager turns adult, the diagnosis changes to Antisocial Personality Disorder. We can then have a full-blown sociopath on our hands—an adult with total disregard for the rules and regulations governing society. It's "every man for himself," get what you can get, regardless of how you get it.

Once these symptoms are set in place and ingrained, they tend to be extremely difficult to change; and the life of the individual tends to be difficult and chaotic. People with conduct disorders and antisocial personalities do not have a good life. They tend to go from crisis to crisis with frequent stops at parties; they also tend to cause trouble for everyone around them. They may not be good providers, they have chaotic relationships and shaky friendships, and they are usually on a first-name basis with the local police. They frequently get tagged by local officials as troublemakers, and eventually the officials lose tolerance for their bad behavior. (For a complete description of the diagnoses we have discussed here consult the *DSM-IV*.)

Living a Dysregulated Life

The individual with ADD is also more vulnerable to peer pressure. They are hungry for acceptance, and if the only way they can be accepted is to associate with the wrong crowd, so be it. They get acceptance where they can. It becomes much like the child who will gladly accept negative attention over no attention at all. They will exhibit more of the wrong behaviors in response to praise from the group or gang. This can escalate until they cross the line, break the law, and find themselves in jail. We have always been amazed by the lengths children will go to get a little acceptance and attention.

We have found many research studies suggesting that adults who were diagnosed ADD/ADHD in childhood have a much greater incidence of a second diagnosis of antisocial behavior than the non-ADD/ADHD. Children do not magically leave their ADD symptoms behind at some arbitrary age. They carry their symptoms with them. So, we end up with an adult who is impatient, impulsive, and disorganized.

These people make poor decisions, are not able to foresee the logical consequences of their actions, and are usually very angry. When this person carries their problems into adulthood, they have more opportunity to get into trouble because they have so many more options open to them as an adult. The late adolescent and the adult remain challenged with impulsivity, poor decision-making, and inability to see the consequences of their actions. They have great trouble being proactive in their life. They go through lives always reacting to the messes they have gotten themselves into.

Results of follow-up studies on adults who were diagnosed ADD/ADHD in childhood do not paint a rosy picture. The results suggest that as many as 65 percent of juvenile ADD/ADHD sufferers carry their symptoms into adulthood. Their level of education is consistently lower than that of non-ADD people.

Antisocial behavior is likely to be seen in as many as 45 percent of these adults; and approximately 25 percent of them actually meet the diagnostic criteria for antisocial personality disorder. We see an ongoing behavioral pattern which keeps them in conflict with others most of their lives.

Brainwave patterns are a significant indicator of behavioral patterns, and there are certain brainwave signature patterns that reflect behavioral problems. Researchers were discussing the relationship of violence to dysfunctional brainwave patterns as early as the 1970s. Investigators at Boston City Hospital identified epileptic-type brainwave patterns in individuals prone to violence. You will recall that we also identified epileptic-type patterns in ADD. In a 1970 research paper, Frank R. Ervin was quoted as saying, "We find that violent-prone persons have a childhood history of hyperactive behavior, multiple fire settings, prolonged enuresis (bed-wetting), cruelty to animals, destructive activities generally out-of-keeping with their peers."[9] He labeled this behavior syndrome episode dyscontrol.

These findings, together with more recent findings by neurofeedback researchers, have been routinely ignored by government officials, politicians, and mainstream physicians. The early research is out there, but we need to build on it. In the meantime, we need to implement treatment programs with professionals well-trained in neurofeedback.

There are neurotherapists out there to treat the people with these devastating disorders. How many individuals and families must continue to suffer while governments ignore this research, only to spend more and more tax dollars to hire more and more police and to build more and more prisons? The criminal justice system is so overwhelmed now that even a small reduction in caseload would be welcomed.

Taking the Brain Dysregulation Model Seriously

It becomes increasingly obvious that dysfunctional brainwave patterns correlate with ADD and antisocial behavior. These dysfunctional patterns are likely to be the product of genetic injury and the type of brain injury that occurs in utero, with birth trauma, poor nutrition, heavy metal toxicity, and in physical head trauma. Parental and societal influences can, to some degree, modify these violent tendencies in either direction; but the most wonderful parenting or the best psychotherapy in the world will not change brainwave-firing patterns. The dysregulated brain is the root cause of most of the negative behaviors we have discussed.

It becomes increasingly obvious that dysfunctional brainwave patterns correlate with ADD and antisocial behavior. These dysfunctional patterns are likely to be the product of genetic injury and the type of brain injury that occurs in utero, with birth trauma, poor nutrition, heavy metal toxicity, and in physical head trauma.

Electroencephalograph (EEG) researchers continue to find associations between abnormal brainwave patterns and violence. In a recent article in the *Journal of Neurotherapy,* Dr. James R. Evans and Suzanne Claycomb reported finding quantitative EEG abnormalities in a group of men with histories of violent behaviors.[10] This type of research confirms the clinical findings of neurotherapists everywhere. There is a growing recognition and acceptance by neurotherapists that EEG biofeedback can treat violent behavior just as successfully as it has treated ADD. Within a matter of weeks a well-trained neurotherapist can reduce violence and antisocial behavior in their patients.

We have successfully treated the types of behaviors discussed here for years. We recognize that dysfunctional brainwave patterns reflect a dysfunctional lifestyle. It is clear that what has been done to eliminate violence in this country has had only marginal success. All too often, children and adults who are diagnosed with ADD are not seen as having a "real problem." But they *do* have a real problem, and if you add in the second diagnosis of aggressive behavior, the problem becomes exponentially larger and affects not only the patient, but the family, the community, and society at large.

It is clear that our treatment emphasis in the past has been on social, family, and environmental conditioning. Contrary to research findings, the concept of brain dysregulation is sometimes viewed as a joke, and at best a novelty. Yet it is very easy to accept the idea that an individual with a brain tumor can climb a tower and begin shooting people. This example makes it vividly clear that brain trauma can and does cause violent behavior.

The concept seems to be discounted unless it is an event of huge magnitude. It does not take a tumor the size of a lemon to cause violent behavior. Violent behavior can be caused by a severe bump on the head, a fall, a birth trauma, and many other types of injury *if* it affects the right spot in the brain. We have seen many patients in our clinic who have unremarkable (no abnormality) conventional imagery such as x-rays, CT scans, and MRIs. Yet when we analyze their EEG biofeedback records we see abnormal brainwave signatures.

One case that stands out involved William, a nineteen-year-old who had been charged with murder. The only head injury we could find in his history was a fall from a ten-foot wall when he was ten years old. This fall resulted in a big bump on his forehead. He was x-rayed and released from the ER with a "He's okay" remark. William's parents noticed subtle changes in his behavior from that time on. He was soon diagnosed with ADD, and he demonstrated more and more oppositional behavior which escalated to conduct disorder. Alcohol and drugs became a regular part of his daily life. At home, he was often difficult to manage. He had a few minor scrapes with the law but nothing serious.

Then one evening while his parents were out, William had friends in. One thing led to another and before long there was a full-blown party going on with lots of drinking and probably drugs. As most often happens at parties of this type, uninvited people showed up. One uninvited guest started trouble. There were words, then scuffles. Finally the stranger passed out.

To get even and to play a bad joke on him, the other boys rolled him in a rug and drove him to an isolated area and put him out, expecting that when he woke up, the joke would be on him and he would be really upset and lost. As it turned out, the joke backfired, the night turned cold, it rained, the ground froze, and the boy died. All three of the boys involved were charged with first-degree murder.

While they were awaiting trial, a family member saw a TV show on the treatment of violent behavior with EEG biofeedback. The family contacted the doctor on the show and he referred them to our clinic. When we first saw William, his psychological testing indicated strong antisocial tendencies. We immediately began neurofeedback treatment, working in as many treatments as possible in the time we had. At the end of twenty treatment sessions, William was tested again.

There was a remarkable drop in his antisocial score. He had completely quit drugs and alcohol. He had secured and maintained steady employment, and his family reported he was like a different person. There were changes in his brainwave patterns—they were beginning to normalize. We were pleased with his progress and continued to treat him until his trial date.

We went into court armed with EEG records and psychological test results. Many witnesses testified to the personality changes. Defense attorneys were not asking the court to forgive his crime, just that he be placed where he could continue to receive treatment, and that he be given some consideration for the positive changes and the good efforts on his part. Sad to say, he received no consideration and was in fact sentenced to a longer term than the other defendants, in spite of the fact that he was promised leniency if he cooperated fully, which he did. We feel our testimony was not taken into consideration, and was in fact treated without regard. This type of ruling seems to reflect the legal system's jaded view of any mental health treatment, and particularly of a treatment that reports such a remarkable change in a defendant's brainwave patterns.

Contrary to the conclusions you might have drawn from media reports about the state of Texas, some Texas institutions have incorporated neurofeedback programs into their criminal justice system that successfully treat violent juvenile offenders. Another such program has been implemented by Drs. Steve Fahrion and Patricia Norris. These doctors are doing some wonderful work in a Kansas prison. Douglas Quirk, Ph.D., a psychologist at the Ontario Corrections Institute in Canada, has been using biofeedback to treat violent offenders since 1959.

Dr. Eugene Peniston, who developed the now-famous Peniston protocol while working in the VA Medical Center in Fort Lyon, Colorado, treats alcoholics with phenomenal success. Dr. Peniston is now training others to treat alcoholics, drug abusers, and people with post-traumatic stress disorder (PTSD) using neurofeedback. The results are startling.

Even the legal system is beginning to take an interest and see the benefits of neurofeedback. Judge John Larsen, state district judge in Missoula, Montana, used a federal grant to purchase a neurofeedback machine for their juvenile justice court.

Not all of the violent behavior that we treat has come to us after a run-in with the law. We once got a call from a tearful mother of a five-year-old boy who had been kicked out of four nursery schools. She was understandably frantic. We generally do not see children under the age of seven for EEG biofeedback treatment, but this mother was so desperate and the conduct disorder so severe, we agreed to evaluate this child. After they arrived at the clinic, it was obvious that we were going to be challenged on this one.

The boy was a handsome, bright-eyed, blond-haired terror. Although he was all over the place and difficult for us to manage, we were finally able to start his treatment. The chief complaint of this child, whom we shall call Rocky, was his aggression. He had a history of assaulting any child he didn't like or who got in his way, and at times for no apparent reason at all.

Initially Rocky was hard to handle, but the more neurofeedback sessions he had, the easier he was to deal with. By the time we terminated Rocky's treatment, he was regularly hugging us and bringing us gifts he had made or pictures he had drawn. His mother now reports he is the model student, the leader on school field trips. He has become easy to talk to, pleasant to be around, and nonviolent. When Rocky's treatment was terminated, his mother was again in tears, not tears of desperation, but tears of happiness and appreciation.

There are *many* success stories like Rocky's. There are also successes with sad outcomes like William's. Every practice where neurofeedback therapists treat ADD and aggressive behavior can relate similar stories of success. (A current list of neurofeedback providers can be found in appendix A. Because this is such a fast-growing field, recent additions to this list may be obtained from the website: www.eegspectrum.com)

There needs to be much more research conducted in this field. In the meantime, we cannot sit back and wait another five, ten, or fifteen years while more data is gathered. We need to act now. Neurofeedback is already available as a powerful treatment that has demonstrated results superior to anything else available.

Not only can it revolutionize the way we treat ADD, antisocial behavior, and alcohol abuse, it could also change the ways these disorders and the people who suffer from them are perceived. We must consider the many lives that will be ruined each year that we fail to implement effective treatment programs. Parents, police officials, educators, social workers, politicians, and the criminal justice system all have a major breakthrough in the treatment of these devastating disorders within their reach.

In summary, ADD, oppositional, aggressive, violent, and addictive behaviors have, at their core, dysfunctional brainwave patterns. They are likely companions of each other: If you see one of them, look for the others. Even many professionals have the tendency to see these disorders as mutually exclusive rather than being a cluster of disorders with a common origin. Parents and professionals must begin to look at these disorders as a cluster and not dismiss ADD as a simplistic problem of not listening in school.

Neurofeedback is a successful treatment modality for this cluster of attentional and behavioral disorders. It is a treatment that is quick, non-invasive, and cost-effective, particularly when compared to years of drug therapy and the possibility of legal trouble in later life. Neurofeedback offers a completely new way of conceptualizing and treating not only ADD, but oppositional, aggressive, and violent behavior. It has also been used successfully to treat problems of addiction. In our opinion, neurofeedback will be the treatment of choice in the future for these vexing problems.

13

Homework: Adjusting Expectations to the Reality of the ADD Child

Homework is and always has been a problem for certain types of children. This is particularly true for children with specific learning disabilities, ADD, and emotional problems. When it is a problem for the child, it often becomes an even greater problem for the parents. When it comes to homework, one size does not fit all. Classroom and homework assignments need to be adjusted to meet the needs of individual students and specific situations.

Some children eagerly approach school, while it becomes an agonizing time in the lives of others. Some children learn quickly, memorize easily, and work rapidly. Other children struggle to pay attention, are not skilled in concentration, exhibit memory problems, and process information slowly. If the teacher assigns all students the same number of math problems or the same number of pages to read, many of the children will experience extreme frustration and failure.

We treat school homework quite differently from the natural order of life. In the workaday world of parents, not everyone is considered equal in ability; not everyone works the same time in a workday or produces at the same rate. We need to be more mindful of individual abilities when it comes to assignments, both in school and with homework.

Children need the daily structured life that school provides. The years spent in school help to mold the patterns that form a bridge between the playful life of a child and the heavy demands of providing for oneself as an adult. Homework is a valuable part of education; it teaches children to work on their own, to be personally resourceful, and to develop problem-solving strategies.

Homework—A Chance to Learn from Mistakes

There are some inherent difficulties in determining how to produce meaningful homework. The difficulties are determining how much homework, what kind, who does it, and what the child learns from it. The brilliant visionary, Buckminster Fuller, was correct when he pointed out that education often misses the mark. Rather than learning to parrot what the teacher said in class, children need to learn from their mistakes.

Mistakes are our course correctors. They guide us. Some teachers will mark a big red "X" on what the child did wrong, but perhaps we should be giving extra points when the child learns something from making those mistakes. The child must be taught to value mistakes rather than be shamed by them. An important part of homework should be learning from the mistakes made while doing it.

We encourage teachers and parents to see mistakes as a joyful way to learn, not a shameful opportunity to punish. When a child makes a mistake, comments like, "Oh, good, you made a mistake. Let's see what we can learn from this," can turn an embarrassment into an adventure. Soon children will learn to use mistakes as a course corrector, reducing the possibility of damaging self-esteem when mistakes are made.

Keep Homework to a Minimum

The function of homework should be to teach self-discipline, self-direction, organization, responsibility, and mastery. The child must organize things on his or her own, do the work and return it to the teacher. If a child gets on the bus at seven-thirty in the morning and gets home at three-thirty in the afternoon, he has worked the equivalent of an adult's eight-hour day. Is it reasonable to ask him to do two hours of homework?

A six- or seven-hour day is more than enough for a young child. In the primary grades, all homework assignments should be short, easy, and fun. Homework, even through the twelfth grade, should not exceed ninety minutes. No child should be asked to work more than an eight- or nine-hour day.

The more fun an assignment is, the more likely it is to be completed. Rather than give a page of math problems, give the student a few relevant problems that have practical applications. Set up a point system so that children can earn privileges over time. Set up team competition with fun prizes. Assignments should relate to real-world situations, not mind-numbing routine. When the projects are fun, children do not mind working extra time. Fun projects become a diversion rather than a continuation of the school day.

Learning is best when learning is fun. It is paramount that we teach children to think creatively rather than routinely; this carries over into adult life and could ultimately change the routine workaday world. People might begin to view problem solving in more creative ways.

Homework Is Often Homework for the Parents

Children in primary school require parental assistance to do homework. Most parents work outside the home, so if they help with two hours of homework, then their day becomes very long, too. Frequently, primary school children come home with a duplicated homework assignment they are unable to read. The parents must read it, explain it, and help the child do it. Although there is nothing wrong with parents helping with their child's education, homework should be for the child.

The best assignments are *clear* and very *doable* for the child. Parents must not fall into the trap of doing the child's homework.

If the assignments are too difficult for the student, the teacher must make adjustments, not the parents.

Practical Recommendations for Homework

Watch Out for Bad Homework Patterns: The most common bad homework patterns are perfectionism, procrastination, and complaining. Have a set time to do the homework. Let the homework start at the same time every day whenever possible. A good time is right after school or just after dinner. Let it be as routine as going to school. For the perfectionistic child, don't let it go on forever. If the child works the sixty to ninety minutes and the work isn't done, have him stop. A note to the teacher about the child's effort should be sufficient.

If the teacher is unrealistic in his assignments, then schedule an appointment with the teacher to explore options. Some school divisions have policies regarding homework. Find out what they are in your school district. For all three problems—procrastination, perfectionism, or complaining—always be caring, firm, and consistent. If the child sees the parent frustrated and angry, what message does that send to the child about learning? Set a good example.

Be available during homework time, but don't do the homework. The parents' role is that of a good coach, tester, and example-giver. Show how to do a similar problem without doing their problem. Remember, you are trying to train skills, not just get through the content. Developing the skills of independent work and organization takes time. Most parents will be involved in the homework through the eighth grade year. In high school, the parents' role should be reduced to consultant. Remember, patterns that are set early have the tendency to last a lifetime.

Have a Designated Space for Homework: Let the homework space be the same all the time. That's where you go when you do homework, and nothing else should be done in that space at that time. Keep homework materials handy in that space. Make sure there are always plenty of extra paper, pencils, pens, crayons, markers, highlighters, rulers, glue, folders, and construction paper in the homework space. This way, the child isn't wasting energy and time looking for supplies and you're not running out to the store every evening to get them.

Think of the homework space as the workspace for your child. The homework space can be a folding card table, the kitchen table, or a permanent space in the house; but it is always the homework space. We seldom recommend the homework space be in the child's bedroom, out of sight. It is too easy to do things other than study if the spot is secluded or behind closed doors.

Your Child Must Invest More in the Homework Than You Do: Avoid power struggles. Your child can frustrate you with statements such as, "That's not the way my teacher does it" or "You don't know how to do it." You are the coach, not the student. Give the examples, test the child, encourage, but then back off. Remember, if your child struggles for a while, they may be more ready to listen to you. The child may have to work out some problems and details with the teacher, and should be encouraged to communicate with their teacher. A good teacher can tell when the assignment was too lengthy or too difficult.

Your job as a parent is to see that the work gets done, not to do it. If the work is too difficult or lengthy, model how to negotiate with the teacher. Learning to negotiate social contracts is an important skill for your child to learn. Only when the teacher is unyielding or too threatening should you enter the picture, and, if you must get involved, model for your child how to negotiate in a respectful way.

Maintain Family Harmony by Disengaging from a Disruptive Scenario: Sometimes parents must find someone else to help with the task, such as an aunt, older sibling, friend, or neighbor. A high school student might want to make some extra money supervising the homework. This action will stop the power struggle immediately. Set the rules and the structure, then disengage. Children will frequently work harder for someone other than their parents. So, when conflicts arise over homework, be prepared to step aside. Many schools offer tutors and after-school assistance—take advantage of these services. If you do find yourself in conflict with your child, model how to have a disagreement in a calm, courteous manner, but be firm and consistent.

Reduce Stimulation: No radios, TVs, or games while homework is being done. These are major distractions that interfere with attention and concentration. Make the environment quiet and calm. It is also not fair to ask one child to work while others are playing. Homework time should be a quiet peaceful time for everyone in the house. Children with ADD frequently request the extra stimuli of television or radio. We recommend peaceful classical music. This may help to calm the hyperactivity and add additional stimuli for that busy mind. Start with Mozart.

Break Homework Down into Small Parts: Children with ADD are frequently overwhelmed with large tasks or too many problems. Put one piece of work, one row of problems, or one task in front of the child at a time. Don't overwhelm him with too much to do. After one problem is completed, give another. If a child can do three of one type of math problems, don't give fifteen additional problems. Keep it simple, keep it organized. You are teaching the child organizational skills and how to prioritize. Repetition is important in building mastery but not in training independent work habits.

For the child with a learning disability such as ADD, it is a torturous process to keep doing the same type of work over and over. Try breaking up the homework period into fifteen- or twenty-minute segments. For example, you may have the child work fifteen minutes on math, stop and work fifteen minutes on spelling words before returning to math. As the child's tolerance for routine work increases, lengthen the time blocks.

Set up a System: A good way to train skills is to set a specific night for a specific subject. For example, Monday night is math. Tuesday night is spelling. Wednesday night is science, etc. This means that you do the regular homework assignments but put extra emphasis on one subject. Work with the teacher(s) by communicating clearly the problems you see at home. By working together, you can reinforce the learning that takes place both at home and at school.

Set up a Feedback Loop: Know when your child has homework, know that it gets turned in, and know how well the student did on the work. Let the teacher know how long the child worked. Let the teacher know when the child feels overwhelmed. Let the teacher know if there are problems or a family crisis. Family problems often cause changes in a student's behavior. This helps the teacher to be alert to possible changes in attitude or effort.

An assignment notebook and quick phone calls to the teacher can be very helpful in knowing the quality of work the child is doing at all times. Again, your job is not to do the child's work, but to be informed and to act as a good in-home historian for the teacher. A good teacher will want to know the child's history as well as a day-to-day history of academic progress.

Establish Good Communications with the Teacher: The teacher and the parent are both responsible for helping the child develop intellectually and emotionally. Work together, stay in communication, and don't get into a power struggle with each other. The child encounters greater risk when this happens. If conflicts arise, model good communications. Homework can be a difficult issue and can turn anyone, child, parent or teacher, into the scapegoat. Our purpose is to help—not hinder—the child's development.

The suggestions given here represent the ideal homework scenario. We realize how difficult it might be for parents to meet all of these goals, especially in the beginning. Creating the ideal work environment takes time and effort. If you cannot effect all these changes at once, don't worry. Often, this is a trial-and-error situation. Realize that any change, no matter how small, will help bring about better homework patterns. Perhaps you can find what works for your ADD child a bit at a time. By building on small successes you can eventually foster sound study habits and homework patterns.

14

Parenting—Good Management Is Crucial in Treating Your ADD Child

If you want to improve your parenting skills, there are a few simple rules to follow. Not only will they be good for your child, they will make life easier for you. This is especially true if your child has attentional or behavioral problems. The most basic rule in parenting is this: to understand what behavior is getting reinforced.

The Importance of Using Appropriate Reinforcement

Reinforcement is the reward we get for the behavior we are doing. Every morning people all over the world get up and go to work. They work all week and at the end of the "pay period" they get paid. That is how the world functions. If they stop getting paid, they stop working. If they get more pay for working longer, they work longer. It is a simple notion, but with our children, we often ignore this basic dynamic. Consider these scenarios.

- "Momma, if you'll buy me the bicycle, I'll make good grades."

- "If you'll just let me play, I'll do my homework later."

- "I need the computer so I can make good grades."

- "Let me go out tonight and I'll do my school paper this week-end."

All too often, we reward our children first and never get the promised work. As the old saying goes, we put the cart before the horse. Reinforcement is not always money. Sometimes it is grades or respect. Frequently, we work hard for intangibles like praise. In parenting we must remember what behavior we want, then decide how best to reinforce it. Remember, rewarding good behavior works better than punishing bad behavior. For example, if you want Tommy to play in the sandbox and not the street, it is more effective to reward sandbox play than to punish street play. Soon, Tommy knows where the reward is and engages in that behavior.

The secret to reinforcement is to know what reward the child wants. Often we instruct parents to spend a week or two studying their child's behavior. How much does he watch TV? How often is she on the phone? How much does she play with her dolls or computer or video games? How frequently does he visit friends? It usually is not very hard to determine what children like and do not like. The reinforcement is not based on what to take away, it is based on what the child earns.

If you study the child's behaviors, you learn what he will work for and what is a wasted offer. After you have a firm understanding of what the child likes and does not like, you set up the reinforcement program. For example, you might set up a behavioral program that rewards one hour of homework with one hour of TV. They work, then get paid for it. Or, for every homework hour, they can play out with their friends.

Recently we treated a seventeen-year-old high school junior. In addition to neurofeedback and parent counseling, we set up a behavioral plan. Every night, Roy had to bring home an assignment notebook signed by every teacher. When the completed homework matched the assignment notebook, Roy got the car keys. At first he hated us, he hated his parents, he hated the world, but after three weeks he was beaming. He was making good grades and he had "control" over his parents. He no longer had to beg for the keys. He produced the work, politely asked for the keys, and went to shoot hoops at the school ground with his buddies.

Roy's parents gave him something he wanted when he had completed the homework they wanted. This does not mean we give up control of where our children go or whom they are with. Parents must maintain control over these issues. It does, however, eliminate the child's begging and the parents' nightly arbitrary decisions.

The attention-deficit child has a greater need for reinforcement than most children do. They generally have low self-esteem and a negative self-focus. When you praise the attention-deficit child, make sure you are praising him only for adequate performance.

In Roy's case, there were two local boys who had been in trouble with the law for drugs, so Roy's parents set the rule that they were not allowed in the car. Violate this rule, you lose the car for a week the first time, a month the second time, and six months the third time. Roy valued the car much more than he valued driving these two around; they never got in the car.

With younger children it may be video games or TV or toy soldiers or sleepovers. With the girls it may be the phone or music or hiding in their room. Whatever the reward, *let them earn it*. Work first, get paid later.

Use Praise as Reinforcement

The attention-deficit child has a greater need for reinforcement than most children do. They generally have low self-esteem and a negative self-focus. Praise them abundantly, but not to the exclusion of other children in the family. Remember, often the child who performs well gets no praise at all because the attention-deficit brother or sister is getting all of the time and attention. When you praise the attention-deficit child, make sure you are praising him only for adequate performance. Never just toss out compliments, because to do this would trivialize praise. There may be times when you have to look hard for a job well done, but it is there, so keep looking; then build on the success.

Learning to condition a child for adequate performance is a long-term process. The child learns over weeks, months and even years that he gets praise only for doing positive things, such as attending and concentrating. Each time he brings in a good report card or a high score on a test, praise him. When he makes a mistake do not punish him, but sit down with him and ask, "What did you learn from this mistake?" Over time, he can learn to use his mistakes and not be shamed by them.

Mistakes Are Course Correctors

Although we covered this topic earlier, we think it is worth repeating. Schools are set up based on a very old system. The teacher lectures, then children are tested on what the teacher said. Mistakes are marked with an "X." It is vital that we teach our children that mistakes are course correctors. Unfortunately, we often use a child's mistakes as weapons against her. She is usually punished for mistakes rather than turning the mistakes into valuable teaching tools.

What we should be doing is teaching children information in creative ways, then letting them work independently or in groups. Afterwards, we can ask them what mistakes they made and what they learned from the mistakes. We all learn much more from our mistakes than we do from perfect performance, particularly if we are taught to examine the mistake rather than hide it in shame.

The Need for Behavioral Management in ADD

Attention can be a problem for all humans. We all have varying degrees of the ability to attend and concentrate, and we concentrate better at some times than at others. Most of us fall within a normal range of the ability to attend to the task at hand.

However, children with attentional and behavioral problems have more trouble focusing than children without these problems. They tend not to fit in and often have low self-esteem. If these problems are not resolved in childhood, the individual may end up becoming an adult with even greater problems.

There are certain behavioral strategies that seem to help manage this attention-deficit type of problem. In addition to understanding reinforcement strategies, there are other things parents and teachers can do to train attentional skills and behavioral control. No matter how intelligent a person is, if she cannot access that intelligence through attention and concentration she may never fulfill her potential.

Drop the Big Myth about Performance: It is a big myth and a mistake to believe that we cannot expect ADD children and adults to perform to some level of adequacy. With time, patience, and training, every child and every adult with ADD can be expected to function within the normal human performance range, both academically and socially. We must take care that a diagnosis does not end up being an excuse for poor performance.

Keep in mind that there are greater and lesser degrees of ADD, and that performance will vary accordingly. With proper training, regardless of the severity, you will see improvement in the symptoms. Neither children nor adults should be excused from appropriate behavior. The symptom checklist we discussed earlier can be used as a goal-setting tool. Do not imagine the checklist as a list of things to be ashamed of or excuses for inadequate performance. Expect your child to try hard academically, and carefully note and praise any improvement. Expect your child to work on dysfunctional social behavior. When behaviors are inappropriate use them to set goals for next time and reward the slightest improvement.

Remember scolding, yelling, or criticizing drives the child deeper into low-frequency brainwaves which are characteristic of attentional and behavioral problems. If a child engages in an ADD-type behavior and you yell at him, it drives the brain to make more low-frequency waves, and forces him into more of that behavior. It is easy for your child to train you to yell all the time by only responding to you when you yell. Learn to speak nicely and politely and be creative with your parenting.

If you excuse poor behavior, what have you reinforced? You have reinforced the bad behavior. It is like your boss saying, "I noticed you didn't come in yesterday. That's just how you are, and I just expect it from you. You're ADD and you can't help it." This is not likely to make you the best employee, is it?

If you excuse disruptive behavior or below-normal academic performance, the child may never learn to conform to normal standards. If you scream and yell at disruptive behavior, you drive the brain deeper into dysfunctional patterns, and you see more of the unwanted behavior. Set up a behavioral plan that gives rewards for good performance. Make your children want to do well to get the reward. Set up your plan so that the child determines what he can do rather than you having to make daily decisions on play activities.

Firmness and Consistency: Firm, consistent parenting is a must. The ADD child requires a well-structured lifestyle. The child expects firm and consistent messages from the parents. If the child is given the same message over and over in a firm but loving manner, he will begin to incorporate these standards and values into his lifestyle.

If the message is not consistent, the child gets mixed messages that do nothing but offer more confusion to an already dysfunctional brain. For example, why is it okay to go out and play today and it was not okay yesterday? Why did you check homework today and you did not check it yesterday? When the rules change, explain the rationale—do not just change the rule.

For example, they can stay up later in the summer when there is no school and must go to bed earlier on school nights. Explain why: "You need eight hours of sleep every night. In the summer you can stay up later because you can sleep later. You need eight hours of sleep because that is what our bodies require to grow and stay healthy." Children like to know the "why" of our decisions. They may not always agree that you have decided correctly, but when you explain your decision logically they have a good model.

Firmness does not mean roughness. You can be very warm, kind, and caring while being firm on what behavior is required. We often find parents who think firmness means they can be rougher and tougher. What we are talking about is "tough love." "No" means "no," not "maybe." The rule is the rule today and it is the same rule tomorrow and the day after that. Rules can always be expressed in a courteous and caring manner. "I just mean you cannot stay up. I do not mean I don't love you. I do love you, and because I love you bedtime is now." Firm but consistent messages are a good parenting must.

Lifestyle Management: Making good lifestyle decisions is an important ability missing from the ADD child's repertoire of intellectual responses. He does not know how to manage his life. He lives completely in the now. If he wants to play, he wants to play now with no thought of the future. He has no concept of the notion of consequences. He will play until he collapses; he will spend until his money is all gone; he risks life and limb with no idea what the consequences are for risk-taking behavior.

For children like this, we have to keep going over the same rule the same firm, consistent way. Our job as parents, teachers, and professionals is to slowly, patiently and carefully teach our children how to begin to manage their lives.

Part of managing life for ADD children is to learn to compensate for the problem areas. When we help these children set goals, we remind them to think about their goals before they respond. For example, "Shirley, tomorrow is a school day, so let's think tonight how you can accomplish your goal of being ready on time and having everything you need." If we teach them to think out loud, they can begin to formulate strategies to accomplish goals. When we think out loud with them, it is a wonderful form of modeling.

No Power Struggles: All too often, we see children from families that are locked in power struggles. Trying to control children with force or will is never a satisfactory strategy. Instead, it often leads to a struggle of wills. The parents are determined to make the child do something and the child determined not to do it. Unfortunately, both parties end up losing in some way. The child has more energy and more tenacity, so adults either give in out of exhaustion or become brutal with their punishments. This leads to guilt on the part of the parent and a sense of abuse or being unlovable on the part of the child.

Whenever you find yourself being pulled into a power struggle, exit gracefully. Someone has to be the adult in these situations, so you be the adult. Figure out what is happening, then look for resolutions that do not end in conflict. Remember what is being reinforced, then think through ways to manipulate the reinforcement so the child acts in an appropriate manner. This does not mean the child gets his way. It means he has to give appropriate behavior to get the reward he wants. It also means you can gracefully exit the power struggle.

Set up rules that reinforce positive behavior and punish negative behavior. Let the system you set up teach the child to get what they want by doing what is expected of her. When you set up a good system you cease to be the bad parent, and the child gets to earn what she wants through positive behavior. We have seen parents construct some very clever systems where the child earns points through behavior, and those points can be used to acquire money, play time, or some other reward. But, always insist: Work first, play later.

Identify the Real Problem: It takes fearless parents to truly look at what is going on in a problem family. Often a child or an adult will be labeled as the problem. This person seems to get blamed for everything and often carries a label like "the problem child." ADD children are often the recipients of such titles. They become the "identified problem" when in fact, this may not be the case.

Family problems need to be examined closely. Disorders like depression can mask ADD. Sometimes there may be no real ADD at all, but there may be an advantage to the child for it to appear that way. We have often seen children who appear ADD when they are not. They look helpless or seem inadequate, but after a careful examination there is something else going on.

For example, Susan acted helpless and inadequate to get attention and to stop her parents from fighting. Once we realized what was going on, we initiated family therapy, and Susan's symptoms began to resolve. She was not ADD after all. It is possible that the child appears to be in trouble so others do not notice when a parent is having trouble. Before we begin labeling children, we want to know exactly what the problem is. If something else is going on in the family, it almost assuredly makes attentional and behavioral problems worse.

Avoid Mixed Messages: Communication with our children is vital, and the messages must be clear, concise, and consistent. Tell an ADD child slowly and descriptively what you want to tell him, and avoid double messages. "Get in there and completely clean up this room and do it fast." Do I thoroughly clean it or clean it fast? Messages like that just confuse and frustrate any child, but it is compounded if the child has ADD. The ADD child has no system for cleaning a room in the first place, so you start them with clear simple instructions. "First make your bed, then hang up your clothes. Call me when you have done those two things." This is not only a clear communication, but it is breaking the job down into doable chunks. Giving an ADD child a lengthy message ensures his failure.

What is the consistent message you would like to give to your child? Figure out which message will motivate him to work hard and try to compensate for his ADD. Then give him the message clearly, consistently, and in understandable chunks.

Respecting Individual Learning Styles: We each have different learning styles. Some of us learn better hearing information, others from seeing, others from touching, and still others learn from combinations. It's important for parents and teachers to study a child to see his specific learning style. How does he learn best?

Once you understand this critical element, you can begin teaching the child with far more success. Every child, even one with the most modest capacity for learning, can be taught appropriate behavior by using his individual style. If your child learns best by doing and touching, do not tell him to clean the room, do it with him until the patterns are formed.

Some children need a list to go by, others need to hear it and see your lips move. Once you have studied your child, you can be a better resource for his teachers. Once you know his learning style, his behavior begins to change because your behavior changed. The best way to change someone else's behavior is to change your behavior.

The Advantage of White Noise: We are frequently asked if it is okay for the child to play the radio or TV while they are studying. In most instances the answer is no. However, TV and radio are often used to drown out other distracting noises. Noise is just formless sound; if you turn on the TV, radio, vacuum cleaner, the dryer, and a mixer at the same time, you do not hear anything in particular. This is called "white noise."

Sometimes turning on noise helps us to concentrate. Often, if things are too quiet we can be distracted by the slightest sound. Have you ever noticed yourself straining to hear when people are whispering? Children are nosy by nature, so noise blocks out the desire to know what the family is doing in the other room. If, however, they have turned on their favorite show or their favorite music while trying to do homework, that is not white noise. If your child is easily distracted, you can purchase sound machines that produce white noise; they usually cost between thirty and sixty dollars. These machines make an unidentifiable noise rather than a sound that will pull their attention.

Sequencing Is a Key: We learn through a process of sequencing information. For example, we don't remember our social security number by 2-4-3-8-1-2-6-0-9. We remember it by chunking the numbers 243-81-2609. That is how we learn our phone numbers, our license plate numbers, and any other number that is important. We also learn almost every other thing by chunking, or sequencing, information.

When you give information or instructions that you want remembered, break the information down into chunks or steps. By breaking instructions into simple steps, you enhance memory and improve the likelihood of getting the desired behavior.

For example, if you want your child to take out the trash, sequence the instructions. First get a trash bag, then go to all the trashcans, start with the one in your bedroom, then your bathroom, then the kitchen. Dump the trash into the bag, then put the bag in the outside can. Then roll the can to the street. Given these instructions over and over again the child will begin to remember in sequence. This is much more productive that just ordering, "Get the trash out." For some children, you may need to give a part of the instruction, and once that is completed, give another part. Sequencing the instructions in a firm, consistent manner will eventually begin to produce results.

Organizing Work: Generally, a child with attention deficit does not have a clue as to how to organize anything. One of the most frequent complaints we get from parents and spouses of those with ADD is, "They are so disorganized." They are disorganized because they do not know how to prioritize, they do not know how to sequence, and they often cannot visualize the end result.

So how do you help with organization? Work on good modeling and organizing out loud. If you want to teach the child to clean up her room in some organized fashion, you do it with her over and over, and you organize out loud, like this:

> "First, I am going to put all the toys in the toy box so we can walk in the room easier. Now I am going to put your games on the shelves. I think we should put the big heavy things on the low shelves so they won't fall and break or fall on us."
>
> "Now, we can put the small game boxes on the higher shelves. We can put the lighter things up there more easily."
>
> "Now let's put all of your dirty clothes in the hamper so we won't step on them."
>
> "Now we can hang up your good coat so it won't get dirty."

By walking through the organization out loud, the child begins to develop a strategy. It takes a long time to train this, but once it is completed you become a coach, not a nag. Over time you will do less and less work and experience less frustration. If you do not help your child learn sequencing and development of organizational ideas, you will face endless years of aggravation and lecturing.

Take the time to organize out loud until the child develops internal strategies. Each evening, help with the organization of the homework until it becomes as routine as going to school. Here is an example:

> "First, let's clean the workspace."
>
> "Now, let's get out our supplies—paper, pencils, ruler, dictionary, etc."
>
> "Now, what do we start with first? You have a spelling test tomorrow. Let's start with spelling words. Then you can do your ten math problems."

You may need to write these steps down or go over them verbally several times. Then you should gracefully exit the homework space—homework is the child's job.

Avoid Overstimulation: If there is a lot of stimulation in the child's environment, it is much more difficult to stay focused. The ADD child begins to pay attention to everything and nothing comes into focus. Think of ADD as a state of hyper-attention. The child's attention is jumping back and forth to anything and everything that moves or makes a sound. He cannot lock in on any one thing. It is like his attention mechanisms are wide open and he sees and hears everything at once, but nothing is clear.

The best way to help with the problem of overstimulation is to begin by reducing the noise level and activity level of the home. Turn volumes down, slow down frantic activity levels, and talk more slowly and softly. Think things out loud.

Eliminate distractions in the child's study area. Have only the essentials on the table or desk; eliminate fancy wallpaper, bright colors, and knickknacks; do not have TVs, stereos, or radios in the study area. Keep the child's room and study area plain and simple. Results from research with colors appear to show that pale blues, greens, and beige are the least stimulating colors. Remember, ADD children notice everything, so give them as little as possible to notice.

Think of ADD as a state of hyperattention. The child's attention is jumping back and forth to anything and everything that moves or makes a sound. He cannot lock in on any one thing. The best way to help with the problem of overstimulation is to begin by reducing the noise level and activity level of the home.

Once again, be a scientific researcher. Study the child and experiment with things like colors, lights, and sounds to see if you can produce better concentration patterns.

Decision-Making Out Loud: Decision-making is always a difficult task for people with ADD. They tend to live in the moment, they want what they want, when they want it, the way they want, and they cannot see consequences. For example, if they see something they want they get it, forgetting they were saving the money for more important things. It is difficult to make good life decisions when you can only see the now. The idea of making good grades for college acceptance is foreign to them. That is too far in the future. Focus on *now.*

We can help build in a mechanism for making decisions by

deciding out loud. Children need to see how we make decisions. Usually they only see the result of the decision and how it impacts their lives. If they listen to you talk through the decision process, they can develop their own decision-making strategy by observing how it is done.

For example, the child requests to spend the night at a friend's, then go to a ball game. Do not just say yes or no. Instead, say:

"Let's think this through. Tomorrow is Saturday, so you do not have school to worry about. Your household chores are through, except mowing the grass. The family is not doing anything tonight or tomorrow. So, mow the grass now. That will take you an hour and a half. Then you can go. Tell your friend to pick you up in two hours. Now you must hurry to be ready."

It is important to point out all the relevant facts in each decision. The next time the family may be busy or it may be a school night, and the decision would be different. By deciding out loud, they understand the "no" answer. The reasoning process gets established when we talk through our decisions out loud.

Managing Impulsiveness: Impulsivity is a major problem in the life of children and adults with ADD. Remember that attention deficit disorder is a neurological disorder. They have excessively low-frequency brainwaves, the type we exhibit when we are asleep, unconscious, or "zoned out." Individuals with ADD are not intentionally being impulsive or disruptive. They are often stimulating themselves so that they feel like they are in the world.

We often stimulate them in negative ways when we could just as easily stimulate them in a positive way by touching them, hugging them, or praising them. A disruptive child will frequently calm down considerably if a parent will just put a hand on his shoulder or hug him. When the parent is calm the child feels safe, the touch lets the child know he is in the world. It is particularly important to be calm and reassuring to an impulsive child.

It is also important to talk out consequences with a child. Use other children as a model or use them as teachers for younger children. We often learn a great deal by teaching others. One method of teaching would be to ask questions. For example, "Heather, what will happen if you spend your lunch money on a toy before lunch time?" This gives Heather a chance to rehearse what the consequences might be. If you see a child being reckless on a bike or skateboard ask the child what consequences might occur.

For example, "John, what could have happened to that boy on the bicycle if the driver in that car had not stopped." Then let John formulate an answer. This gives John a chance to teach himself, and removes you from being the nag or the lecturer.

We frequently avoid mistakes by rehearsing what we will say or do later. Rehearsing builds in automatic responses. If we say something over and over or we think a scenario through over and over, when the time comes, we may do it the way we rehearsed it.

Help your child rehearse appropriate responses that inhibit impulsive, risk-taking behavior. Do not miss any opportunity to have him formulate an answer. If their answer is inappropriate, try leading him to answer. For example, "John, if the car had not stopped, the car might have hit the boy. What could have happened to him then?"

Prioritizing the Chores: ADD children and adults never seem to get chores done correctly and in a timely manner. This is in part due to their disorganization and poor decision-making ability. They are also so easily distracted that almost anything can pull them off task. Adults with ADD frequently have many projects going at the same time, and they seldom complete anything, and the workspace of a person with ADD is usually in chaos.

So the first thing we have to look at is what is getting reinforced. Make sure you put the horse before the cart. As we said earlier, do the work, then get paid. If the child cleans her room, she can spend the night with a friend. Keep the rules simple and never become hostile, we certainly do not want to give them that model to follow. So what if the child takes ten hours to clean the room? When the child gets tired of spending ten hours cleaning, she will become more efficient.

It is important in every task to teach the child to think out loud. Model how to organize and how to prioritize each chore. At first, stay with the same chore until there is some level of mastery. Then you can add or change chores. If the chores are constantly changing, the child gets even more confused.

Getting around Procrastination: This is not only a sign of ADD but also a symptom of being passive-aggressive. Often procrastination is a child's only safe way to protest. What are they protesting? They may be protesting having ADD, always feeling stupid, or they may be protesting against parents they feel are treating them unfairly. Procrastination, if left unchecked in childhood, may lead to a lifetime of putting things off, waiting until the last minute, and/or never getting important things done. The more you protest the more they procrastinate. Therefore:

- Don't fuss at them
- Don't get upset
- Eliminate power struggles
- Notice what is getting reinforced
- Praise for the simplest positive action
- Build their self-worth
- Remember that the best punishment is not getting what they want until they have done what they are supposed to do
- Try to make tasks into games
- Teach them to try to beat the clock by getting a reward if the task is done in a specific time period

Overcome Boredom with Brainwave Stimulation: Boredom is a major problem for people with ADD. Part of the reason for the ADD child's boredom is due to the effort it takes to pull himself out of low-frequency brainwaves. Often it is just too much trouble, requiring too much energy to generate activity.

Encourage your child to find activities that activate him. Cut off the TV and video games. Don't permit the child to sleep all day. Have a set time for going to bed and getting up. It is important to suggest activities, but do not do the activities for the child. You may even get an activity started but let him take over. Using appropriate reinforcement challenges boredom.

On Not "Leaving the Planet": In the middle of a sentence or middle of an activity, the ADD child often goes off into daydreaming or fantasy. It is as though he leaves the planet, so you need to teach the child a strategy for returning. For example, if the child is reading, teach him to put his finger on the sentence he is reading, so when he returns he knows where he is. It is perfectly okay for the child to follow what he is reading with his finger. You can help by reorienting him when he comes back, i.e., "Billy we were talking about your math homework. What do you think about it?"

If leaving the planet appears to be a chronic problem, make sure that seizure activity is ruled out.

Do Not Rescue, Pamper, or Overprotect: Our job as parents and teachers is to teach our children strategies for overcoming problems, not teach them to wait for a rescuer. We do this by exploring strategies with them, helping them to list options and explore the consequence of each option. Then we must step out of the way and allow them to make mistakes.

We see far too many children with ADD and other problems who are overprotected. When you rescue, you deprive them of a learning opportunity. It is, however, okay to rescue them if the situation is one that would be better handled by an adult. Parents and teachers have to walk a thin line between protecting the child and not overprotecting the child. This requires maturity on the part of the adult. As a parent or teacher, you may need to monitor the situation unobtrusively, being ready to step in if necessary. You may need to offer a solution or provide an answer to the child's problem, then debrief him and find out what he learned from the situation. This trains him to think for himself.

Avoid the Crisis Mentality: If a child is a difficult one, he does not make the grades the other children do, is not as quiet as other children, is not as well behaved as other children—do not make this a crisis. Be creative. Teach the child ways to compensate. Your calm consistent teaching will pay off in the long run. Remember, most of the scrapes our children get in are nowhere near a crisis. Anything this side of death and dismemberment is a tool to teach problem solving and strategy planning.

If you remember from literature, any time the young King Arthur escaped danger or got out of a predicament and told Merlin, the old wizard always said, "I'm glad." When Arthur protested the wizard's comments, Merlin would explain that he was glad Arthur was safe and he was glad the young Arthur was learning to take care of himself. Training the child to think improves the child's chances of being independent and successful as an adult.

Don't Be Surprised: The ADD child is predictably unpredictable. Often when the ADD child performs in an appropriate way, socially or academically, we act surprised. We often exhibit frustration, disappointment, or rage. Learn to prepare yourself for the myriad unpredictable behaviors your child will exhibit, and do not be surprised by anything. Take it in stride.

One thing that promotes anxiety in the ADD child is the reaction of the parents. It is difficult enough having ADD, because you never quite know what to expect from yourself. That is bad enough, but if you are always afraid your parent will act inappropriately to your inappropriate behavior, you could become constantly anxious.

As a parent, project what your child might do today and how you might handle it. For example, today is the company picnic. Last year Jack ran into people, spilled drinks, talked too loudly, and fell in the fountain. Ask yourself, "How can I keep him more focused and occupied? If he does get in trouble, how can I stay calm and not overreact?"

This is a form of rehearsal for you. You can also help the ADD child rehearse behaviors, but do not be surprised when the best laid plans fall apart because Jack got distracted. Never be surprised by anything you can predict—you can always predict the ADD child will be unpredictable.

Practice Brief Instructions and Good Listening: Never give long-winded explanations to a child with ADD. You will be just talking to yourself. Figure out how to give him the answer in the fewest number of words. A long-winded explanation is a perfect opportunity for this child to leave the planet. Do not make any rule too long, too complex, or too difficult. We want to program for success, so give rules that they can understand and achieve quickly and easily.

On the other hand, it is okay to have long conversations and for the most part let the child do the talking. It is a wonderful way to get to know your child. We always learn more listening than talking. So, when we lecture, we really do not get to know our children. Listening helps us know what they like, what motivates them, what scares them, and how they feel. So, listen often and listen long. When you do give instructions, make them brief, consistent, and firm.

No Yelling: We have seen time and time again in our clinic that yelling, criticism, stress, and pressure cause children to make more low-frequency brainwaves. They start to go unconscious if you yell at them. So, avoid yelling, screaming, criticism, and threatening. Not only does yelling drive them deeper into their ADD, but it is rude. No child ever got changed by a lecture or by being screamed at. They change by observing correct behavior. Children are beautiful gifts and should be treated with the greatest respect.

Stay Relaxed: The suggestion we offer is don't take things too seriously. When the parent is hyper, anxious, and stressed out, the child picks it up. Children are very sensitive—they feel things deeply. If something is wrong, they feel responsible. The worst thing we can do for ADD children is add to their problems. Learn to be the relaxed, reassuring teacher.

Teach children to relax and focus on problem solving. Teach them to learn from their mistakes, to experiment, to find joy, and to love themselves and others. They will learn these things best by seeing these behaviors in you. So, follow these three important rules:

1. Don't take things too seriously.

2. Don't take things too seriously.

3. And, don't take things too seriously.

Afterword

Getting Started with Neurofeedback

For those struggling with ADD and for parents of children with ADD, there are treatment choices other than medications. As we've demonstrated throughout this book, neurofeedback is a safe, natural treatment for ADD, and one that addresses its underlying causes. Treatment with neurofeedback commonly leads to significant and far-ranging improvements in attention and behavior. After treatment with neurofeedback, most ADD people are able to either decrease their doses of medication or stop taking drugs for ADD altogether.

The fact that neurofeedback is not better known or not yet embraced by mainstream medicine does not detract from its ability to improve serious and chronic problems. Not everyone improves, but the majority of those treated gain significant benefits that extend to school or job, health, relationships, and personal life.

Those who have ADD and the parents of children with ADD may choose to get more information about this treatment option. We suggest that in addition to reading about neurofeedback, you arrange to talk with neurofeedback practitioners, with people who have been treated, and parents of children who were treated more than a year ago. While such evidence may be considered anecdotal, the genuine enthusiasm you will hear is often an important intangible. This enthusiasm has a distinct character that results from experiencing or witnessing an important, authentic outcome. It is unlike the brief cheerfulness that a placebo provides. (See appendix A for a list of neurofeedback clinicians. They will be able to help you get in contact with people who have been treated with neurofeedback.)

Be cautious of clinicians who are unfamiliar with neurofeedback, yet claim that it has not been proven to be effective. Many accepted, widespread treatments in medicine are not scientifically "proven" to work. Medicine is not an exact science that proceeds by scientific proof upon scientific proof. Though neurofeedback uses rigorous scientific methods inasmuch as is possible, it is an evidence-based, outcome-based discipline.

There is a wealth of evidence and outcome data that supports neurofeedback's safety and effectiveness. Do not blame your doctor if he or she is completely unaware of the documented evidence concerning neurofeedback. No one can keep abreast of everything in the major journals, much less even be aware of what is being reported in the smaller journals where neurofeedback is discussed. Those of us who have learned about neurofeedback feel most fortunate, as it has more often been by a chance encounter that we became aware of this powerful treatment, and not from a natural progression of study in our field.

Neurofeedback is a safe, natural treatment for ADD, and one that addresses its underlying causes. Treatment with neurofeedback commonly leads to significant and far-ranging improvements in attention and behavior. After treatment with neurofeedback, most ADD people are able to either decrease their doses of medication or stop taking drugs for ADD altogether.

While this book is intended primarily to introduce you to neurofeedback, another important purpose is to relay our belief that the optimal treatment of ADD is not as simple as taking a pill. Treatment should consist of a wider strategy that seeks to improve brain functioning. Proper nutrition and freedom from toxic substances will help support optimal brain activity in anyone, and these are much more important in a person with ADD.

We are aware that providing good nutrition for their children seems like such an uphill battle for so many of the parents who come to our clinic. Our observation is that a gradual change in diet patterns over time seems to be the approach most likely to succeed.

A careful evaluation of possible toxicity should be considered for anyone with a history of possible exposure and anyone not responding to neurofeedback. Possible exposures include frequent courses of antibiotics, prednisone, nonsteroidal anti-inflammatories, or acid-blockers, the presence of silver fillings in the mouth, untested water supply, proximity to industrial fumes or engine exhausts, pesticide/herbicide spraying, or mold-resistant paints. The list is actually much longer, but these are among the more common sources.

Neurofeedback, optimal nutrition, heavy metal detoxification, and yeast treatment are only a few of the many safe and effective methods now approaching mainstream medicine. The huge upsurge of interest in, and the utilization of, alternative forms of treatment for a wide range of diseases is an indication of the benefits many are realizing. The growth of alternative approaches has probably been more the result of heartfelt testimonials to friends and relatives than from the dissemination of the scientific studies that have been done.

Given this, there are two reasons for not waiting for more conclusive findings before considering an alternative treatment. The first is that many natural or unpatentable treatments will likely never be conclusively studied due to the enormous amount of money required to perform such studies. The money spent on large studies is an investment, and like any investment, it is intended to produce profits. This requires that treatments be patentable.

The second reason is that many of the alternative treatments are safe and support healthy, normal body functioning. They are often "good for you" whether or not they help reduce the symptoms. Those of us who have neurofeedback equipment use it routinely on ourselves and our families to promote healthy brain functioning.

For those of us who use neurofeedback in our clinical practices, there is seldom anything as gratifying as the consistent and dramatic improvements in our patients' lives. Certainly the most poignant moments for us are when parents, after seeing their children's lives restored, talk about the anguish and heartache they had lived with for so many years. Many tell us about having had fears their children would never come close to realizing their potential, and would go on to live lives of disappointment, self-doubt, and loneliness. Often, parents tell us about experiencing a moment that reveals to them in no uncertain terms the extent of the changes that neurofeedback has helped bring about in their child's life.

For those of us who use neurofeedback in our clinical practices, there is seldom anything as gratifying as the consistent and dramatic improvements in our patients' lives. Often, parents tell us about experiencing a moment that reveals to them in no uncertain terms the extent of the changes that neurofeedback has helped bring about in their child's life.

The father of a seven-year-old boy said simply, solemnly, "Robbie was invited to a birthday party." While this might seem routine to many parents, for Robbie's father it symbolized that his son's tormented journey was ending and a new life was beginning.

Here's another example. The mother of a fourteen-year-old girl called to describe how, months after her daughter's treatment was completed, she opened the medicine cabinet looking for an eye dropper and found herself face-to-face with three shelves of medications Brandi had taken for years. They were mostly pain medications for her headaches, but there were also stimulants, tranquilizers, and sleeping pills. She told us when she realized that Brandi had not had a pill of any kind in over six months, she stood in front of that medicine cabinet and wept.

Witnessing the relief and gratitude of the parents of the children we treat is a gift, and brings home the realization of what a privilege it is for us to be in a position to offer such a hopeful, effective solution to so many people.

Our memories of patients we have treated are rich with snapshots of their successes that they have recounted to us over the years:

- Kerri, a personable mid-teen, was an aggressive point guard on her high school basketball team, but was suspended from the team due to academic failures. The next season, after intensive neurofeedback treatment over the summer, not only did her grades improve, but she became a better player. She felt her court vision improved and her coach reported that she was able to remember and execute more complex tactics. She is now in her junior year of college, majoring in law enforcement with plans to become an FBI agent.

- Shawn is a fifth-grader who would not spend the night at a friend's house or go camping due to his fear of wetting the bed, which occurred with distressing regularity at home. He was treated for ADD with neurofeedback and has not had a single episode of enuresis in eleven months.

- Bradley is a middle school principal with adult ADD whose life was dominated by strategies he used to help him remember what he needed to do and where he needed to be. He had Post-It notes everywhere; he was constantly programming his watch to beep to remind him of things; his computer was loaded with reminder messages. He drank a pot of coffee each day, and was unable to cut his smoking down to less than a pack a day. Though his friends and colleagues found his methods and his breakneck pace amusing, we knew of the anguish he and his wife were experiencing due to the tremendous burden he was under just to get from day to day. His response to neurofeedback was a wonderful demonstration to us of how a well-regulated brain allows a person to access his inborn abilities. Today, Bradley is a relaxed man with a peaceful demeanor. He is a highly organized administrator and, with the spare time and energy he finds himself with, has begun to pursue two lifelong aspirations; he has taken up the saxophone and is making preliminary plans to run for a local office.

We could go on with stories such as those we have told you in this book—as could other neurofeedback practitioners could tell you, as well—but we have provided enough case histories and information to help you in your search for a better, more productive life for you or your child, so we wish you well in your endeavors.

An ADD Glossary

ADD: Attention deficit disorder.

ADHD: Attention deficit/hyperactivity disorder.

Amplitude: Scope or range; width of range of a quality. Usually of a wave or vibration, measured from the extreme to median positions. Half of a wavelength.

APGAR score: A numerical expression of the condition of a newborn infant, determined at one minute and at five minutes after birth, being the sum of points gained on an assessment of the heart rate, respiratory effort, muscle tone, reflex irritability, and color.

Brainwaves: A rhythmical fluctuation of electrical potential in the brain.

Classical conditioning: Learning in which a response is elicited by a neutral stimulus made directly effective by its repeated association with a stimulus normally evoking the response.

Concomitant: Existing or occurring together.

Continuum: A coherent whole made up of elements which vary only by minute degrees.

Derivative: A chemical substance derived from another substance either directly or by modification or partial substitution.

Dizygotic: Derived from two separate fertilized eggs, or zygotes (as fraternal twins).

Dopamine: A neurotransmitter used in the functioning of the sympathetic and central nervous systems.

Epilepsy: A disorder of cerebral function marked by attacks of unconsciousness with or without convulsions.

Etiologic: Pertaining to the causes of diseases.

Etiology: The study or theory of the factors that cause disease and the method of their introduction to the host.

EMG (electromyography): The recording and study of the intrinsic electrical properties of skeletal muscle.

Functional injury: An injury affecting function, as opposed to structure.

Glucose: A simple sugar containing six carbon atoms. Glucose is an important source of energy in the body and the sole source for energy in the brain.

Hertz: A unit of frequency equal to one cycle per second.

Hypoglycemia: A deficiency of glucose in the bloodstream, causing muscular weakness and incoordination, mental confusion and sweating.

In utero: Within the uterus.

Layperson: One without training or skills in a profession or branch of knowledge.

Monozygotic: Pertaining to or derived from one fertilized ovum, as identical twins.

Norepinepherine: A hormone closely related to epinephrine and with similar actions, secreted by the medulla of the adrenal gland and also released as a neurotransmitter by sympathetic nerve endings.

Operant: In psychology, any response that is not elicited by specific external stimuli but that recurs at a given rate in a particular set of circumstances. To condition a response by giving an appropriate reward.

Paradigm: Any pattern or example.

Peripheral: Pertaining to the outer part or surface; away from the center.

Probands: The original person presenting with or likely to be subject to a mental or physical disorder and whose case serves as the stimulus for a hereditary or genetic study.

Psychostimulant: A drug producing an increase in psychomotor activity.

Rhythmic activity: Measured movement; the recurrence of an action or function at regular intervals.

Schizophrenia: Any of a group of emotional disorders characterized by a disintegration of the process of thinking, of contact with reality, and of emotional responsiveness.

Serotonin: A compound widely distributed in the tissues, particularly in the blood platelets, intestinal wall, and central nervous system; acts as a neurotransmitter, especially concerned with the process of sleep.

Tachycardia: An increase in the heart rate above normal.

Tardive dyskinesia: A form of impairment of the power of voluntary movement marked by involuntary repetitive movements, induced by antipsychotic agents, and may persist after withdrawal of the agent.

Tinnitus: Any noise (buzzing, ringing, etc.) in the ear.

Appendix A

A List of Neurofeedback Providers by State and Country

UNITED STATES

ARIZONA

Mesa
Alberto J. Texidor, Ph.D., P.C.
East Valley Neurofeedback Center
1855 W. Baseline Road, Suite 170
Mesa, AZ 85202
(480) 899-0238; fax (480) 899-8139
Texidor@doitnow.com

Parker
Sharon Moehle Hansen, Ed.S., Licensed
Psychologist
9495 Hilltop Drive
Parker, AZ 85344
(520) 667-1619
sghansen@redrivernet.com

Peoria
Bud Leikvoll
Arrowhead Psychological Resources
11361 N. 99th Ave., #102
Peoria, AZ 85345-5469

(623) 974-0357
bedoc@msn.com
http://providers.eegspectrum.com/US/BudLeivkoll
www.arrowheadpsychological.com

Phoenix
Dennis DeWayne Andrew
New Hope
2432 W. Peoria Avenue, Suite 1040
Phoenix, AZ 85029
(602) 870-0020
dewane.andrew@worldnet.att.net

Scottsdale
Sanford J. Silverman, Ph.D., BCIA, Licensed
Psychologist
Center for Attention-Deficit and Learning
Disorders
10505 N. 69th St., Suite 1100B
Scottsdale, AZ 85253
(480) 314-4299; fax (480) 314-4994
info@centerforadd-az.com
www.centerforADD-AZ.com

ARKANSAS

Fayetteville
Rick Kirkpatrick, LCSW
Health South Rehabilitation Hospital
153 E. Monte Painter
Fayetteville, AR 72703
(501) 444-2270

CALIFORNIA

Calabasas
Stephen A. Kibrick, Ph.D.
4766 Park Grenada, #208
Calabasas, CA 91302-1546
(818) 222-2024

Chico
P. David Graham, M.A.; Judy Brislain, Ed.D.
Brislain Learning Center
1550 Humboldt Road, Suite 3
Chico, CA 95928
(530) 342-2567; fax (530) 342-2578
grahampd@aol.com
JAB_shrink@aol.com

Cupertino
John L. Doonan, MFCC
10070 Pasadena
Cupertino, CA 95014
(408) 314-2618
johnldd@home.com

Del Mar
Mary Lou Connoly, RN, MSN
Del Mar, CA 92014
(619) 733-5559
bconnol1@san.rr.com

Diamond Bar
Karen S. Kiefer, M.S., D.O.; Greg Maddex, D.O.
S.M.A.R.T. Medical
1111 S. Grand Ave, Suite J
Diamond Bar, CA 91765
(909) 861-2291; fax (909) 861-0194
KSKieferDO@aol.com
http://providers.eegspectrum.com/US/kiefer.htm

Encinitas
Fred Fortado

EEG Spectrum of Encinitas
336 Encinitas Blvd., #120
Encinitas, CA 92024-3723
(760) 942-6368
fredsr@pacbell.net
http://providers.eegspectrum.com/US/FredFortado

Encino
Susan Othmer, BCIA, NRNP; Leigh Siverton,
Ph.D., Licensed Psychologist; Harold Burke, Ph.
D., Licensed Neuropsychologist
EEG Spectrum (Home Office)
16500 Ventura Blvd., Suite 418
Encino, CA 91436
(818) 789-3456; (818) 788-2083; fax (818) 728-0933
clinic@eegspectrum.com

Lorraine Barak, MFCC; Martha Widawer, Ph.D.
Encino Center for Counseling and Psychotherapy
16550 Ventura Blvd., Suite 405
Encino, CA 91436
(818) 501-4435
mwidawer@ix.netcom.com

Fontana
Gregory B. Johnson, LMFT
GBJ Counseling Services
1050 Cherry Avenue, Suite R
Fontana, CA 92337
(626) 391-4674

Fullerton
Scott Kambak, M.A.
Success Unlimited Center
1235 N. Harbor Blvd., Suite 100
Fullerton, CA 92632
(714) 447-4422
skambak@earthlink.net
www.successunlimitedcenter.com

Glendale
Sharon Rae Deacon, Ph.D.; EveLynn McGuiness, Ph.D.
Sharon Rae Deacon and Associates
3245 Verdugo Road
Glendale, CA 91208
(818) 957-5166
emcguin@earthlink.net
http://providers.eegspectrum.com/US/SharonRaeDeaconAssociates

Half Moon Bay

Jane Kingston, M.S., MFCC
625 Miramontes, Suite 105
Half Moon Bay, CA 94019
(650) 726-6774
jane@igc.org
http://providers.eegspectrum.com/US/JaneKingston

Huntington Beach

Lisa Enneis, M.A., MFT
18700 Beach Blvd., Suite 230
Huntington Beach, CA 92647
(714) 375-0568; (714) 965-9207
lisaenn@aol.com

Veronika Tracy-Smith, Ph.D., Penny P. Irwin, Ph.D.
Huntington Psychological Services
16052 Beach Boulevard, Suite 228
Huntington Beach, CA 92647
(714) 841-3465; fax (714) 960-0701
drtracy@surfcity.com
pepi@ix.netcom.com

Irvine

Jeffrey Wilson, Ph.D.
20 Corporate Park, Suite 125
Irvine, CA 92606
(949) 955-0565
jefwil@pacbell.net

La Canada

Leonard R. Baker, M.D.
Descanso Medical Center for
Development and Learning
1346 Foothill Blvd., #301
La Canada, CA 91011
(818) 790-1587
lbakermd@dmcl.com

La Jolla

Ain Roost, Ph.D.
4180 La Jolla Village Dr., #250
La Jolla, CA 92037-9142
(619) 552-0500; fax (619) 552-0510
ainroost@aol.com

Los Angeles

Thomas M. Brod, M.D.
12304 Santa Monica Blvd., Suite 210
West Los Angeles, CA 90025

(310) 207-3337
tbrod@ucla.edu
www.bol.ucla.edu/~tbrod

Jim Incorvaia, Ph.D.
Reiss-Davis Child Study Center
3200 Motor Ave.
Los Angeles, CA 90034
(310) 204-1666, ext. 316; fax (310) 838-2791

Elizabeth Kim, Ph.D.
Brain Fitness Center
2727 W Olympic Blvd., Suite 208
Los Angeles, CA 90006-2640
(213) 384-8700
elizabjkim@digiis.com
http://providers.eegspectrum.com/US/ElizabethKim

Caroline Grierson R.N., B.S.N., C.B.T., C.N.T
Train Your Brain (Westwood Village)
100 UCLA Medical Plaza, Suite 760
Los Angeles, CA 90095
(310) 264-7246, ext. 104; fax (818) 988-1616
GrierEEGBF@aol.com
http://providers.eegspectrum.com/US/TrainYourBrain

Los Gatos

Mark Steinberg, Ph.D. and Associates
14601 South Bascom Ave., #250
Los Gatos, CA 95032
(408) 356-1002; fax (408) 356-4430
Mark Steinberg: mark@marksteinberg.com
Drew Pierson: imethos@pacbell.net
www.marksteinberg.com

Marina Del Rey

Allen Darbonne, Ph.D.
4676 Admiralty Way, #409
Marina Del Rey, CA 90292
(310) 578-6400
soulzat@earthlink.net

Menlo Park

Lilian Marcus, MFT
Biofeedback Associates
825 Oak Grove Ave., C-502
Menlo Park, CA 94025
(650) 328-5580; fax (650) 321-8608
lilianmarcus@earthlink.net
www.brainwavetherapy.com

Merced

Karen Carlquist-Hernandez, Ed.D. and
Associates
3319 North M Street
Merced, CA 95348
(209) 385-3585
http://providers.eegspectrum.com/US/KarenCarlquistHernandez

Palmdale

Barbara A. Linde, Ph.D.; Roberta Japka, Ph.D.
3031 East Avenue R-12
Palmdale, CA 93550
(661) 947-2537; fax (661) 947-4127
eeglinde@hughes.net
http://providers.eegspectrum.com/US/MindMediaInstitute

Palm Springs

Life's Journey Center
291 E. Camino Monte Vista
Palm Springs, CA 92262
(760) 864-6363; fax (760) 864-6360

Pasadena

Kent S. Kinzley, M.A., M.F.T.
595 E. Colorado Blvd., Suite 506
Pasadena, CA 91101
(626) 440-7322
kkinzley@earthlink.net
www.camftmembers.com/neurofeedback

Jan Aura, Ph.D.
120 S. Euclid Ave., #8
Pasadena, CA 91101
(310) 559-0200
jaura@mindspring.com

Kathleen M. Power, D.C.
151 South El Molino Ave., Suite 301
Pasadena, CA 91101
(626) 793-7161; fax (626) 793-8447
kathleenpower@compuserve.com

Placentia

John E. Kelley, Ph.D.
The Anxiety and Stress Center
151 N. Kraemer Blvd., Suite 105
Placentia, CA 92870-5044
(714) 985-4700; fax (714) 523-1637
johnekelley@earthlink.net

Rancho Mirage

Julie A. Madsen, Psy.D.; Mark Bilkey, Psy.D.
42600 Bob Hope Drive, Suite 409
Rancho Mirage, CA 92270
(760) 346-3312
drjameeg@msn.com

Ruth A. Bolton, R.N., Ph.D.
Medical Psychology Group, Inc.
39000 Bob Hope Drive
Kiewit Prof. Building, Suite 302
Rancho Mirage, CA 92270
(760) 341-2900

Redlands

Carol Hindman, R.N., M.F.T.; Donna Maehre, C.B.T
Center for Wellness and ADD Treatment Center
101 East Redlands Boulevard, Suite 251
Redlands, CA 92374
(909) 792-2216; fax (909) 795-9931
cbhindman@compuserve.com

Steve Johnson, M.S., M.F.T.
Redlands-Yucipa Guidance Center
1323 W. Colton Ave., Suite 105
Redlands, CA 92373
(909) 792-0747; fax (909) 792-1057
solardrawn@aol.com

Redondo Beach

Lisa Cavallaro, Psy.D.
1711 Via El Prado, Suite 204
Redondo Beach, CA 90277
(310) 540-5514; fax (310) 540-5527

Sacramento

Leonteen Chevreau, Ph.D.
Neurofeedback Valley Associates
7501 Hospital Drive, Suite 207
Sacramento, CA 95823
(916) 681-4141; fax (916) 689-8383
neurofb@aol.com
http://providers.eegspectrum.com/US/NeurofeedbackValleyAssociates

San Diego

Sarah F. Luth
Transpersonal Counseling and Hypnotherapy
1045 Mead Ave.
San Diego, CA 92116
(619) 296-2895

The Center for Neurofeedback and Research
Midway Medical Center
3405 Kenyon Street, Suite 105
San Diego, CA 92110

San Francisco
Jonathan D. Miller, D.C.
Lapis Light Natural Health
345 West Portal Ave., Suite 120
San Francisco, CA 94127
(415) 504-8770; fax (415) 504-8771
drmil@pacbell.net

San Jose
Patricia Nylander, R.N.
The Neuro Connection
5369 Camden Avenue, Suite 288
San Jose, CA 95124
(408) 445-9743
tnc6@excite.com

San Mateo
Jane Kingston, M.Sc., M.F.T.
100 South Ellsworth, Suite 806
San Mateo, CA 94401-3926
(650) 347-5456
jane@igc.org
http://providers.eegspectrum.com/US/JaneKingston

Santa Barbara
Clark Elliott, Ph.D.; John Broberg
Santa Barbara Neurofeedback Center
923-B Laguna Street
Santa Barbara, CA 93101
(805) 560-7690; fax (805) 739-9229
claelliott@aol.com

Melinda Horn, M.A., MFCC
Santa Barbara Neurotherapy Center
25 Crestview Lane
Santa Barbara, CA 93108
(805) 689-8061
melhorn@aol.com

Santa Maria
Clark Elliott, Ph.D.; Angeles Ramirez, M.D.
1107 South Broadway
Santa Maria, CA 93454
(805) 560-7690; fax (805) 739-9229
claelliott@aol.com

Frank Schlosser, M.F.T.
1107 So. Broadway
Santa Maria, CA 93454
(805) 922-2989

Santa Paula
Sandy Talbott, R.N.
854 E. Main Street
Santa Paula, CA 93060
(805) 701-8884; fax (805) 647-0072
talbott@dpsworld.com

Simi Valley
Bruce Watson, LCSW
Conejo Neurofeedback and Counseling
1687 Erringer Road, #202B
Simi Valley, CA 93065
(805) 373-0233
blwatson@gte.net
http://providers.eegspectrum.com/US/BruceWatson

Tahoe City
John Finnick, M.A., LEP
Center for Human Development
P.O. Box 5815
Tahoe City, CA 96145
(530) 581-1506; fax (530) 581-2878
info@braintrainers.com
www.braintrainers.com

Torrance
Gary J. Schummer, M.Div., Ph.D.
A.D.D. Treatment Center
24050 Madison St., Suite 111
Torrance, CA 90505
(310) 378-0547; fax (310) 378-0347
ADDCenters@cs.com
www.dr-add.com

Valley Village
Jeannine L. Calaba, Psy.D.
4820 Gentry Ave.
Valley Village, CA 91607
(818) 763-3361

Walnut Creek
Ali Hashemian, Ph.D., BCHT
39 Quail Court, Suite 101
Walnut Creek, CA 94596
(925) 280-9100; fax (925) 280-9131
ali@idealu.com

Westlake Village

Harold L. Burke, Ph.D.
Clinical Neuropsychology
2277 Townsgate Rd., Suite 220
Westlake Village, CA 91361
(805) 449-8777
hburke@gte.net

Beverly Cross, M.A., M.F.T.
2535 Townsgate Rd., #209
Westlake Village, CA 91361
(805) 379-1009
Psychsaver@aol.com

CONNECTICUT

Middletown

Robert F. Reynolds, Ph.D., Clinical Director
Connecticut Educational Services
770 Saybrook Rd., Building B
Middletown, CT 06457
(860) 343-0227; fax (860) 343-8511
rrenold@ct-ed.com
www.ct-ed.com

Waterford

Henry Mann, M.D.
Advanced Options
567 Vauxhall Street, Ext #201
Waterford, CT 06385
(860) 439-0237
hank7503@aol.com
http://providers.eegspectrum.com/US/HenryMann

West Hartford

Rae Tattenbaum. M.S.W., C.S.W.
Inner Act
68 South Main Street
West Hartford, CT 06107
(860) 561-5222
RTinneract@aol.com
http://providers.eegspectrum.com/US/tattenbaum.htm
www.inner-act.com

FLORIDA

Boca Raton

Dr. Wayne Clayman
Florida Mental Fitness Center
109090 Skyridge Circle

Boca Raton, FL 33498
(561) 414-6782; fax (954) 590-5159
flmentalfit@aol.com

Ft. Myers

Barbara K. Carlin, M.S.
Neurofeedback and Biofeedback Therapy Pain
and Stress Management Center
4066 Evans Ave., #24
Ft. Myers, FL 33901
(941) 768-0821; fax (941) 768-5802
bcarlin801@aol.com
www.neurofeedbackandbiofeedback.com

Jacksonville

Ann Grenadier, LMHC, CBT, CEEG; Ivy
Caldarelli, M.S.
Biofeedback Associates of NE Florida
8130 Bay Meadows Circle West, Suite 308
Jacksonville, FL 32256
(904) 733-2038; fax (904) 739-3266
ivyives@aol.com

Melbourne

Henry Owens, Ph.D.
1351 Bedford Drive, Suite 103
Melbourne, FL 32940
(321) 757-6799; fax (321) 757-6792
howens46@hotmail.com

Miami

Samuel E. Roura, M.D.; Isa Pilote-Baker, M.S.W.
Drs. and Associates
8045 Northwest 36th Street, Suite 510
Miami, FL 33166
(305) 718-9800; fax (305) 718-9080
sampecori@aol.com
kalisab@aol.com

Pembroke Pines

Jean Menendez, AANC; Perry Vitale, Ph.D.
Assoc. for Human Development P.A.
2231 North University Drive, Suite C
Pembroke Pines, FL 33024
(954) 989-8818; fax (954) 989-8812
jean_menendez_neurofeedback@hotmail.com

South Miami

Mindy S. Kopolow
7600 Red Road, Suite 302
South Miami, FL 33143
(305) 663-9180
dockop18@aol.com

Tallahassee

Jack Golden, Ph.D.
2807 Capital Medical Blvd., P.O. Box 15754
Tallahassee, FL 32308
(850) 656-1129
golden263@aol.com
http://providers.eegspectrum.com/US/golden.htm

Linda R. Young, Ph.D.
EEG Neurofeedback Clinic
1638 North Plaza Drive
Tallahassee, FL 32308
(850) 656-1404
toppernole@myexcel.com

Venice

Patricia Jo Ryan, Ph.D.
333 South Tamiami Trail, Suite 203
Venice, FL 34285
(941) 486-1930; fax (941) 966-5407
anapjr@acun.com
http://providers.eegspectrum.com/US/PatriciaJoRyan

West Palm Beach

Leslie Coates, LCSW
Palm Beach Mental Fitness Institute
600 Sandtree Drive, Suite 206C
Palm Beach Gardens, FL 33403
(561) 799-0088; fax (561) 799-6872
www.eegbraintrain.com

GEORGIA

Decatur

Stephen J. Johnson, Ph.D.
The Center for Cognitive Rehabilitation
1276 McConnell Drive, Suite C
Decatur, GA 30033-3506
(404) 321-1441; fax (404) 321-5876
CCR1276@aol.com
www.rehabgeorgia.com

Gainesville

David Bailey, Ed.D.
Affiliated Psychological and Medical Consultants
200 S. Enota Drive NE, Suite #400
Gainesville, GA 30501
(770) 535-1284; fax (770) 536-3888
drdavidbailey@aol.com

Thomasville

Catherine B. Howell, Ph.D.
Associates In Wellness
421 North Crawford Street
Thomasville, GA 31792
(912) 228-5192; fax (912) 228-5139
catherine_howell@compuserve.com

HAWAII

Honolulu

Amanda S. Armstrong, Ph.D.
Armstrong and Bradford, LLC
1600 Kapiolani Boulevard, Suite 1650
Honolulu, HI 96814-3806
(808) 951-5540; fax (808) 951-5545
aloha-amanda@hawaii.rr.com
http://providers.eegspectrum.com/US/AmandaSArmstrong

Kailua

Demi Wood, M.A., M.F.T.
32 Kainehe Street, #207
Kailua, HI 96734
(808) 262-8606; fax (808) 262-8706
demi@hawaii.rr.com

Kamuela

Anita Gerhard, M.D.
Box 6705
Kamuela, HI 96743
(808) 885-8989; fax (808) 885-8484
gerhard@aloha.net

IDAHO

Boise

Dr. Sara LaRiviere
1412 W. Washington
Boise, ID 83712
(208) 331-7711
slarivi@bsu.idbsu.edu

Rigby
Fran Bryson
3881 E. 400 North
Rigby, ID 83442
(208) 745-5774; fax (208) 749-5759

ILLINOIS

Champaign
Janne Gingrich Crass, BSN, MSN
2718 Valley Brook Drive
Champaign, IL 61822
(217) 352-7654; fax (217) 278-4015
joannagc@aol.com

Charleston
Andy Hogan Ph.D.
Midwest Neurofitness
126 Sixth St., P.O. Box 584
Charleston, IL 61920
(217) 348-1086
ahogan@lincweb.com

Chicago
Ann Richman, M.A.
Richman Discovery Clinic
6305 N. Milwaukee Ave.
Chicago, IL 60646
(773) 774-0909; fax (773) 774-8213
rdc@web-town.com
http://providers.eegspectrum.com/US/RichmanDiscoveryClinic

Highland Park
William Levin, Ph.D.
1803 St. Johns Ave.
Highland Park, IL 60035
(847) 432-5270

Hoffman Estates
Alexander A. Eschbach, Ph.D.
1000 Grand Canyon Parkway, Suite 105
Hoffman Estates, IL 60194
(847) 755-0555; (847) 755-0580
docesch@aol.com
http://providers.eegspectrum.com/US/AdvancedBiofeedbackCenter

Matteson
Rosita Butler, R.N., NCC, LCPC;
Barbara Meagher, M.A., CCC., SLP/L
Transitions
20320 Crawford Ave.

Matteson, IL 60443
(708) 748-6000; fax (708) 748-6173
eegattrans@wmol.com

Northbrook
Joy Lunt, R.N.; Jeanne M. Berger, M.S.W.
EEG Spectrum-Northshore, Inc.
3701 Commercial Avenue, Suite 15
Northbrook, IL 60056
(847) 509-5099; fax (847) 205-0642
eegjoy@aol.com
http://providers.eegspectrum.com/US/JoyLunt

IOWA

Des Moines
Ladell Lybarger, R.N.
1221 Birch Lane
Des Moines, IA 50315-3019
(515) 244-1883; fax (515) 244-0406
LybargerRn@aol.com

Mount Pleasant
Rita Davis, R.N., M.A.
Reegeneration
812 Lincoln Street
Mount Pleasant, IA 52641
(319) 986-4187
Reegener@interl.net

KANSAS

Topeka
Thomas V. Matthews, Ph.D.
2709 SW 29th St.
Topeka, KS 66614
(785) 273-8461
thinkwell@biofeedback.org
http://providers.eegspectrum.com/US/ThomasMatthews

LOUISIANA

Slidell
Debbie Piacsek, APRN, MSN, CS
Center for Better Living
951 Gause Blvd.
Slidell, LA 70458-2937
(504)641-0505; fax (504) 641-6440
dpiacsek@bellsouth.net
www.centerforbetterliving.com

MARYLAND

Cantonsville
Marianne S. Becker, Ph.D.
Adoption Resource Center
6630 Baltimore National Pike
Cantonsville, MD 21228
(410) 465-1066
beckermsw@aol.com

Chevy Chase
Michael Sitar, Ph.D.
5480 Wisconsin Ave., Suite 221
Chevy Chase, MD 20815
(301) 718-3588
michaelasitar@cs.com

Olney
Robin Moore, LCPC
2707 Olney Spring Road
Olney, MD 20832
(301) 924-1909
Robinmoore@erols.com

MASSACHUSETTS

Andover
Richard N. Shulik, Ph.D.
35 Clark Road, P.O. Box 3067
Andover, MA 01810
(978) 475-3599; fax (603) 437-5588
shulik@mediaone.net

Great Barrington
Jamie Deckoff-Jones, M.D.
New England Hyperbaric Center
42 West Sheffield Road
Great Barrington, MA 01230
(413) 528-9977
jdj@newenglandhyperbaric.com
www.newenglandhyperbaric.com

Greenfield
Josephine Queneau, B.S.N.
416 Leyden Road
Greenfield, MA 01301
(413) 774-4688
woodsong55@aol.com

Medford
Georgianna Saba, M.Ed.
Irlen Diagnostic Center and EEG Biofeedback
Boston
25 A Mabelle Avenue
Medford, MA 02155
(781) 396-3321
eegboston@aol.com

Northampton
Sebern Fisher, M.A.
34 Elizabeth Street
Northampton, MA 01060
(413) 586-4230
sebern@earthlink.net

Catherine Rule, M.Ed., CAGS, CRC; Brian Norris,
M.Ed.; Barry Sparkes, D.Ed.
Optimal Brain Institute
16 Center Street, Suite 301
Northampton, MA 01060
(413) 584-5108; fax (413) 585-9974
cathryn@javanet.com
www.optimalbrain.com

Paula Murphy, LICSW, LMT; Dona Wheeler,
LICSW, MS
16 Center Street, Suite 301
Northampton, MA 01060-3130
(413) 586-6680
pmurphy@javanet.com
donawheeler@cs.com
www.optimalbrain.com

Katharine Hazen, MSW, ACSW, LICSW
49 Hubbard Ave.
Northampton, MA 01060
(413) 586-8352
khazen@map.com
http://providers.eegspectrum.com/US/hazen.htm

Patricia Lyons R.N., MS, CS
16 Center St., Suite 218
Northampton, MA 01060
(413) 587-0775; fax (413) 586-6550
patmikel@aol.com
www.optimalbrain.com

Petersham

Susan Ott, Ph.D.; Terry Burch, M.A., LMHC
Birch Spring Clinical Services
110 North Main Street
Petersham, MA 01366-9501
(978) 724-8892
burterry@netscape.net

Waltham

Jill-Laurie Crane, M.A.; Joseph C. Crane, M.A.
633 Trapelo Road
Waltham, MA 02452
(716) 647-9089
josephc637@aol.com

Wellesley

Jolene Ross, Ph.D.
Wellesley Neurotherapy
140 Bristol Road
Wellesley, MA 02181
(781) 431-9115; fax (781) 431-8725
jolenefr@mediaone.net
http://providers.eegspectrum.com/US/JoleneRoss

West Barnstable

Paul Goldring, Ph.D.
EEG Feedback of Cape Cod
1074 Route 6A
West Barnstable, MA 02666
(508) 362-1180
paulg@capecod.net
http://providers.eegspectrum.com/US/PaulGoldring

MICHIGAN

Ann Arbor

Charles F. Spinazola, Ph.D., Director, Licensed
Clinical Psychologist
Michigan Neurotherapy Center Ann Arbor
2345 South Huron Parkway
Ann Arbor, MI 48104
(734) 761-1757
drspinazola@provide.net
http://providers.eegspectrum.com/US/CharlesSpinazola

Eve Avrin, Ph.D.
3300 Washtenaw Ave., Suite 285
Ann Arbor, MI 48104
(734) 913-9870

Ann Arbor/Dexter

Robert Egri, M.A., CSW, MFT
Counseling Resources of Ann Arbor
2479 Peters Road
Dexter-Ann Arbor, MI 48130
(734) 665-5050

Ann Arbor/Saline

Jane Doner, M.A.
Neurofeedback Learning Center
439 Woodgrove
Ann Arbor, MI 48103
(734) 944-9994
jldoner@earthlink.net
http://providers.eegspectrum.com/US/JaneDoner

East Lansing

Martha Bristor, Ph.D.
5909 Shadowlawn Drive
East Lansing, MI 48823
(517) 332-3391; fax (517) 432-3320
bristorm@msu.edu

Lansing

Lynn M. Darling, Ph.D.; Richard Dombrowski,
Ph.D.; Kathleen Bowers, MSW, ACSW
Riverwind Psychology Associates
6639 Centurion Drive, Suite 150
Lansing, MI 48910
(517) 703-0110
darling7@msu.edu
rdphd@juno.com
katbwrs@aol.com

St. Joseph

William A. Schnell, M.A.; Jane Schnell
2517 Niles Ave.
St. Joseph, MI 49085
(616) 982-0046; fax (616) 983-1600
billandjanes@prodigy.net

MINNESOTA

Grand Marais

Kathleen Lee Stewart, BSN, R.N., CFNP;
Karl Hansen, B.A.
North Shore Neurofeedback
P.O. Box 275
Grand Marais, MN 55604-0275
(218) 387-2983; fax (218) 387-3153
solarkarl@boreal.org

Minneapolis

Michael Joyce, M.A., NLP, BCIAC-EEG; Barb
Moffett; Michele Repk; Karen Sternal, BA
A Chance to Grow
1800 2nd Street NE
Minneapolis, MN 55418
(612) 789-1236; fax (612) 706-5555
mjoyce@mail.actg.org
http://providers.eegspectrum.com/US/MichaelJoyce

North Mankato

Al Mumma, M.S., Licensed Psychologist
723 Park Avenue
North Mankato, MN 56003
(507) 388-5224
almumma@mctcnet.net
http://providers.eegspectrum.com/US/AlMumma

Stillwater

W. Roy Evans, M.A., Licensed Psychologist
6381 Osgood Avenue North, Bldg C
Stillwater, MN 55082-6118
(651) 439-2301; fax (651) 439-7368
highbeta@baldwin-telecom.net

MISSOURI
Columbia

Wiley Miller, Ph.D.
Hiesberger and Associates
3201 Providence
Columbia, MO 65203
(573) 875-0077
millerwi@missouri.edu

Kansas City

Robert L. McRoberts, Ph.D.
222 W Gregory, Suite 229
Kansas City, MO 64114
(816) 444-4887

MONTANA
Great Falls

Audrey Thompson, Ed.D., LCPC
2300 12th Street South
Great Falls, MT 59405
(406) 761-5671
athompson@in-tch.com

Helena

Bernadette Pedersen, B.A., BCIAC
Brainworks
2001 11th Ave., Suite 20
Helena, MT 59601
(406) 495-1122
bp@brainworksllc.com
www.brainworksllc.com

Missoula

Z'eva Singer, M.A.
Singer Associates, P.C.
5190 Old Marshall Grade
Missoula, MT 59802
(406) 721-3351; fax (406) 721-9742
singer@montana.com

Whitefish

Clare Chisholm, M.A., LPC
Neurofeedback Clinic
244 Spokane Ave., Suite 3
Whitefish, MT 59937-2600
(406) 863-9767; fax (406) 862-0039
cclpc@digisys.net

NEBRASKA
Hastings

Virginia K. White, R.N., M.S. Eds;
Ann Pattno, M.S.
Professional Counseling Associates
Landmark Center, 2727 W. 2nd Street, #330
Hastings, NE 68901
(402) 461-4917; fax (402) 461-4103
vwhite@cnweb.com
pattnoann@yahoo.com

Lincoln

Andrea J. Sime, LCSW, BCIA;
Sandy Lamberson, BSN, R.N.
First Step Wellness Center
1919 S 40th St., Suite 212
Lincoln, NE 68506-5243
(402) 441-9280; fax (402) 441-9279
Andrea Sime: asime@inetnebr.com
Sandy Lamberson: braintrainer1@aol.com

B.J. Wheeler, Ph.D.; Barbara Ellis, R.N., A.P.R.N.
The Quest, Connections in Mind and Body
6759 Bermuda Drive
Lincoln, NE 68502
(402) 476-6759
bjwheeler@neb.rr.com
bjellis@neb.rr.com

Milford

Dixie Placek, M.A., LMFT, CNP
Affiliates in Individual and Family Growth
2605 Yankee Hill Road
Milford, NE 68405-8457
(402) 761-3069
ai45325@navix.net

NEVADA

Henderson

Judith DeGrazia Willard, Ph.D.
Advanced Neuro and Psychological Specialties
1701 E Green Valley Pkwy, Build #2, Suite A
Henderson, NV 89014
(702) 650-0590
jdwillard@anps.com
http://providers.eegspectrum.com/US/JudithDeGraziaWillard
http://anps.com

NEW HAMPSHIRE

Londonderry

Edward Jacobs, Ph.D.
12 Parmenter Road
Londonderry, NH 03053
(603) 437-2069; fax (603) 437-5588
ehjpsych@aol.com

NEW JERSEY

Atlantic Highlands

Betty Jarusiewicz, Ph.D., CADC
Atlantic Counseling Center, Inc.
51 Memorial Parkway (Hwy 36)
Atlantic Highlands, NJ 07716
(732) 872-8700
bjarus@home.com

Audubon

Michael J. Colis, Ph.D.
408 S White Horse Pike

Audubon, NJ 08106
(856) 310-9696; fax (856) 546-7362
Mjcphd@snip.net
http://providers.eegspectrum.com/US/MichaelColis

Tenafly

Anya Luchow, Ph.D.
111 E. Clinton Ave.
Tenafly, NJ 07670
(201) 569-4585; fax (201) 567-6183

NEW YORK

Bronx

Julie Weiner, M.S. (Nutrition), BCIAC, Fellow
Biofeedback Learning Center
5997 Riverdale Ave.
Bronx, NY 10471
(718) 601-4569; fax (303) 479-9727
jweiner1@netzero.net

Brooklyn

Katherine Leddick, Ph.D., DCIAC-EEG; David Yourman, Ph.D.
54 Montgomery Place
Brooklyn, NY 11215
(718) 623-1173

Ithaca

Judith Abrams, PAC, LAC
342 DeWitt Building
Ithaca, NY 14850
(607) 277-7713
jask@clarityconnect.com

Kingston

Carol S. Kessler, Ph.D., DAC, LAC, MS, LMT
187 Pine Street
Kingston, NY 12401
(845) 334-9340; fax (845) 334-9343
carolskessler@aol.com

Liverpool

James Terry
Pathway Counseling Center
326 1st Street
Liverpool, NY 13088
(315) 451-4815
mosesjet@aol.com

New York City

Leslie Seiden, BCIAC; Hal Rosenblum, BCIAC
Braincare, Inc.
133 E. 91st Street
New York, NY 10128
(212) 828-1188; fax (212) 423-3045
Braincare@aol.com
www.braincare.com

Merlyn Hurd, Ph.D., BCIAC-EEG
88 University Place, 8th floor
New York, NY 10003
(212) 807-8690; fax (212) 645-3076
merlynh@aol.com

Katherine Leddick, Ph.D., BCIAC-EEG;
David Yourman, Ph.D.
164 W. 80th St., Lower Level
New York, NY 10024
(212) 787-8155
KHL7400@ nyu.edu
dby2@earthlink.net
http://providers.eegspectrum.com/US/KatherineLeddick

Deborah Pines, CSW
451 West End Avenue, Suite 1D
New York, NY 10024
(212) 799-3888; fax (212) 501-9045
ploughman7@mindspring.com

Saratoga Springs

Kathy Zilbermann, Ph.D.
4 Franklin Square, Suite D
Saratoga Springs, NY 12866
(518) 587-4350
kzlib@nycap.rr.com

NORTH CAROLINA

Asheville

Philip Ellis, Ph.D.; Susan Grant, M.A.
Focus: Center for Neurofeedback
189 E. Chestnut Street
Asheville, NC 28801
(828) 281-2299, Philip Ellis
(828) 273-2044, Sue Grant
wncphil@msn.com
grasu53@aol.com

Ed Hamlin, Ph.D.; Cynthia Ackrill, M.D.
The Pisgah Institute
158 Zillicoa Street
Asheville, NC 28801
(828) 254-9494; fax (828) 254-0161
edh9494@aol.com
cackrillmd@home.com

Thea Schulze, MSW, LCSW
31 Clayton Street
Asheville, NC 28801
(828) 251-2681; fax (828) 669-0756

Greensboro

Gail Sanders Durgin, Ph.D.
2311 West Cone Blvd., Suite 227
Greensboro, NC 27408
(336) 540-1972; fax (336) 540-1973
nyuphd@aol.com

Greenville

Judy Carlson-Cataland, Ed.D., R.N., CS, FNP,
BCIAC
2415 Charles Boulevard
Greenville, NC 27858
(252) 353-8022; fax (252) 353-8055
healthinnovations@earthlink.net

OHIO

Centerville

Fred Sinay, M.Ed., LPCC
EEG Spectrum of Centerville, Ohio
537 Windsor Park Drive
Centerville, OH 45459
(937) 434-4882
fsinay@msn.com

Chagrin Falls

Alan Bachers, Ph.D.; Mark C. Brown, Ph.D.
Center for Better Living
7160 Chagrin Road Suite 150
Chagrin Falls, OH 44023-1101
(440) 247-7465; fax (440) 247-9978
bonkers@oh.verio.com
http://providers.eegspectrum.com/US/CenterforBetterLiving

Cincinnati

Justine Ritter
Cincinnati Neurotherapy Center
8228 Winton Road, Suite 100A
Cincinnati, OH 45231
(513) 521-5483
wandjritter@earthlink.net

Piqua

Carla Bertke, Ph.D.
Rehabilitation Center for Neuro Development
850 S. Main Street
Piqua, OH 45356-3836
(937) 773-7630

Toledo

Gregory E. Forgac, Ph.D., Inc.
3900 Sunforest Court
Sunforest Medical Building, Suite 200
Toledo, Ohio 43623
(419) 474-4471; fax (419) 475-9312
ge4jack@aol.com

Wadsworth

Glen P. Martin, LPCC; Beth Martin, LPT;
Rosemary Herron, LPC
Neurotherapy Counseling Center
One Park Centre, Suite 15
Wadsworth, OH 44281
(330) 336-8300; fax (330) 336-1222
neurotherapy@msn.com
http://providers.eegspectrum.com/US/GlenMartin

OKLAHOMA

Ada

Dana Hargus, M.Ed., LPC
Biofeedback and Counseling, Inc.
119 North Broadway, Suite 105
Ada, OK 74820
(580) 436-7120; fax (580) 436-7121
hargus118@cs.com

Altus

Dane Nielsen, MBS; Mary Keuhn, OT
Brainwave Biofeedback, Inc.
1121 N. Spurgeon
Altus, OK 73521
(580) 480-1345
cir@ionet.net

Enid

William Schlagel
St. Mary's Hospital Cardiorespiratory and
Neurology
305 S. 5th
Enid, OK 73701
(580) 249-3071; fax (580) 548-5002
bschlagel@okla.smhs.com

Lawton

Kenneth L. Jones, M.A.; Judith Jones, LPC
Brainwave Biofeedback, Inc.
1930 NW Ferris, Suite 12
Lawton, OK 73507
(580) 250-1545; fax (580) 355-3414
kjones@msn.com
catballou@yahoo.com

Norman

Sally Church, Ph.D.
1300 McGee Dr., Suites 101A and 102
Norman, OK 73072-5858
(405) 360-0048
SWMLC1@aol.com
http://providers.eegspectrum.com/US/SallyChurch

Oklahoma City

Paula Clinton, M.Ed., LPC, LMFT; Thomas R.
Thomson, M.Ed.
Transformational Choice Therapies, Inc.
4334 New Expressway, Suite 224
Oklahoma City, OK 73116
(405) 843-8588, (405) 843-5443
trthomson@home.com
http://providers.eegspectrum.com/US/TransformationalChoiceTherapies

OREGON

Ashland/Medford

Phil Miller, MS; Susan Berryhill, M.A., MPH, LPC
129 S. Laurel Street
Ashland, OR 97520
(541) 482-2780; fax (541) 482-3709
PhilMiller@EEGpower.com
SBerryhill@EEGpower.com
http://providers.eegspectrum.com/US/PotentialUnlimited
www.EEGpower.com

Eugene

Matthew Fleischman, Ph.D.
Center for Attention and Learning
915 Oak Street, Suite 300
Eugene, OR 97401
(541) 343-9221; fax (541) 343-6410
MFleischman@worldnet.att.net
http://providers.eegspectrum.com/US/MatthewFleischman

Klamath Falls

Chauncey Farrell, M.S.
Mind Body Connection
1310 McClellan Drive
Klamath Falls, OR 97603
Cfarrell@cdsnet.net

Lake Oswego

John McManus, Ph.D.
Abilities Center
15100 SW Boones Ferry Road, Suite 700
Lake Oswego, OR 97035
(503) 636-0111; fax (503) 977-9583
Abilitiescenter@inetarena.com
www.abilities-center.com

Lebanon

Lila McQueen, Ph.D.
1711 S. Main Street
Lebanon, OR 97355
(541) 259-5400
mcqueenphd@centurytel.net
http://home.centurytel.net/mcqueenphd

Portland

Kayle Sandberg-Lewis, LMT, M.A.
6315 SE 15th Ave.
Portland, OR 97202
(503) 234-2733
StressLess@att.net

PENNSYLVANIA

Bucks County

Barry Belt, M.A., Licensed Psychologist
Attention Deficit Specialists
Floral Vale Professional Park
503 Floral Vale Blvd.
Yardley, PA 19067
(215) 497-0240; fax (215) 497-0259
BABelt@aol.com

http://providers.eegspectrum.com/US/ads.htm
www.addsolutions.com

Carlisle

Henry M. Weeks, Ph.D.
211 Echo Rd.
Carlisle, PA 17013-9510
(717) 249-8382
hweeks@epix.net

Downingtown

Kathleen J. West, Ph.D.
506 E. Lancaster Avenue
Lower Level West
Downingtown, PA 19335
(610) 518-6020; fax (610) 518-3892
brknhll@aol.com

Exton

Barbara Tury, M.A.
Neurofeedback and Counseling Connection
47 Marchwood Road
Suite 2-H
Exton, PA 19341
(610) 280-9555; fax (610) 280-9532

Philadelphia

Marged Lindner, Ph.D.
Park Drive Manor #C2, 633 W. Rittenhouse St.
Philadelphia, PA 19144
(215) 849-0735
mlindner@voicenet.com
http://providers.eegspectrum.com/US/MargedLindner

Swarthmore

Kathryn N. Healey, Ph.D.;
Frank Masterpasqua, Ph.D.
211 N. Park Ave.
Swarthmore, PA 19081
(610) 499-1234; fax (610) 499-4625
Kathryn.N.Healey@widener.edu
Frank.j.masterpasqua@widener.edu

Trooper

Mitchell M. Sadar, Ph.D.
Sadar Psychological Services
124 Woodlyn Ave.
Trooper, PA 19043
(610) 933-9440; fax (610) 933-8567
sadar@rcn.com

RHODE ISLAND

Narragansett

Peter Seuffert, M.S., LMFT
Alternative Unlimited
23 Lauderdale Drive
Narragansett, RI 02882
(401) 782-2980
pseuf@cs.com

Providence

Laurence M. Hirshberg, Ph.D.
Two Regency Plaza
Providence, RI 02903
(401) 351-7779; fax (401) 333-3820
lhirshberg@home.com

SOUTH CAROLINA

Beaufort

Royce V. Malphrus, Ph.D.
Sea Island Pain and Stress Management Clinic
989 Ribault Road, Suite 260
Beaufort, SC 29902
(843) 522-8569
malph@hargray.com

Mount Pleasant

Dr. Michael C. Mithoefer
208 Scott Street
Mt. Pleasant, SC 29464
843-849-6899

TENNESSEE

Franklin

Carole Kendall, Ph.D.
1107A Lakeview Dr,
Franklin, TN 37067
(615) 791-1332
CaroleKend@aol.com

Germantown

Cliff Heegel, Ph.D.
2199 S. Germantown Road
Germantown, TN 38183
(901)758-4070; fax (901) 626-7549
cheeg@askdrcliff.com
www.askdrcliff.com

Knoxville

Joel F. Lubar, Ph.D.
Judith O. Lubar, L.C.S.W.
6423 Deane Hill Drive
Knoxville, TN 37919
(615) 584-8721

TEXAS

Austin

Edward C. (Neil) King, Jr., MSSW (Director)
EEG Spectrum of Austin
4131 Spicewood Springs Road, Suite Q-2
Austin, TX 78759
(512) 338-4095; fax (512) 338-4070
qeeg@bga.com
http://providers.eegspectrum.com/US/EdwardKing

Jan Ford Mustin, Ph.D., PC; Al K. Mustin, Ph.D.,
Director
4407 Bee Caves Road, Suite 411
Austin, TX 78746
(512) 347-8100; fax (512) 347-8200
doctor@mustin.com
www.mustin.com

Corpus Christi

Burton Kittay, Ph.D.; Manuel A. Vara, L.P.C.
Psychological Wellness Center
5350 S Staples Street, Suite 200
Corpus Christi, TX 78411-4654
(361) 992-2244
BurtKittay@aol.com
http://providers.eegspectrum.com/US/PsychologicalWellnessCenter

Houston

Nancy White, Ph.D.
The Enhancement Institute
4600 Post Oak Place, Suite 301
Houston, TX 77027
(713) 961-5243; fax (713) 552-0752
nancywhite@enhancementinstitute.com

Carol Kershaw, Ed.D.; J. William Wade, M.Div.,
LPC, LMFT
Institute for Family Psychology
2012 Bissonnet Street
Houston, TX 77005-1647
(713) 529-4588; fax (713) 529-4589
hypnopsych@aol.com
www.mhehouston.com

Plano

John H. Millerman, Ph.D., Clinical Director
Achievement Plus
1825 E. Plano Parkway, Suite 110
Plano, TX 75074-8570
(972) 422-1399; fax (972) 881-7410
drjohnm@iamerica.net
http://providers.eegspectrum.com/US/JohnH.Millerman

Round Rock

Sheila Martel, M.Ed., LPC, QEET,
Executive Director
Biofeedback Therapies
1100 Round Rock Ave., Suite 107
Round Rock, TX 78681
(512) 266-1475; fax (512) 310-8370
biofeedback@jump.net
http://providers.eegspectrum.com/US/SheilaMartel

UTAH

Clearfield

Heber C. Kimball, Ph.D.
Family Connection Center
1360 E. 1450 South
Clearfield, UT 84015
(801) 773-0712
famcon@davis.uswest.net

Salt Lake City

Steve Szykula, Ph.D.
Comprehensive Psychological Services
1200 E. 3300 South
Salt Lake City, UT 84106
(801) 483-1600; fax (801) 483-1610
compsych@zzlink.net

VIRGINIA

Abingdon

Robert W. Hill, Ph.D.
The Oaks
16501 Jeb Stuart Highway, P.O. Box 2077
Abingdon, VA 24210
(276) 628-1378
http://providers.eegspectrum.com/US/RobertW.Hill

Ronald Brill, Ph.D.
Tamarack Center
390 Commerce Drive, Box 8
Abingdon, VA 24211
(276) 628-1496; fax (276) 628-7985
rbrill@naxs.com

Alexandria

Deborah A. Stokes, M.Ed.
Behavioral Medicine Consultants
2121 Eisenhower Avenue, Suite 200
Alexandria, VA 22314
(703) 684-0334; fax (703) 960-5934
dstokes@cox.rr.com
www.neurofeedbackconsult.com

Ashland

Carol C. Hughes, Ed.D., LPC
303 Caroline Street
Ashland, VA 23601
(804) 798-2555; fax (804) 798-1178
chughes@rmc.edu

Newport News

F. Lanier Fly, LMFT
Family Therapy
718 J. Clyde Morris Boulevard
Newport News, VA 23601
(757) 873-8566
fly@widomaker.com

Adrianne Ryder-Cook, LLD, ML, MCL, MS.JD
Riverside EEG Biofeedback Services
11815 Rock Landing Drive
Newport News, VA 23006
(757) 594-3399; fax (757) 594-3503
neurotherapy@rivhs.com

Richmond

Glenn Weiner, Ph.D.
Dominion Behavioral Healthcare
703 N. Courthouse Rd., #101
Richmond, VA 23236
(804) 794-4482; fax (804) 379-7578
glennweiner@att.net
http://providers.eegspectrum.com/US/GlennWeiner
www.childneurofeedback.com

Troutdale

Eduardo Castro, M.D.
Mount Rogers Clinic of Troutdale
799 Ripshin Road
Troutdale, VA 24378
(276) 677-3631; fax (276) 677-3843
edcastro@netva.com

Warrenton

Linda F. Harrover, R.N.
The Harrover Group, Inc.
7296 Forrest Road
Warrenton, VA 20187
(540) 349-1415; fax (540) 349-9563
frankhar@erols.com

WASHINGTON

Bellevue

Steven Rothman, Ph.D.,
Licensed Clinical Psychologist
1800 112th Ave. NE, Suite 210W
Bellevue, WA 98004
(425) 454-4266
steverothman@seanet.com
http://providers.eegspectrum.com/US/StevenRothman

Burlington

Christie M. Betz, R.N.
Northwest Neurofeedback
160 Cascade Drive, Suite 215
Burlington, WA 98233
(360) 404-2005; fax (360) 404-2008
cbetz@casproctr.com

Colville

Gregg D. Sharp, D.O.
Colville Healing Arts Center
143 Garden Homes Drive
Colville, WA 99114
(509) 685-2300
info@healingartscenter.com
www.healingartscenter.com

Edmonds

Stephanie Harris, R.N.C.
Biofeedback Clinic of Edmonds
8523 224th Street SW
Edmonds, WA 98026
(425) 672-1676

C3Beta@msn.com
http://providers.eegspectrum.com/US/StephanieHarris

Everett

Tim Buckley, B.S., M.D.
Pacific Crest Family Consultants
2731 Wetmore Avenue, Suite 220
Everett, WA 98201
(425) 252-7716; fax (425) 258-9536
tim@tuf-kids.com
www.tuf-kids.com

Mount Vernon

Rosemary MacGregor, R.N., M.S.
Stress Management and Biofeedback Center
2114 Riverside Drive, # 205
Mt. Vernon, WA 98273
(360) 428-0134
rosemary@pacificrim.net
http://providers.eegspectrum.com/US/RosemaryMacGregor

Seattle

Thomas DuHamel, Ph.D.
ABCD, Inc.
2611 NE 125th St., #225
Seattle, WA 98125-4357
(206) 361-6884
duhamelt@maxxconnect.net

Steven Rothman, Ph.D., Licensed Clinical
Psychologist
Lake City Professional Center
2611 N.E. 125th Street, Suite 117
Seattle, WA 98125
(425) 454-4266
steverothman@seanet.com
http://providers.eegspectrum.com/US/rothman.htm

Elizabeth Walker, Ph.D.
5134 S. Willow
Seattle, WA 98118
(206) 725-6926
ecwalker@aol.com

Snohomish

Betty Hunholz, R.N.
Clearview Medical Center
18122 Highway 9 S.E.
Snohomish, WA 98290

(425) 481-8811, (360) 668-6519;
fax (425) 481-5734

WEST VIRGINIA

Bluefield

Teresa Paine, Ph.D.
New Horizons Comprehensive Counseling
Services
1601 1/2 Bland Street, Suite #1
Bluefield, WV 24701
(304) 327-8362; fax (304) 327-8361
newhorizons@stargate.net

WISCONSIN

Oconomowoc

Anne Felden, Ph.D.; Marta C. Muller, M.D.
Oconomowoc Developmental Training Center
36100 Genesee Lake Road
Oconomowoc, WI 53066-9201
(414) 569-5515
afelden@odtc-wi.com
mmuller@odtc-wi.com

Wauwatosa

Peter J. Hansen, Ph.D., BCIA, Licensed Clinical
Psychologist
Family Care Psychological Services
Mayfair Professional Building
2500 Mayfair Road, #560
Wauwatosa, WI 53226
(414) 771-5002

ARGENTINA

Buenos Aires

Dr. Esther Romero Tannenhaus Rosario
Rosario 478-2nd floor
Buenos Aires (1424)
Argentina 54
011 4902-1473; fax 54 011 4901-8911
esther@unifax.com.ar
www.neuroterapia.com.ar

AUSTRALIA
WESTERN AUSTRALiA

Como

Roger P. Lavell, MAPS, Clinical Psychologist (B.
Psych, M.App. Psych, Dip. Clin. Hypnosis)
Suite 2, Como Corporate Center
11 Preston Street
Como, WA 6152
08 9367 0610; fax 08 9368 1600
rlavell@cygnus.uwa.edu.au

Claremont

Dr. Susan Priest, Clinical Psychologist, M.Psych
(Clin.), Ph.D.
Health Care Systems Australia P/L
Medical Consulting Rooms
Bethesda Hospital
25 Queenslea Drive
Claremont, WA 6010
08 9340 6380
spriest@iinet.net.au

Cottesloe

Dr. Kerry Monick, MBBS, DPM, FRANZCP.
Consultant Psychiatrist
Neurofeedback West
"Cottesloe Chambers"
Suite 10—136 Railway Street
Cottesloe, WA 6910
08 9384 8595; 08 9384 8535;
fax 08 9385 6336
kmonick@iinet.au

Fremantle

Denis McCarthy, M.App. Psych
Whole Life Center
9 Holland Street
Fremantle, WA 6160
08 9430 7777; fax 08 9430 4305
gaianet@cygnus.uwa.edu.au

Joondalup

Dr. Rama Naidoo, Consultant Pediatrician
Suite 204—Specialist Medical Centre
Joondalup Health Campus
Shenton Road
Joondalup, WA 6027
08 9400 9911
sairama@aol.com

West Leederville

Carol Smith, M.Psych (Clin.) (Child)
Clinical and Child Psychologist
7 Rosslyn Street
West Leederville, WA 6007
08 9382 8955; fax 08 9382 8755

SOUTH AUSTRALIA

Adelaide

Dr. Tim Hill
86 South Terrace
Adelaide, SA 5000
08 8410 6500
tcrhill@senet.com.au

Greg Ireland
School of Psychology, University of So. Australia
GPO Box 2471
Adelaide, SA 5001
618 302 2468; fax 618 302 2956
greg.ireland@unisa.edu.au

Dr. Peter Thomas
48 Carrington Street
Adelaide, SA 5000
08 8212 4005
ttg@iweb.net.au

Greenwith

Ed Zahra, B.Com., Dip.App.Psych.,
M.App.Psych., M.A.S.H.
Access Psychology
Clinical and Educational Psychology
Greenwith—St. Agnes
Tel: 08 8289 7766
ed@accesspsychology.com.au
www.accesspsychology.com.au

Kent Town

Stephen Dunstone, Psychologist
33 Dequetteville Terrace
Kent Town, South Australia 5067
08 8364 5342; fax 08 8331 3814
dunstone@senet.com.au

QUEENSLAND

Brisbane

Tamara Lorensen

The Neurotherapy Centre
P.O. Box 144
Kelvin Grove D.C.
Queensland 4059 Australia
61 (0)7 3352 7755
tamara@tpgi.com.au

Cairns

Rob Buschkens
The Neuro Training Clinic
29 Headrick Street
Manunda—Cairns
61 (0)7 4041 7516; fax 61 (0)7 4093 7403
eeg@austarnet.com.au

Coorparoo

Brian O'Hanlon, Psychologist, MAPS
Fellow (Aust. College of Clin. Psych.)
PO Box 313
Coorparoo Qld 4151
(07) 3397 8250
bohanlon@uq.net.au

Gympie

Don Brinkworth; Del J. Sherlock, Ph.D.
37 Tamaree Road
Gympie, Queensland 4570 Australia
61 07 5482 9298; fax 61 07 5482 6116
delsh@tpgi.com.au
dbrinkw@tpgi.com.au

Rockhampton

Dr. Alan Keen, Psychologist
A&M Psychological Services
123 Denham Street
Rockhampton
Queensland 4700
07 4927 2153; fax 07 4927 2230
a.keen@cqu.edu.au

Sunshine Coast (Maroochydore)

Mark Darling, B Soc Sc (Hons)(Psych)
Level 1, 9 First Avenue
Maroochydore
Queensland 4558
61 (0)7 5451 9922; fax 61 (0)7 5443 1785
mdarling@powerup.com.au

NEW SOUTH WALES

Artarmon
Jan Osgood; Jodi Osgood
Action Potential Neurotherapy
25 Onyx Road
Artarmon, NSW 2064
61 02 9419-6683
josgood@ozemail.com.au

Bass Hill
Rosemary Boon
Learning Discoveries
104 Chester Hill Rd.
Bass Hill NSW 2197
02 9727 5794
rboon@iprimus.com.au
home.iprimus.com.au/rboon

Bowral
Geraldine Knights, R.N.
Highlands Neuro-Biofeedback Centre
Shop 2, 371 Bong Bong Street
Bowral, NSW 2576
61 02 4862 4482; fax 61 02 4862 4417
knights@ozemail.com.au

Charlestown
Sr. Patricia Wilson
Stroke and Disability Information (Hunter)
17 James Street
Charlestown, NSW 2290
61 02 4943 9786; fax 61 02 4942 3481

Crows Nest
Alex Sevitt Psychologist
ADD/ADHD National Diagnostic P/L
Level 1, 48 Albany Street
Crows Nest NSW 2065
02 9437 5071; fax 02 9936 5438
rolex@geko.net.au

Fairfield West
Wellbeing and Integrated Neurotherapy Services
10 Dyson Place
Fairfield West, NSW Australia 2165
612 9604 6937; fax 612 9604 1307

Granville
Terry Cook, M.D.
15 Carlton St

Granville—NSW 2142
61 2 9682 7057
hamelin@orangemail.com.au

Milton
John Hegg, MA Psych Syd Uni, BA Beh Sci LSC
Vermont
South Coast Neurotherapy Services
137 Princess Hwy
Milton—NSW 2538
02 4455 5970
jonhegg@bigpond.com

Sydney
Dana Adam, MA, M App Psych, MAPS
Active Support Centre
Suite 501, Level 5
149 Castlereagh Street
Sydney, NSW 2000
61 (0)2 9262 9408
dana_adam@hotmail.com

Wentworthville
Angelo Schibeci, Ph.D., MAPS, MACCP, MAAAPB
Josephine Capitani, BA, M. Appl. Psych., MAPS,
MACCP, MSNR
Health Plus
52 Dunmore Street
Wentworthville NSW Australia 2145
612 9631 8944; fax 612 9631 2984
shekinah@ihug.com.au

VICTORIA

Leopold
Guylene Kayler-Thomson, BA, RN
Neurofeedback Australia
15 Ferguson Rd
Leopold
Victoria 3224
61 (0)3 5250 1755
shum@bigpond.com

Melbourne
Moshe Perl, Ph.D.
Clinical and Forensic Psychologist
650 Glenhuntly Road
Caulfield South Melbourne Victoria 3162
Australia
03-9533-0555
mperl@ozemail.com.au

Jacques Duff, BA (psych) Grad. Dip. Psych.
MAAAPB
Behavioural Neurotherapy Clinic
82 Blackburn Road
East Doncaster 3109
Australia
613 9842 0370
info@adhd.com.au
www.adhd.com.au

CHILE

Santiago

Fernando Morgado, M.D., Jane Crossley
Neurofeedback Clinic, Apoquindo Medical Bldg.
Apoquindo 4100, Room 1009
Santiago, Chile
(562) 212-9011
fmorgado@ctc-mundo.net

COSTA RICA

San José

Dr. Francisco Jimenez Marten, M.D., Director
Psicologa; Evelyn Diaz, C.N.
Latin American Institute of Neurotherapy
Instituto Latinoamericano de Neuroterapia Plaza
Cristal, 100 mts south, 50 West, 25 south
Curridabat, San José, Costa Rica, Central
América
(Mailing address) PO Box 025216, SJO-872,
Miami, FL 33102-5216
(506) 224-6176
inslatne@sol.racsa.co.cr

CZECH REPUBLIC

Prague

Jiri Tyl, Ph.D., Clinical Psychologist Chair;
Wendy Tylova, Ph.D. EEG Biofeedback, Clinical
Psychology
EEG Biofeedback Institute of the Czech Republic
University Hospital Policlinic
Lannova 2 Prague
Czech Republic CZ-110 00
 + 420 2 2480 2349;
Personal: + 420 602 224 964
Tyl@eegbiofeedback.cz
www.eegbiofeedback.cz

Ing. Josef Tomek, President
Tak Co., Ltd.
Holandska 1
101 00, Praha
Czech Republic
011 420 2 724187

GERMANY

Altotting

Dr. Ronald Schmidt; Thomas Fuchs
Sozialpadiatrisches Zentrum Inn-Salzach
Vinzenz-von-Paul
Strabe 10
84503, Altotting
49 06 71-509-247; fax 06 71-509244

Berlin

Avi Sonnenschein
Ludwigkirschstrasse 10A
10719 Berlin, Germany
011 49 30881 5620

Munchen

Wolfgang Keeser, Ph.D.
Leopoldstrasse 59
D-80802, Munchen, Germany
49-89-331694 or 49-89-334003; fax 49-89-332942
wolfgang.keeser@p-net.de

ISRAEL

Haifa

Ernesto Miselevich, M.D., Child, Adolescent and
Family Psychiatrist—Psychotherapist; Lena
Davis Solomon, Neuropsychologist and
Rehabilitation Psychologist
1, Litanis St, P.O. Box 6490
Haifa 31064, Israel
(972) 4 8375748
neurofeed@yahoo.com
http://providers.eegspectrum.com/Intl/ErnestoMiselevich

Jerusalem

Naomi Palmor, Ph.D., C.C.C.
Or Sharga 17/2
Ramot D., Jerusalem, Israel
011-972-2-587-2424
eegbio@actcom.co.il

Tel Aviv

Ernesto Miselevich, MD., Child, Adolescent and Family Psychiatrist—Psychotherapist; Lena Davis Solomon, Neuropsychologist and Rehabilitation Psychologist
77, Bialik St, Apart. 16
RAMAT-GAN
(972) 3 6121811; fax (972) 4 8375748
neurofeed@yahoo.com
http://providers.eegspectrum.com/Intl/ErnestoMiselevich

KOREA

Seoul

Sooyoon Kim, M.D.
International Clinic
737-37 Hannam-Dong, Yong San-Ku
Seoul, Korea
82 2 790 0857
sky114@thrunet.com
www.internationalclinic.co.kr

MEXICO

Cuernavaca Morelos

Michael Seifert, C.N.P.,
Administrator/Neurofeedback Specialist
Centro de Neuroterapia de Cuernavaca
(Neurotherapy Center of Cuernavaca)
Avenida Palmas # 811, Suite 2
Colonia Bellavista
Cuernavaca, Morelos, Mexico
U.S. Telephone dialing: 011-527-313-9410
Mexico Dialing: 91 (73) 13-94-10
Cncspectrum@cableonlive.com.mx

Mexico City

Georgina Blasquez, Psychologist and Family Therapist
Crece Neurofeedback
Tesoreros 86
Mexico City, D.F. 041000
(525) 606 39 17
creceneuro@yahoo.es

NETHERLANDS

Almelo

J. Fekkes, MA, Clinical psychologist/psychotherapist
Twenteborg Hospital Department of Clinical Psychology
Almelo, The Netherlands
00(31) 564 833240
j.fekkes@twenteborg.nl

Hengelo

Institute for Neurofeedback (private practice)
Hengelo, The Netherlands
00 (31) 74 2568968
Psy.Fekkes@net.HCC.nl

Institute for Neurofeedback (private practice)
Mitchamplein
7556 SC
Hengelo, The Netherlands
00 (31) 523 266153
wzwaag@xs4all.nl

Groningen

B. Reitsma, Ph.D., Clinical psychologist/psychotherapist
University Hospital Groningen Department of Medical Psychology Pain Expertise Centre
Groningen, The Netherlands
00 (31) 50 3614133
b.reitsma@med.rug.nl

Doezum

Institute for Neurofeedback (private practice)
Doezum, The Netherlands
00 (31) 594 612701

Hardenberg

W.D. van der Zwaag, MA., Clinical psychologist/psychotherapist
Hardenberg Medical Centre
Hardenberg, The Netherlands
00 (31) 523 287878
wzwaag@ssch.nl

Meppel

B. van Twillert, MA., Health psychologist
Diaconessenhuis
Meppel (Medical Centre), Department of
Psychology and Psychotherapy
Meppel, The Netherlands
00 (31) 522 233354
twillert@diacmeppel.nl

Zwolle

Institute for Neurofeedback (private practice)
Zwolle, The Netherlands
00 (31) 38 4232337
twillert@diacmeppel.nl

NEW ZEALAND

Wellington

Jan Bowers, B.A.(psyc/educ), NZRN, MNZAC,
Nat. Reg. Neurofeedback Providers (USA)
Audra Centre Associates
Level 6, 75 Ghuznee Street
Wellington 6001 New Zealand
011-64-4-801-6610
JanBowers@xtra.co.nz

NORWAY

Oslo

Øystein Larsen
Ungplan as.
Gjerdrumsvel 12 a-f
0486 Oslo
Norway
23008530; fax 23008531
oystein@ungplan.no
www.ungplan.no

Treningssenter i Oslo:
Ungplan as.
Gjerdrumsvei 12 A-F
0486 Oslo
47 23008530; fax 47 23008531

Treningssenter i Sandefjord:
Ungplan as.
Museumsgaten 47,
3210 Sandefjord
47 33429910; fax 47 33429911

Treningssenter i Skien
Ungplan Telemark
Blekebakkveien 3
3725 Skien
47 35913880; fax 47 35913899

Treningssenter i Arendal:
Ungplan Sørlandet
Havnegata 2
4836 Arendal
47 37027591; fax 47 37027955

Toensberg

Medicus as
Arne Tveten, M.D., Psychiatrist;
Mette Hesby, R.N., Psychiatric Nurse
Moellegt. 8, 3111
Toensberg, Norway
47 33 31 37 80; fax 47 33 31 37 28
medicus@c2i.net

Ulvik

Ulvik Neurofeedback Center
Geir Flatabo, M.D.
P.O. Box 88
N-5731 Ulvik, br
Norway
47 5652 6504; fax: 47 5652 6566

SINGAPORE

Kenneth Kang, Ph.D.
Spectrum Learning Pte Ltd.
583 Orchard Road, #16-01/17-01 Forum
Singapore 238884
65-834-9476; fax 65-733-1416
kanghh@merlion.singnet.com.sg

Prof. Yu Wei Shin, Ph.D.
Nanyang Technological
University School of MPE. NTU, Nanyang Ave.
Singapore 639798
65 7905519; fax 65 7757735
mwsyu@ntu.edu.sg

SPAIN

Madrid

Ana Diez-Bolanos, Psy.D.

EEG-Biofeedback Services
Travesia Santa Maria de la Cabeza, n.5, 1
28220 Majadahonda—Madrid—Spain
011 34 916 388 973
anadiez@eegspain.com
www.eegspain.com

Santander

Ana Diez-Bolanos, Psy.D.
Centro de Neuropsicologia Cibernetica
Isabel II n 10, 2, Izda.
39002 Santander, Spain
011 34 942 364 241; fax 011 34 942 364 530
anadiez@retemail.es
empresas.mundivia.es/braincenter/ana1.html

Sevilla

Luise Jaki, M.S.
Valparaiso 21, B-3 Pl.4
E-41013 Sevilla, Spain
011 34 95 4232 872
lujaki@teleline.es
http://providers.eegspectrum.com/Intl/LuiseF.Jaki

SWITZERLAND

Chur

Dr. Andreas Müller
Schulpsychologischer Dienst GR
Quaderstrasse 15
Chur, Switzerland, 7000
0041 81 257 27 42; fax 0041 81 257 21 93
andreas.mueller@spd.gr.ch

Zurich

John Styffe
Focus Fitness
Weberstrasse 8 8800
Thalwil, Switzerland
41 1 722 18 28
jstyffe@dplanet.ch

Dipl. Psych. Maximilian Teicher
Praxis fuer Integrative Psychoterapie
Neurofeedback und Biofeedback
Limmatquai 70
CH-8001 Zurich
41 1 262 85 85
bioneuro@cs.com

UNITED KINGDOM

St. Albans

Surinder Kaur
EEG Neurofeedback Services
Dolphin Lodge Dolphin Yard
Holywell Hill
St. Albans, Herts
AL11EZ UK
01 727 839533

Cambridgeshire

Beverly Steffert
Dyslexia Associates
35 Madingley Road
Cambridgeshire, England CB3 0EL
01144 (0) 1223 528755
DrSTEFFERT@aol.com

VENEZUELA

Caracas

Alvaro Villegas, M.D.; Kenya Correa, M.D.; Jaime
Paez, M.D.
Clinica Santa Maria
Av. Aristides Calvani No. 10 Qta.
Santa Maria-Los Chorros
Caracas, Venezuela 1071
212-2322421; fax 212-2375125
Alvaro Villegas villegasa@cantv.net
Kenya Correa kenyacorre@cantv.net
Jaime Paez jaime1402@cantv.net

Humana

Dr. Pedro Delgado, Psychiatrist;
Maria Delgado
Caracas, Venezuela
58 212 5500425/0829; fax 58 212 550 2713
humana@eldish.net

Centro Clinico Professional Caracas
Sarita Kramer, Clinical Psychologist
Ave Panteon
San Bernardino
Conultorio 412
Caracas- Venezuela
(58-2) 5742975; fax 5742975
saritakramer@compuserve.com
www.neurospa.com

Appendix B

Hidden Sources of MSG

This list is taken from Dr. Blaylock's excellent book, *Exictotoxins* (Santa Fe: Health Press; 1997).

Additives containing MSG:

monosodium glutamate
hydrolyzed vegetable protein
hydrolyzed protein
hydrolyzed plant protein
plant protein extract
sodium caseinate
calcium caseinate
yeast extract
textured protein
autolyzed yeast
hydrolyzed oat flour

Additives that frequently contain MSG:

malt extract
malt flavoring
bouillon
broth
stock
flavoring
natural flavoring
natural beef or chicken flavoring
seasoning
spices

The Hill-Castro Checklist

There are different score totals for each category of symptoms. This is because different categories have varying numbers of associated symptoms. To limit the symptom list to a pre-selected number of symptoms would limit the scope and perspective of the checklist. That is another reason we went to a percentage score rather than having a different cut-off score for each category.

VI - Aggressive/Sadistic Behavior

	not present 0	very mild 1	mild 2	moderate 3	severe 4	very severe 5
Bullies, threatens or intimidates others						
Often initiates fights						
Has used a weapon that could harm others						
Has been physically cruel to others						
Has been physically cruel to animals						
Has stolen while confronting victim						
Has forced someone into sexual activity						
Deliberate fire setting						
Broken into the property of others						
Lies to obtain goods or favors						
Stolen without confronting victim						
Does not respect anyone						
Bosses others around						
Makes derogatory remarks about others						
Seems to enjoy being in trouble "a hero"						
Delights in failure of others						
Pushes or shoves others						
Cheats at games						
Preoccupied with death, guns, killing						
TOTAL						

95 = ___%

VII - Tic Disorders

Motor Tics (sudden jerky type motions)

	not present 0	very mild 1	mild 2	moderate 3	severe 4	very severe 5
Facial tic: eye blinking, eye rolls, squinting, grimacing, lip licking, biting tongue, grinding teeth						
Head and neck: hair out of the eyes, neck jerking, tossing head around, shoulder shrugging						
Arms and hands: Flailing arms, extending arms, biting nails, finger signs, flexing fingers, picking skin, popping knuckles						
Diaphragm: unusual inhale, exhale, gasping for breath						
Legs: Kicking, hopping, skipping, jumping, bending, stooping, stepping backward						
Feet: tapping, shaking, toe curling, tripping, turning feet						
Others: blowing, smelling, twirling hair, jerking, kissing, hitting self, chewing, scratching, shivering, pulling						

Vocal Tics

	not present 0	very mild 1	mild 2	moderate 3	severe 4	very severe 5
Throat clearing, coughing						
Grunting, snorting, animal noises						
Yelling, screaming						
Sniffing, burping						
Barking, honking						
Motor or jet noise						
Spitting						
Squeaking, "huh"						
Humming						
Stuttering						
Deep breathing, sucking breath in						
Repetitive cursing, "fu", "sh"						
TOTAL						

95 = ___%

VIII - Depression

	not present 0	very mild 1	mild 2	moderate 3	severe 4	very severe 5
Seems sad, does not smile very much						
Seems unusually quiet						
Poor sense of humor						
Grouchy, irritable						
Sullen						
Looks flat						
Withdrawal from family/activities						
Tearful						
Frequently seems lonely						
Moodiness, unpredictable mood swings						
A loner, withdrawn						
Depressed						
No interest						
Problems with sleep						
Thinks about death or dying						
Suicidal						
TOTAL						

80 = ___%

IX - Anxiety

	not present 0	very mild 1	mild 2	moderate 3	severe 4	very severe 5
Panic attack type symptoms						
Frequently nervous						
Often upset						
Is fearful of many things						
Fearful of being alone						
Fearful of a specific object						
Jumpy, hypervigilance						
Timid						
Worries excessively						
Persistent thoughts						
Repetitive behaviors (hand washing, counting)						
Exaggerated startled response						
Shaking, trembling						
Tearful						
Fear of death or dying						
Tense muscles						
Always on edge						
TOTAL						

85 = ___%

X - Low Self-Esteem

	not present 0	very mild 1	mild 2	moderate 3	severe 4	very severe 5
Doesn't trust self						
Frequently puts self down						
Refuses to try new things						
Poor performance even when they have the ability						
Always takes a back-seat position						
Timid and reserved						
Often shy around others						
Trouble answering questions in front of others						
Sees the worst in self						
Hangs around with less capable friends						
Easily embarrassed						
Seems satisfied with poor school performance						
Does not compete with others						
Gives up easily						
Shows no self confidence						
TOTAL						

75 = ___%

XI - Sleep

	not present 0	very mild 1	mild 2	moderate 3	severe 4	very severe 5
Difficulty going to bed						
Difficulty going to sleep						
Wakes up frequently						
Early awakening						
Restless sleep						
Talking in sleep						
Walking in sleep						
Wakes up in terror						
Restless legs						
Bed wetting or soiling						
Nightmares						
TOTAL						

55 = ___%

XII - Developmental & Learning Disorder(s)

	not present 0	very mild 1	mild 2	moderate 3	severe 4	very severe 5
Mental Retardation						
Reading Disorder						
Mathematics Disorder						
Disorder of Written Expression						
Developmental Coordination Disorder						
Expressive Language Disorder						
Mixed Receptive/Expressive Language Disorder						
Phonological Disorder (articulation)						
Stuttering						
Autistic Disorder						
Retts Disorder						
Childhood Disintegrative Disorder						
Aspergers Disorder						

(List any learning disorders on the front)

I - Attention Deficit

	not present 0	very mild 1	mild 2	moderate 3	severe 4	very severe 5
Does not seem to listen when spoken to						
Makes careless errors in schoolwork						
Avoids or dislikes tasks requiring sustained attention						
Short attention span						
Disorganized						
Loses things						
Trouble keeping up with personal property						
Easily distracted						
Forgetful in daily activity						
Difficulty completing tasks						
Gets bored easily						
Stares into space/daydreaming						
Low energy, sluggish or drowsy						
Apathetic or unmotivated						
Frequently switches from one activity to another						
Trouble concentrating						
Falls asleep doing work						
Failure to hand in work						
Trouble doing homework						
Trouble following directions						
Excited in the beginning but doesn't finish						
Difficulty learning						
TOTAL						

110 = ___%

II - Hyperactivity

	not present 0	very mild 1	mild 2	moderate 3	severe 4	very severe 5
Fidgets with hands and feet						
Squirms in seat						
Frequently leaves seat inappropriately						
Runs, climbs or moves excessively						
Difficulty working or playing quietly						
On the go						
Driven						
Talks excessively						
Can't sustain eye contact						
Needs a lot of supervision						
Pays attention to everything						
Frequently "rocks"						
Excitability						
Lacks patience						
In trouble frequently						
Restless						
TOTAL						

80 = ___%

III - Impulsivity

	not present 0	very mild 1	mild 2	moderate 3	severe 4	very severe 5
Cannot see consequences of behavior						
Blurts out answers or comments						
Difficulty waiting turn						
Frequently interrupts						
Butts into others' conversations						
Engages in physically dangerous activity						
Acts before thinking						
Frequently takes risks						
Takes all dares						
Frustrated easily						
TOTAL						

50 = ___%

IV - Immaturity

	not present 0	very mild 1	mild 2	moderate 3	severe 4	very severe 5
Delayed physical development						
Prefers to play with younger children						
Plays with toys below age level						
Behavior resembles younger children						
Immature responses to situations						
Talks "baby talk"						
Whining and clinging like younger person						
Inappropriately messy						
Difficulty understanding age appropriate directions						
TOTAL						

45 = ___%

V - Oppositional Behavioral

	not present 0	very mild 1	mild 2	moderate 3	severe 4	very severe 5
Oppositional and disrespectful toward authority						
Often loses temper						
Argumentative						
Often defies rules						
Frequently refuses adult request						
Deliberately does things that annoy others						
Blames others for his mistakes or behavior						
Touchy or easily annoyed by others						
Angry and resentful						
Spiteful or vindictive						
Swears or uses obscene language						
Shows provocative behavior						
Shows excessive stubbornness						
Lies frequently						
Must have his own way						
Plays tricks on or teases others						
Doesn't keep promises						
Resists being disciplined						
Cannot take teasing						
Refuses to take suggestions						
Has an *I don't care* attitude						
Runs away from home						
Often truant from school						
Stays out all night against parents rules						
TOTAL						

120 = ___%

Child/Adolescent Version

Name _____

Date _____ Age _____

Rater _____

I.	Attention deficit	____%
II.	Hyperactivity	____%
III.	Impulsivity	____%
IV.	Immaturity	____%
V.	Oppositional Behavior	____%
VI.	Aggressive/Sadistic Behavior	____%
VII.	Tic Disorders	____%
VIII.	Depression	____%
IX.	Anxiety	____%
X.	Low Self-Esteem	____%
XI.	Sleep	____%
XII.	Developmental & Learning Disorders	____%
	Total	____%

VI - Aggressive/Sadistic Behavior

	not present 0	very mild 1	mild 2	moderate 3	severe 4	very severe 5
Bullies, threatens or intimidates others						
Often initiates fights						
Has used a weapon that could harm others						
Has been physically cruel to others						
Has been physically cruel to animals						
Has stolen while confronting victim						
Has forced someone into sexual activity						
Deliberate fire setting						
Broken into the property of others						
Lies to obtain goods or favors						
Stolen without confronting victim						
Does not respect anyone						
Bosses others around						
Makes derogatory remarks about others						
Seems to enjoy being in trouble *a hero*						
Delights in failure of others						
Pushes or shoves others						
Cheats at games						
Preoccupied with death, guns, killing						
TOTAL						

95 = ____%

VII - Tic Disorders

Motor Tics (sudden jerky type motions)

	not present 0	very mild 1	mild 2	moderate 3	severe 4	very severe 5
Facial tic: eye blinking, eye rolls, squinting, grimacing, lip licking, biting tongue, grinding teeth						
Head and neck: hair out of the eyes, neck jerking, tossing head around, shoulder shrugging						
Arms and hands: Flailing arms, extending arms, biting nails, finger signs, flexing fingers, picking skin, popping knuckles						
Diaphragm: unusual inhale, exhale, gasping for breath						
Legs: Kicking, hopping, skipping, jumping, bending, stooping, stepping backward						
Feet: tapping, shaking, toe curling, tripping, turning feet						
Others: blowing, smelling, twirling hair, jerking, kissing, hitting self, chewing, scratching, shivering, pulling						

Vocal Tics

	not present 0	very mild 1	mild 2	moderate 3	severe 4	very severe 5
Throat clearing, coughing						
Grunting, snorting, animal noises						
Yelling, screaming						
Sniffing, burping						
Barking, honking						
Motor or jet noise						
Spitting						
Squeaking, "huh"						
Humming						
Stuttering						
Deep breathing, sucking breath in						
Repetitive cursing, "fu", "sh"						
TOTAL						

95 = ____%

VIII - Depression

	not present 0	very mild 1	mild 2	moderate 3	severe 4	very severe 5
Seems sad, does not smile very much						
Seems unusually quiet						
Poor sense of humor						
Grouchy, irritable						
Sullen						
Looks flat						
Withdrawal from family/activities						
Tearful						
Frequently seems lonely						
Moodiness, unpredictable moodswings						
A loner, withdrawn						
Depressed						
No interest						
Problems with sleep						
Thinks about death or dying						
Suicidal						
TOTAL						

80 = ____%

IX - Anxiety

	not present 0	very mild 1	mild 2	moderate 3	severe 4	very severe 5
Panic attack type symptoms						
Frequently nervous						
Often upset						
Generally fearful						
Fearful of losing control						
Fearful of a specific object or event						
Jumpy, hypervigilance						
Timid						
Worries excessively						
Persistent thoughts						
Repetitive behaviors (hand washing, counting)						
Exaggerated startled response						
Shaking, trembling						
Tearful						
Fear of death or dying						
Tense muscles						
Always on edge						
TOTAL						

85 = ____%

X - Low Self-Esteem

	not present 0	very mild 1	mild 2	moderate 3	severe 4	very severe 5
Doesn't trust self						
Frequently puts self down						
Refuses to try new things						
Poor performance even when they have the ability						
Always takes a back-seat position						
Timid and reserved						
Often shy around others						
Trouble answering questions in front of others						
Sees the worst in self						
Hangs around with less capable friends						
Easily embarrassed						
Seems satisfied with poor performance						
Does not compete with others						
Gives up easily/expects failure						
Shows no self confidence						
TOTAL						

75 = ____%

XI - Sleep

	not present 0	very mild 1	mild 2	moderate 3	severe 4	very severe 5
Difficulty going to bed						
Difficulty going to sleep						
Wakes up frequently						
Early awakening						
Restless sleep						
Talking in sleep						
Walking in sleep						
Wakes up in terror						
Restless legs						
Night sweats/Hot flashes						
Nightmares						
TOTAL						

55 = ____%

XII - Other
(List on front page)

	not present 0	very mild 1	mild 2	moderate 3	severe 4	very severe 5
Mental Retardation						
Learning Disorder (list type)						
Studdering						
Autistic Disorder						
Allergies						
Chemical Sensitivity						
Addiction(s) (list)						
Anorexia (nervosa)						
Bulimia (nervosa)						
Stroke						
Seizure Disorder						
Head Injury						
Migraine Headaches						
Tension Headaches						
PMS						
Menopause						
Other:						

I - Attention Deficit

	not present 0	very mild 1	mild 2	moderate 3	severe 4	very severe 5
Does not seem to listen when spoken to						
Makes careless errors						
Avoids or dislikes tasks requiring sustained attention						
Short attention span						
Disorganized						
Loses things						
Procrastinates						
Easily distracted						
Forgetful in daily activity						
Difficulty completing tasks						
Gets bored easily						
Stares into space/daydreaming						
Low energy, sluggish or drowsy						
Apathetic or unmotivated						
Frequently switches from one activity to another						
Trouble concentrating						
Falls asleep doing work						
Failure to meet deadlines						
Underachiever						
Trouble following directions						
Excited in the beginning but doesn't finish						
Difficulty learning/remembering						
Works best under deadlines/pressure						
TOTAL						

$\overline{115}$ = ____%

II - Hyperactivity

	not present 0	very mild 1	mild 2	moderate 3	severe 4	very severe 5
Fidgets with hands and feet						
Squirms in seat						
Frequently leaves seat inappropriately						
Moves excessively						
Difficulty working quietly						
On the go						
Driven						
Talks excessively						
Can't sustain eye contact						
Needs a lot of supervision						
Pays attention to everything						
Frequently "rocks"						
Excitability						
Lacks patience						
In trouble frequently						
Restless						
TOTAL						

$\overline{80}$ = ____%

III - Impulsivity

	not present 0	very mild 1	mild 2	moderate 3	severe 4	very severe 5
Cannot see consequences of behavior						
Blurts out comments						
Difficulty waiting turn						
Frequently interrupts						
Butts into others' conversation						
Engages in physically dangerous activity						
Acts before thinking						
Frequently takes risks						
Takes all dares						
Frustrated easily						
TOTAL						

$\overline{50}$ = ____%

IV - Immaturity

	not present 0	very mild 1	mild 2	moderate 3	severe 4	very severe 5
Delayed physical development						
Prefers to be with younger people						
Buys "things" below age level						
Behavior resembles a younger age						
Immature responses to situations						
Talks "silly"						
Whining and clinging						
Inappropriately messy						
Difficulty accepting responsibility						
TOTAL						

$\overline{45}$ = ____%

V - Oppositional Behavioral

	not present 0	very mild 1	mild 2	moderate 3	severe 4	very severe 5
Oppositional and disrespectful toward authority						
Often loses temper						
Argumentative						
Often defies rules						
Frequently refuses request						
Deliberately does things that annoy others						
Blames others for his mistakes or behavior						
Touchy or easily annoyed by others						
Angry and resentful						
Spiteful or vindictive						
Swears or uses obscene language						
Shows provocative behavior						
Shows excessive stubbornness						
Lies frequently						
Must have his own way						
Plays tricks on or teases others						
Doesn't keep promises						
Resists being disciplined						
Cannot take teasing						
Refuses to take suggestions						
Has an "I don't care" attitude						
Doesn't come home on time						
Often absent from work						
Frequent trouble at work						
Can't hold a job						
TOTAL						

$\overline{125}$ = ____%

Adult Version

Name _____

Date_____Age_____

Rater_____

I.	Attention deficit	____%
II.	Hyperactivity	____%
III.	Impulsivity	____%
IV.	Immaturity	____%
V.	Oppositional Behavior	____%
VI.	Aggressive/Sadistic Behavior	____%
VII.	Tic Disorders	____%
VIII.	Depression	____%
IX.	Anxiety	____%
X.	Low Self-Esteem	____%
XI.	Sleep	____%
XII.	Other	____%
	Total	____%

Appendix D

The Feingold Association of the United States List of Food Additives

---

Additives to avoid:

tartrazine (yellow 5)
quinoline yellow
yellow 2G
sunset yellow FCF
cochineal, carminic acid
carmoisine (red)
amaranth (red no.2)
ponceau (red no.4)
erythrosine (red no.3)
red 2G
allura red AC (red no.40)
patent blue
indigo carmine (blue)
brilliant blue FCF

black
brown FK
chocolate brown HT
TBHQ (preservative, may also be listed as "antioxidant")
BHA (preservative, may also be listed as "antioxidant")
BHT (preservative, may also be listed as "antioxidant")
sulphites (sulfites)
nitrites
adipic acid (often included in "flavoring")
MSG

Additives that do not cause problems for most people:

curcuma or tumeric
riboflavin (vitamin B2)
chlorophyll
caramel
carotene
annatto
betanin
calcium carbonate
titanium dioxide
iron oxide
sorbic acid and sorbates
acetic acid
lactic acid
propionic acid
sodium proprionate
calcium propionate
potassium propionate
carbon dioxide
ascorbic acid (vitamin C) and salts of ascorbic acid
tocopherols (vitamin E)
lecithin
lactates (unless lactose intolerant)

citric acid
sodium citrate
potassium citrate
calcium citrate
tartaric acid
sodium tartrate
potassium citrate
potassium bitartrate (cream of tartar)
niacin (vitamin B3)
alginic acid and alginates
carrageenan
carob-bean flour
tamarind-seed flour
guar gum
xanthan gum
sorbitol
mannitol
pectin
galatine
powdered cellulose
sodium caseinate (avoid if milk-sensitive)
calcium silicate
stearic acid

Much more information may be obtained by contacting the Feingold Association web site at www.feingold.org

Appendix E

Laboratory Testing for Heavy Metals

We use the King James Medical Laboratory for DMSA challenge testing and for hair analysis screening:

The King James Medical Laboratory, Inc.
24700 Center Ridge Road
Cleveland, Ohio 44145
800-437-1404; fax 440-835-2177
www.kingjamesomegatech-lab.com

Appendix F

Nutritional Recommendations

Vitamins and Minerals

Stephen J. Schoenthaler, M.D., has done extensive research on the effects of simple, low-cost vitamin-mineral supplementation on the intelligence, academic performance, and behavior of schoolchildren.

The following is a formulation he used in a study that resulted in an average IQ increase of 3.7 points in a group of approximately 150 schoolchildren for twelve weeks. For those of you familiar with vitamin-mineral supplementation, you will note these amounts are surprisingly modest—none are above the very conservative U.S. Recommended Daily Allowances (RDA).

vitamin A	5000IU
vitamin B1 (thiamine)	1.7mg
vitamin B2 (riboflavin)	1.7mg
vitamin B3 (niacin)	20mg
vitamin B5 (pantothenate)	10mg
vitamin B6 (pyridoxine)	2mg
vitamin B12	6mcg
vitamin C	60mg
vitamin D	400IU
vitamin E	15IU
vitamin K	50mcg
biotin	300mcg
folic acid	400mcg

calcium	200mcg
chromium	100mcg
copper	1mg
iodine	150mcg
iron	9mg
magnesium	80mg
manganese	2.5mg
molybdenum	250mcg
selenium	100mcg
zinc	15mg

Protein

Peter W. Lemon of Kent State University is perhaps the foremost nutritional researcher of protein requirement, especially in athletes. He notes that the current RDA for protein was calculated for sedentary individuals. Athletes commonly require approximately double the RDA. Children and adolescents are obviously more likely to have requirements more similar to athletes than to sedentary adults.

A relatively simple estimate, based on Peter Lemon's work is for children to eat at least 0.5 grams of protein per pound of body weight.

Essential Fatty Acids

Fish oils and flax seed oil are the best sources for supplementing omega-3 fatty acids. Other sources with omega-3 have too much omega-6 content to improve the ratio between omega-3 and omega-6 fatty acids.

There are numerous products containing fish liver and flax seed oils. Fish oils may have contaminants or a high percentage of oxidized fats. For cost per unit dose, and considering the stringent production requirements of omega-3 fatty acids, we use Dale Alexander's emulsified Norwegian cod liver oil. Since the oil is dispersed in water, it is creamy rather than oily, and has a natural orange or mint flavor that adequately masks the taste for most people. Three teaspoons per day are adequate for most older children and adults. Pregnant or lactating women would benefit from one tablespoon per day.

If the taste of this cod liver oil is unacceptable, we recommend a similar amount of flax seed oil.

The omega-3 products from AMNI and Douglas Laboratories have high quality omega-3 capsules. Make sure you are getting 500mg of DHA; pregnant and lactating women aim for 1,000mg of DHA per day.

Appendix G

Glycemic Index

The glycemic index of a food approximates how rapidly that food will be broken down to sugar and absorbed into the bloodstream. The higher the number, the more rapidly that food will increase glucose levels in the blood. A glycemic index above 80 is relatively undesirable. Those below 60 are more desirable for keeping blood glucose and insulin levels in a more favorable range.

maltodextrin	150	croissant	96	orange juice	74
dates	146	rye crisps	93	carrots	70
glucose	137	couscous	93	baked beans	69
russet baked potato	134	macaroni and cheese	92	peas	68
puffed rice	132	sucrose (table sugar)	92	grapes	66
gluten-free wheat bread	129	beets	91	lactose	65
corn flakes	119	raisins	91	sweet potatoes	63
microwaved potato	117	muffins	88	orange	63
pretzels	116	ice cream	87	peach	60
vanilla wafers	110	pizza	86	apple juice	58
waffles	109	white rice	83	pinto beans	55
doughnuts	108	honey	83	plum	55
French fries	107	pita	82	tomato soup	54
graham crackers	106	popcorn	79	pear	53
mashed potatoes	104	fruit cocktail	79	plain yogurt	51
bagel	103	brown rice	79	garbanzo beans	47
white bread	100	spaghetti	78	skim milk	46
wheat biscuits	100	corn	78	soy milk	43
cream of wheat	100	oat bran	78	milk	39
shredded wheat	99	banana	77	grapefruit	36
cornmeal	98	pound cake	77	fructose	32
whole wheat bread	97	kiwi	75	cherries	32
taco shells	97	kidney beans	74		

QEEG and Continuous Performance Tests

Quantitative Electroencephalography

The quantitative electroencephalograph, qEEG, measures the electrical activity of the brain. Small electrodes placed on the surface of the scalp, often nineteen in number, read the tiny voltages produced by brain activity. These signals are amplified and digitally analyzed, then interpreted in a spectral display—color-coded brain maps. The brain maps provide information about the brain wave activity on various sites on the head. The most useful information comes from comparing the brain wave activity of the patient to a large database to see if and how the patient's brain waves vary from the norm. The computer analysis is able to provide information about all the brain wave bands—delta, theta, alpha, and beta—simultaneously and individually.

The qEEG is able not only to aid significantly in the diagnostic process, but to inform and guide the decision-making process for neurofeedback treatment. For example, a child with ADD may show a characteristic increase in slow brain wave activity in the theta range (4Hx-8Hz) in the frontal areas of the brain. Another child may have a normal qEEG while sitting quietly, but show an inappropriate increase in theta while performing a math calculation, rather than the expected increase in the faster beta frequencies (12Hz-60Hz +). A child may reveal an abnormality that is a relatively less common finding in ADD—excessive coherence of alpha (8Hz-

12Hz) on both sides of the brain, for example. A treatment protocol that trains the brain to decrease the coherence may produce progress that would otherwise be difficult if only the standard protocols were used.

Some clinicians use qEEG on each patient they treat; others obtain a qEEG on the patient only if there is inadequate progress with neurofeedback treatment. Both approaches are sound. It appears that at least 60 percent of patients with ADD respond well to the usual neurofeedback protocols without the need for the more sophisticated evaluation qEEG provides.

Continuous Performance Testing

Many clinicians refer a patient with suspected ADD to a licensed psychologist for a full battery of psychological testing. Traditional psychological testing evaluates a wide range of psychological functions, and it can reveal whether the patient's behavior is consistent with ADD. Such testing, however, does not specifically measure attention. Although these tests may be useful for determining if there is significant depression, anxiety disorder, or learning disability that may accompany ADD, their usefulness in actually making the diagnosis of ADD is limited.

The psychological testing instrument that specifically measures attention is the continuous performance test. This computer-based testing accurately measures attention and assesses multiple components of attention. Specifically testing attention, when considering a diagnosis of *attention* deficit disorder, is indispensable for both diagnosing and later for tracking treatment progress, if in fact ADD is present.

Continuous performance testing takes between fourteen and twenty-two minutes to administer, and the computer analysis is available shortly after the completion of the test. Parameters measured include the speed of responses, accuracy, and the types of errors committed. Scores are compared to a large database to determine how the patient's scores compare to a reference group.

The results of continuous performance testing provide information on how a patient's attention compares to a group that is the same age and sex as the patient. Problems with attention are classified as to whether errors are due more to impulsivity or to daydreaming, or to both. Types and quantities of errors and response time can also shed light on the presence of conduct disorder or neurological impairment.

There are three continuous performance test instruments that are worthwhile at this time: the Test of Variables of Attention (TOVA), the Integrated Visual and Auditory Continuous Performance Test (IVA), and Connors' Continuous Performance Test, not to be confused with Connors' Checklist.

Although all three instruments are useful, we prefer the TOVA. The TOVA is longer, is simpler, has excellent timing precision ($\pm$ 1msec), and has the largest reference database with which to compare the patient's scores. These features enhance a clinician's ability to pick up subtler evidence of inattention. The length of the test lends itself to standardization of data over four quadrants, which gives information about a person's flow of attention, information not available from shorter tests. It is non-language based, uses auditory and visual signals in separate tests, and uses midline stimuli, not right-to-left. These features help elucidate information about the function of attention without uncertainty as to whether other functions, such as memory, may be playing a role in the patient's performance on the test.

References

Chapter 1

1. The American Psychiatric Association, *Diagnostic and Statistical Manual of Mental Disorders. 4th Ed* (Washington, DC: The American Psychiatric Association, 1994).

2. J. H. Satterfield, M. E. Dawson, "Electrodermal correlates of hyperactivity in children." *Psychophysiology,* 1971;8:191-197.

3. J. H. Satterfield, et al., "EEG aspects in the diagnosis and treatment of minimal brain dysfunction." *Annals of New York Academy of Science,* 1973;205:274-282.

4. L. S. Budd. *The Active Alerter Newsletter,* (St. Paul, Minnesota). (To order: *Active Alerter* Subscription, c/o Linda Budd, Ph.D., 2301 Como Ave., Suite 204, St. Paul, MN 55108.)

Chapter 2

1. R. T. Brown, K. A. Borden, "Hyperactivity at adolescence: Some misconceptions and new directions." *Journal of Clinical Child Psychology,* 1986;15:194-209.

2. R. Gittelman, et al., "Hyperactive boys almost grown up." *Archives of General Psychiatry,* 1985;42:937-947.

3. G. Weiss, L. Hechtman, *Hyperactive Children Grow Up.* (New York: Guilford Press, 1986).

4. D. Comings, "The genetics of addictive behaviors: The role of childhood behavioral disorders." *Addiction and Recovery,* November/December 1991.

5. A. I. Alterman, R. E. Tarter, "The transmission of psychological vulnerability: Implications for alcoholism etiology." *Journal of Nervous Mental Disorders,* 1983;171:147-154.

6. E. G. Peniston, P. J. Kulkosky, "Alpha-theta brainwave training and beta endorphine levels in alcoholics." *Alcoholism: Clinical and Experimental,* 1989;13:271-279.

7. E. G. Peniston, P. J. Kulkosky, "Alcoholic personality and alpha-theta brainwave training." *Medical Psychotherapy: An International Journal,* 1990;3:37-55.

8. ———, "Alpha-theta brainwave neurofeedback therapy for Vietnam veterans with combat-related post-traumatic stress disorder." *Medical Psychotherapy: An International Journal,* 1991;4:47-60.

9. D. Miller, K. Blum, *Overload.* (Kansas City, Missouri: Andrews and McMeel, 1997).

Chapter 3

1. G. F. Still, "Some abnormal psychological conditions in children." *Lancet,* 1902;1(2):1008-1012.

2. M. Rutter, "Syndromes attributed to 'minimal brain dysfunction' in childhood." *American Journal of Psychiatry,* 1982;139:21-33.

3. J. S. Miller, "Hyperactive children: a ten-year study." *Pediatrics,* 1978;61:217-222.

4. J. S. Schmitt, "The minimal brain dysfunction myth." *American Journal of Diseases of Children,* 1975;129:1313-1318.

5. B. Feingold, *Why Your Child Is Hyperactive,* (New York: Random House, 1975).

6. D. Cantwell, *The Hyperactive Child: Diagnosis, Management, Current Research,* (New York: Random House, 1975).

7. J Biederman, et al., "High rates of affective disorders in probands with attention deficit disorders and in their relatives. A controlled family study." *American Journal of Psychiatry,* 1987;144:330-333.

8. J. R. Morrison, M. A. Stewart, "A family study of the hyperactive child syndrome." *Biological Psychiatry,* 1971;3:189-195.

9. R. Goodman, J. Stevenson, "A twin study of hyperactivity: II. The aetiological role of genes, family relationships, and perinatal adversity." *Journal of Child Psychology and Psychiatry,* 1989;30:691-709.

10. D. E. Comings, *Tourette's Syndrome and Human Behavior,* (Duarte, California: Hope Press, 1995).

11. L. B. Hohman, "Post-encephalitic behavior in children." *Johns Hopkins Hospital Bulletin,* 1922;33:372-375.

12. C. S. Hartsough, N. M. Lambert, "Medical factors in hyperactive and normal children: Prenatal, developmental, and health history findings." *American Journal of Orthopsychiatry,* 1985;55:190-210.

13. M. B. Denckla, M. LeMay, C. A. Chapman, "Few CT scan abnormalities found even in neurologically impaired learning disabled children." *Journal of Learning Disabilities,* 1985;18:132-135.

14. H. H. Jasper, P. Solomon, C. Bradley, "Electroencephalographic analysis of behavior problems in children." *American Journal of Psychiatry,* 1938;95:641-658.

15. C. Bradley, "The behavior of children receiving Benzedrine." *American Journal of Psychiatry,* 1937;94:577-585.

16. J. H. Satterfield, M. E. Dawson, "Electrodermal correlates of hyperactivity in children." *Psychophysiology,* 1971;8:191-197.

17. H. Satterfield, et al., "EEG aspects in the diagnosis and treatment of minimal brain dysfunction." *Annals of New York Academy of Science,* 1973;205:274.282.

18. M. B. Sterman, L. Friar, "Suppression of seizures in an epileptic following sensorimotor EEG feedback training." *Electroencephalograpy and Clinical Neurophysiology,* 1972;33:89-95.

19. M. B. Sterman, L. R. MacDonald, R. K. Stone "Biofeedback training of the sensorimotor EEG rhythm in man: Effect on epilepsy." *Epilepsia,* 1974;15:395-416.

20. M. B. Sterman, "Effects of sensorimotor EEG feedback training on sleep and clinical manifestations of epilepsy." in J. Beatty, H. Legewie, eds. *Biofeedback and Behavior,* (New York: Plenum Press, 1976:167-200).

21. ———, "Sensorimotor EEG operant conditioning and experimental and clinical effects." *Pavlovian Journal of Biological Science,* 1977;12(2):65-92.

22. M. B. Sterman, L. R. MacDonald. "Effects of central cortical EEG feedback training on seizures in poorly controlled epileptics." *Epilepsia,* 1978;19:207-222.

23. M. B. Sterman, "EEG biofeedback in the treatment of epilepsy: an overview circa 1980." in L. White, B. Tursky, eds. *Clinical Biofeedback: Efficacy and Mechanisms,* (New York: The Guilford Press, 1982).

24. J. F. Lubar, M. N. Shouse, "EEG and behavioral changes in a hyperactive child concurrent training of the sensorimotor rhythm. A preliminary report." *Biofeedback and Self-Regulation,* 1976;1:293-306.

25. J. O. Lubar, J. F. Lubar, "Electroencephalographic biofeedback of SMR and beta for treatment of attention deficit disorders in a clinical setting." *Biofeedback and Self-Regulation,* 1984;9(1):1-23.

26. J. O. Lubar, "Electroencephalographic biofeedback and neurological applications." in J.V. Basmajian, ed. *Biofeedback, Principles and Practice for Clinicians,* (Baltimore: Williams and Wilkins, 1989).

Chapter 4

1. J. F. Lubar, M. N. Shouse, "EEG and behavioral changes in a hyperkinetic child concurrent with training of the sensorimotor rhythm (SMR): a preliminary report." *Biofeedback and Self-Regulation,* 1976;3:293-306.

Chapter 5

1. P. S. Jensen, "A 14-month randomized clinical trial of treatment strategies for Attention-Deficit/Hyperactivity Disorder." *Archives of General Psychiatry,* 1999;56(12):1073-1086.

2. Drug Enforcement Administration, Office of Diversion Control. Conference Report. *Stimulant Use in the Treatment of ADHD,* (Washington, DC: Drug Enforcement Administration, 1996).

3. Drug Enforcement Administration, Office of Diversion Control. *Methylphenidate Review: Eight Factor Analysis,* (Washington, DC: Drug Enforcement Administration, 1995).

4. M. E. Llana, "Methylphenidate: Increased abuse of appropriate use?" *Journal of the American Pharmaceutical Association,* 1999;39(4):526-530.

5. E. Cherland, R. Fitzpatrick, "Psychotic side effects of psychostimulates: a 5-year review." *Canadian Journal of Psychiatry,* 1999;44(8):811-813.

6. J. R. Kramer, et al., "Predictors of adult height and weight in boys treated with methylphenidate for childhood behavior problems." *Journal of the American Academy of Child and Adolescent Psychiatry,* 2000;39(4):517-524.

7. JG Millichap, "Methylphenidate role in Tourette's syndrome prevalence." *Journal of the Royal Society of Medicine,* 1999;92(3):156.

8. V. Gross-Tsur, et al., "Epilepsy and attention-deficit/hyperactivity disorder: Is methylphenidate safe and effective?" *Journal of Pediatrics,* 1997;130(4):670-674.

9. C. R. Talley, ed., *American Journal of Health-System Pharmacy,* 1996;53:610.

10. V. W. Fisher, H. Barner, "Cardiac findings associated with methylphenidate." *Journal of the American Medical Association,* 1977;238:1497.

11. T. A. Henderson, V. W. Fisher, "Effects of methylphenidate on mammalian myocardial ultra-structure." *The American Journal of Cardiovascular Pathology,* 1995;5(1):68-78.

Chapter 6

1. M. B. Sterman, L. Friar, "Suppression of seizures in an epileptic following sensorimotor EEG feedback training." *Electroencephalography Clinical Neurophysiology,* 1972;33:89-95.

2. M. B. Sterman, L. R. MacDonald, R. K. Stone, "Biofeedback training of the sensorimotor EEG rhythm in man: Effect on epilepsy." *Epilepsia,* 1975;15:395-416.

3. M. B. Sterman, "Effects of sensorimotor EEG feedback training on sleep and clinical manifestations of epilepsy." in J. Beatty, H. Kegewie, eds.: *Biofeedback and Behavior,* (New York: Plenum Press; 1976:167-200).

4. ———, L. R. MacDonald, "Effects of central cortical EEG biofeedback training on seizure incidence in poorly controlled epileptics." *Epilepsia,* 1978;19:207-222.

5. ———, M. N. Shouse, "Sensorimotor mechanisms underlying a possible common pathology in epilepsy and associated sleep disturbances." in *Sleep and Epilepsy,* (New York: Academic Press, 1982).

6. ———, "EEG biofeedback in the treatment of epilepsy: an overview circa 1980." in L. White, B. Tursky, eds., *Clinical Biofeedback: Efficacy and Mechanism,* (New York: The Guilford Press; 1982).

7. J. F. Lubar, M. N. Shouse, "EEG and behavioral changes in a hyperactive child concurrent training of the sensorimotor rhythm (SMR). A preliminary report." *Biofeedback and Self-Regulation,* 1976;1:293-306.

8. J. O. Lubar, J. F. Lubar, "Electroencephalographic biofeedback of SMR and beta for treatment of attention deficit disorders in a clinical setting." *Biofeedback and Self-Regulation,* 1984;2(1):1-23.

9. M. A. Tansey, R. L. Bruner, "EMG and EEG biofeedback training in the treatment of a 10-year-old hyperactive boy with a developmental reading disorder." *Biofeedback and Self-Regulation,* 1983;8:25-37.

Chapter 7

1. S. Othmer, S. Othmer, *EEG Biofeedback Training for Hyperactivity, Attention Deficit Disorder, Specific Learning Disabilities, and Other Disorders,* 1998. (Available through EEG Spectrum, Inc., Encino, California.)

2. M. B. Sterman, "Physiological origins and functional correlates of EEG rhythmic activities: Implications for self-regulation." *Biofeedback and Self Regulation,* 1996;21(1):3-33.

3. C. A. Mann, et al., "Quantitative analysis of EEG in boys with attention-deficit/hyperactivity disorder: Controlled study with clinical implications." *Pediatric Neurology,* 1992;8(26):30-36.

4. M. B. Sterman. "Power spectral analysis of EEG characteristics during sleep in epileptics." *Epilepsia,* 1981;22:95-106.

Chapter 9

1. L. E. Spieth, et al., "A low-glycemic index diet in the treatment of pediatric obesity." *Archives of Pediatrics and Adolescent Medicine,* 2000;154(9):947-951.

2. A. H. Lichtenstein, et al., "Effects of different forms of dietary hydrogenated fats on serum lipoprotein cholesterol levels." *New England Journal of Medicine,* 1999;340(25):1933-1940.

3. J. R. Burgess, et al., "Long-chain polyunsaturated fatty acids in children with attention-deficit/hyperactivity disorder." *American Journal of Clinical Nutrition,* 2000;71(suppl. 1):S327-S330.

4. A. J. Richardson, M. A. Ross, "Fatty acid metabolism in neurodevelopmental disorder: a new perspective on associations between attention-deficit/hyperactivity disorder, dyslexia, and the autistic spectrum." *Prostaglandins Leukotrienes and Essential Fatty Acids,* 2000;63(1-2):1-9.

5. M. Xiang, et al., "Long-chain polyunsaturated fatty acids in human milk and brain growth during early infancy." *Acta Paediatrica,* 2000;89(2):142-147.

6. M. Makrides, M. A. Neumann, R. A. Gibson, "Is dietary docosahexznoic acid essential for term infants?" *Lipids,* 1996;31(1):115-119.

7. P. J. Reeds, et al., "Protein nutrition of the neonate." *The Proceedings of the Nutrition Society,* 2000;59(1):87-97.

8. S. J. Schoenthaler, et al., "The effect of vitamin-mineral supplementation on the intelligence of American schoolchildren: a randomized, double-blind placebo-controlled trial." *Journal of Alternative and Complementary Medicine,* 2000;6(1):19-29.

9. S. J. Schoenthaler, I. D. Bier, "The effect of vitamin-mineral supplementation on juvenile delinquency among American schoolchildren: a randomized, double-blind placebo-controlled trial." *Journal of Alternative and Complementary Medicine,* 2000;6(1):7-17.

10. R. M. Carlton, et al., "Rational dosages of nutrients have a prolonged effect on learning disabilities." *Alternative Therapies in Health and Medicine,* 2000;6(3):85-91.

11. W. J. Walsh, et al., *Elevated Blood Copper/Zinc Ratios in Assaultive Young Males,* Neuroscience Annual Meeting, Miami Beach, Fla. Abstract of Papers. 1994.

12. Autism Research Review. 1998;12(2):4.

13. W. Walsh, et al. "Elevated blood copper/zinc ratios in assaultive young males." *Physiology and Behavior,* 1997;62(2):327-329.

14. D. O. Kennedy, A. B. Scholey, K. A. Wesnes, "The dose-dependent cognitive effects of acute administration of *Ginkgo biloba* to healthy young volunteers." *Psychopharmacology* (Berlin), 2000;151(4):416-423.

15. M. Boris, F. S. Mandel, "Foods and additives are common causes of the attention-deficit/hyperactive disorder in children." *Annals of Allergy,* 1994;72(5):462-468.

16. T. J. Maher, R. J. Wurtman, "Possible neurologic effects of aspartame, a widely used food additive." *Environmental Health Perspectives,* 1987;75:53-57.

17. D. P. Potenza, R. S. el-Mallakh, "Aspartame: clinical update." *Connecticut Medicine,* 1989;53(7):395-400.

18. L. D. Stegink, et al., "Blood methanol concentrations in one-year-old infants administered graded doses of aspartame." *Journal of Nutrition,* 1983;113(8):1600-1606.

19. J. W. Olney, "Excitotoxins in foods." *Neurotoxicology,* 1994;15(3):535-544.

20. J. W. Daly, B. B. Fredholm, "Caffeine—an atypical drug of dependence." *Drug and Alcohol Dependence,* 1998;51(1):199-206.

21. I. D. Menzies. "Disturbed children: The role of food and chemical sensitivities." *Nutrition and Health,* 1984;3(1-2):39-54.

Chapter 10

1. H. Hu, "Exposure to metals." *Primary Care,* 2000;27(4):983-996.

2. C. F. Bearer. "Environmental health hazards: How children are different from adults." *Future of Children,* 1995;5(2):11-26.

3. U.S. Department of Health and Human Services, Public Health Service, Centers for Disease Control, *Preventing Lead Poisoning in Young Children,* (Atlanta: Centers for Disease Control, 1991).

4. Agency for Toxic Substances and Disease Registry, *Top 20 Hazardous Substances,* (Atlanta: Agency for Toxic Substances and Disease Registry, Environmental Protection Agency; 1999).

5. ———, *Toxicological Profile for Mercury,* (Atlanta: Agency for Toxic Substances and Disease Registry, Environmental Protection Agency, 1992).

6. ———, *Toxicological Profile for Cadmium,* (Atlanta: Agency for Toxic Substances and Disease Registry, Environmental Protection Agency, 1992).

7. K. Cooke, M. H. Gould. "The health effects of aluminum—a review." *Royal Society of Health Journal,* 1991;111(5):163-168.

8. Agency for Toxic Substances and Disease Registry. *Toxicological Profile for Arsenic,* (Atlanta: Agency for Toxic Substances and Disease Registry, Environmental Protection Agency; 1989).

9. Environmental Protection Agency. *Health Assessment Document for Nickel,* (Cincinnati: Environmental Criteria and Assessment Office, Office of Health and Environmental Assessment, Office of Research and Development; Publication EPA/600/8-83/012F, 1985).

10. W. G. Crook, "Ear infections, hyperactivity, and the yeast connection." *International Health Foundation Healthline,* 1989;1(1).

11. ——, "Pediatricians, antibiotics, and office practice." *Pediatrics,* 1985;76(1):139-140.

12. T. L. Perry, S. Hansen, R. G. Christie, "Amnio compounds and organic acids in CSF, plasma, and urine of autistic children." *Biological Psychiatry,* 1978;13(5):575-586.

13. W. G. Crook, "A controlled trial of nystatin for the candidiasis hypersensitivity syndrome." *New England Journal of Medicine,* 1991;324:1592-1594.

Chapter 11

1. J. Lull, ed. *World Families Watch Television,* (Newberry Park, Calif.: Sage, 1988:636).

2. J. Lippman, "Global village is characterized by a television in every home." *Grand Rapids Press;* 1992, October 25.

3. G. Gerbner, *Women and Minorities on Television: A Study in Casting and Fate,* (Report to the Screen Actors Guild and the American Federation of Radio and Television Artists). 1993.

4. ——, M. Morgan, N. Signorielli, *Television Violence Profile No. 16: The Turning Point from Research to Action,* (Philadelphia: University of Pennsylvania; 1993:636-637,640).

5. A. C. Huston, et al., *Big World, Small Screen: The Role of Television in American Society,* (Lincoln, Nebr.: University of Nebraska Press; 1992:636).

6. L. Berkowitz, "Control of aggression." in B. M. Caldwell, H. N. Ricciuti, eds. *Review of Child Development Research (Vol,III), Child Development and Social Policy,* (Chicago: University of Chicago Press; 1973).

7. A. Bandura, D. M. Ross, S. A. Ross, "Imitation of film-mediated aggressive models." *Journal of Abnormal and Social Psychology,* 1963;66:3-11.

8. A. C. Nielsen Company, *Nielsen Report on Television 1990,* (Northbrook, Ill.: Nielsen Media Research, 1990).

9. Peter D. Hart Research Associates. "Would you give up TV for a million bucks?" *TV Guide,* 1992;(40:41):10-17.

10. B. S. Centerwall, "Exposure to television a risk factor for violence." *American Journal of Epidemiology,* 1989;129:636.

11. K. Moody, *Growing up on Television,* (New York: Times Books; 1980).

12. J. Mander, *Four Arguments for the Elimination of Television,* (New York: Morrow Quill; 1978).

13. E. Olsen, "Fit kids, smart kids—new research confirms that exercise boosts brainpower." *Parents Magazine,* October 1994; 33-35.

14. J. M. Healy, *Endangered Minds,* (New York: Touchstone; 1990).

15. J. Beentjes, T. Van der Voort, "Television's impact on children's reading skills: a review of research." *Reading Research Quarterly,* 1988;23(4):389-413.

16. D. Coleman, "Infants under 2 seem to learn from TV." *The New York Times,* November 22, 1988.

17. F. Emery, M. Emery, *A Choice of Futures: To Enlighten or Inform?* (Canberra: Center for Continuing Education, Australian National University; 1975).

18. A. Luria, *Language and Cognition,* (New York: Wiley; 1982).

19. P. T. Rankin, "The importance of listening ability." in *English Journal,* Nov. 1981:623-630.

20. Inter-University Consortium for Political and Social Research. *American's Use of Time Project,* (Ann Arbor, Mich.: Inter-University Consortium for Political and Social Research; 1993).

21. I. Rosenfield, *The Invention of Memory,* (New York: Basic Books, 1988).

22. J. C. Pierce, *Evolution's End,* (New York: HarperCollins, 1992).

23. K. A. Buzzell, *The Neurophysiology of Television Viewing, A Preliminary Report,* (Fryeborg, Maine: 1987). Unpublished research paper (obtainable through Dr. Keith Buzzell, 14 Portland Street, Fryeborg, ME, 04037).

Chapter 12

1. U.S. Department of Justice, Bureau of Justice Statistics. *National Crime Victimization Survey,* (Washington, DC: Federal Bureau of Investigation, Uniform Crime Reporting Program Supplementary Homocide Reports, 1998).

2. Centers for Disease Control. *First Biennial Youth Risk Behavior Study,* (Atlanta: Centers for Disease Control, 1991-1999).

3. P. Kaufman, et al., *Indicators of School Crime and Safety,* (Washington, DC: U.S. Department of Education and Justice, Publication NCES98-251/NCJ-17225; 1998).

4. J. Garbarino, "Viewpoint: some kids are orchids." *Time,* Dec. 20, 1999:51.

5. G. E. Barnes. "The alcohol personality: a reanalysis of the literature." *Journal of Studies on Alcohol,* 1979;40:7.

6. E. Weiss, L. Hechtman, *Hyperactive Children Grown Up,* (New York: Guilford Press; 1986).

7. R. Gittelman, "Parent questionnaire of teen behavior." *Psychopharmacology Bulletin,* 1985;21:923-924.

8. ———, "Self-evaluation (teenager's) self report." *Psychopharmacology Bulletin,* 1985;21:925-926.

9. A. Rosenthal, "Violence is predictable." *Today's Health,* 1970;45:56-57,71-72.

10. J. R. Evans, S. Claycomb, "Abnormal QEEG patterns associated with dissociation and violence." *Journal of Neurotherapy,* 1999;3(2):21-27.

Index

About the Authors

Eduardo Castro, M.D., is the medical director of Mt. Rogers Clinic in Trout Dale, Virginia, one of the leading alternative and complementary medical clinics in the United States for more than twenty-five years. He established the Neurofeedback Center in Charlottesville, Virginia.

Robert W. Hill, Ph.D., founded The Oaks Psychological Service in Abingdon, Virginia, where he specializes in health psychology and behavioral medicine using hypnosis, behavior modification, and biofeedback. Dr. Hill has used brain wave biofeedback to treat ADD/ADHD disorders for ten years and has trained with many pioneers in the field.

Hampton Roads Publishing Company

. . . for the evolving human spirit

Hampton Roads Publishing Company
publishes books on a variety of subjects,
including metaphysics, health, integrative medicine,
visionary fiction, and other related topics.

For a copy of our latest catalog, call toll-free
(800) 766-8009, or send your name and address to:

Hampton Roads Publishing Company, Inc.
1125 Stoney Ridge Road
Charlottesville, VA 22902

e-mail: hrpc@hrpub.com
www.hrpub.com